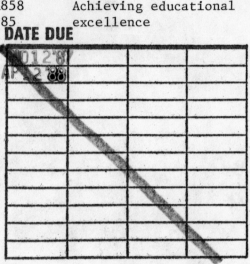

Achieving
Educational Excellence

A Critical Assessment
of Priorities and Practices
in Higher Education

Alexander W. Astin

Achieving
Educational Excellence

 Jossey-Bass Publishers

San Francisco • Washington • London • 1985

ACHIEVING EDUCATIONAL EXCELLENCE
*A Critical Assessment of Priorities
and Practices in Higher Education*
by Alexander W. Astin

Copyright © 1985 by: Jossey-Bass Inc., Publishers
433 California Street
San Francisco, California 94104
&
Jossey-Bass Limited
28 Banner Street
London EC1Y 8QE

Library of Congress Cataloging in Publication Data

Astin, Alexander W.
Achieving educational excellence.

(The Jossey-Bass higher education series)
Bibliography: p. 229
Includes index.
1. Education, Higher—United States—Aims and
objectives. 2. College student development programs—
United States. 3. Talented students—United States.
4. Educational equalization—United States. I. Title.
II. Series.
LA227.3.A858   378.73   84-43025
ISBN 0-87589-636-7

Manufactured in the United States of America

The paper in this book meets the guidelines for
permanence and durability of the Committee on
Production Guidelines for Book Longevity of the
Council on Library Resources.

JACKET DESIGN BY WILLI BAUM

FIRST EDITION

Code 8511

The Jossey-Bass
Higher Education Series

In memory of my father, Allen V. Astin

Preface

Excellence and quality are perhaps the most fashionable concepts in education these days. And while many individuals and organizations are seeking better ways to promote excellence in our schools and colleges, very few have taken the trouble to define what they mean by excellence in the first place. Despite this inattention to definition, there are several conceptions of excellence that are *implicit* in our time-honored educational policies and practices. This book examines these traditional beliefs critically and finds them wanting on several counts: They are not necessarily consistent with the *educational* mission of institutions, they interfere with our efforts to expand educational opportunity, and their use does not promote greater excellence in the system as a whole. *Achieving Educational Excellence* proposes a very different view of excellence—the talent development approach—and discusses how we might go about implementing this alternative approach and how it might serve to improve the quality of our higher education system.

Since this is an intensely personal book, some brief biographical notes may help the reader to understand my approach. My interest in educational excellence originated more
than twenty years ago when I accepted a research position with
the National Merit Scholarship Corporation. An issue of special
interest to me and my fellow researchers was the college-choice
behavior of the Merit Scholars and Finalists. Even though these
exceptionally talented students qualified for admission to
almost any college or university, their choices tended to be confined to a relatively small number of institutions. When we
made a list of these most-preferred institutions, it was limited
largely to the most famous or prestigious institutions in the
country. The fact that each new crop of Merit Finalists produced an almost identical list of most-preferred institutions convinced me of two facts: (1) We Americans have developed a
folklore about our higher education system in which the different institutions are organized hierarchically into a kind of pecking order; and (2) highly able students manifest their belief in
this folklore by choosing the "best" or "most excellent" institutions at the top of the pecking order.

Most of my research at National Merit focused on the impact that different types of colleges have on the student's personal and intellectual development. One of the first things I no-
ticed from these studies was that the "best" colleges at the top
of the institutional pecking order did not always turn out to
have the "best" impact on the student's personal development.

When I was invited in 1965 to head up the research program of the American Council on Education in Washington,
D.C., I jumped at the chance, since the council is the principal
place where the top administrators and policy makers in higher
education congregate. I felt, on the one hand, that the research
would benefit from the involvement and counsel of these educational leaders and, on the other hand, that *they* would benefit
from a better knowledge of how their institutions were actually
affecting their students.

It was at the council that my colleague Robert Panos and
I set up the Cooperative Institutional Research Program (CIRP),
which was designed primarily as a continuing series of large-

scale longitudinal studies of how students are affected by their institutions. The CIRP, which has so far involved more than five million students, one hundred thousand faculty members, and twelve hundred institutions, has provided a rich source of data for continuing studies of American higher education. Much of what we now know about institutional impact on student development has come from CIRP data.

My research on students has covered the entire spectrum of student "talent," from National Merit Scholars to disadvantaged and "open admissions" students. These studies have looked at literally dozens of student outcomes, including retention, cognitive development, affective development, and career progress. I have at different times focused my analyses on a wide variety of institutional types: research universities, elite private colleges, "invisible" colleges, state colleges, single-sex colleges, technological institutions, denominational colleges, community colleges, and historically black colleges. And I have personally visited perhaps two hundred different college campuses and had an opportunity to present my research findings before most of the major national associations and professional societies in the field of higher education.

Practitioners and policy makers, however, have not always been receptive to the findings of these studies, particularly when those findings fail to support our conventional notions of excellence in higher education. The experience of trying to disseminate these findings convinces me that the time has come to take a critical look at our traditional beliefs and theories of excellence. One problem is that these theories are seldom stated explicitly; rather, they are more often implicit in our actions and policies. By stating these theories explicitly and by showing how they influence our institutional values and priorities, I hope that some faculty members, administrators, and policy makers may be motivated to consider alternative definitions of excellence that are more consistent with higher education's educational mission.

Since most of us share a concern about excellence in higher education, this book is intended for a broad audience. College administrators and faculty members, for example, are

interested in how we define and measure institutional excellence and in the relationship of quality to admissions policies,
pedagogical techniques and theories, and the academic reward
system. Counselors, advisers, and other student-affairs personnel
have a common concern with enhancing students' development
—one of the main foci of the book. And trustees and state and
federal policy makers are typically interested in issues such as
expanding access, developing human capital, and the relationship
between resources and educational quality.

Chapter One describes the American higher education
system, particularly its hierarchical aspects. The hierarchy of
institutions is seen as providing the principal basis for our conventional notions about excellence. Several "models" of higher
education (such as the industrial production model and talent
development model) are discussed. It is argued that the most
valid conception of excellence is one that is most consistent
with the purposes of higher education. The chapter concludes
with a consideration of the benefits of higher education and of
how these benefits relate to notions of quality and equity.

Traditional concepts of excellence—the reputational, resources, outcome, and content approaches—are reviewed in
Chapter Two. Although the two most widely held views—reputation and resources—are found to be mutually reinforcing, they
fail to satisfy three fundamental requirements: Neither is necessarily consistent with an institution's primary educational purpose; neither contributes to the expansion of educational opportunities; and adherence to either view offers little possibility
of enhancing the overall quality of higher education in the
United States. While the outcomes view suffers from some of
the same limitations as the reputational and resources views, its
use does offer some possibility of improving the quality of institutions. The final traditional view—the content approach—is
difficult to evaluate because of the lack of research evidence.

An alternative to traditional views of excellence—the talent development approach—is presented in Chapter Three. The
talent development approach to excellence emphasizes the intellectual and personal development of students as a fundamental institutional purpose. According to this view, an excellent

institution is one that facilitates maximum growth among its students and faculty. Unlike the reputational and resources approaches, the talent development view does not limit either educational opportunities or the overall excellence of the system by identifying only a limited number of colleges and universities as "the best." Any institution can be "excellent" if it deploys its resources wisely and effectively to facilitate the intellectual and personal development of its students and faculty.

Chapter Four reviews a number of issues related to educational equity: the meaning of equity, the availability of educational opportunities, testing and tracking, educating underprepared students, and the "conflict" between excellence and equity. Data are presented showing that the "highest-quality" educational opportunities are not equally available to low-income and minority students. While traditional testing and selective admissions practices support the reputational and resources views of excellence, they also serve to deny equal educational opportunities to low-income, underprepared, and minority students. The talent development view of excellence, on the other hand, tends to broaden opportunities because it values the educational development of *all* students and does not necessarily favor the well-prepared student over the underprepared student. Unlike the reputational and resources views of excellence, which generate conflict between the goals of excellence and equity, the talent development approach offers a means of achieving both goals simultaneously.

Chapter Five examines the role of teacher training and education schools in the academy. Data are presented showing that the pool of students aspiring to teaching careers has been declining in both quantity and quality at all levels (primary, secondary, and postsecondary). These declines may be attributed in part to the attitudes and policies of faculty members, administrators, and institutions: the low status accorded schools and departments of education within academia, the low value placed on teaching careers at the precollegiate level, the refusal of the most selective institutions to offer an undergraduate major in education, and the low priority given to excellent teaching in the academic reward system of most universities. To a certain extent, these attitudes and practices reflect the reputational and resources conceptions of excellence, which value the best-prepared students over other students and which value scholarship over teaching. Many of these problems could be ameliorated by embracing a talent development view of excellence. Outstanding teachers would receive the same rewards as outstanding scholars, pedagogy and teacher training would be elevated to higher status within the academy, and larger numbers of the better-prepared students would be encouraged to take up careers in teaching.

Chapter Six presents a theory of student learning and development—the involvement theory—which is designed to assist institutions in fulfilling their talent development mission. *Involvement* refers to the quality and quantity of the physical and psychological energy that the student invests in the college experience. The theory holds that the effectiveness of any educational policy or practice in developing student talent is directly related to the capacity of that policy or practice to increase student involvement. One special strength of the involvement theory is that it seems to explain much of what we know about effective teaching and about institutional practices that facilitate student retention and development. The theory of student involvement can be regarded as a useful *tool* to be used by both faculty members and administrators as they attempt to design more effective environments to facilitate talent development.

Specific suggestions for enhancing the educational excellence of our colleges and universities are presented in Chapter Seven. The chapter first presents specific strategies for increasing students' involvement through changes in instructional methods, student-life activities, and methods of assessment and feedback. Next, the discussion turns to what educational policy makers can do in four areas—student involvement, teacher training, admissions, and research—to promote the talent development mission of higher education. The chapter then considers two types of institutions—the research university and the community college—that pose special problems when it comes to enhancing students' involvement and implementing the talent development conception of excellence. The following section examines various sources of inertia and conservatism that make institutions highly resistant to change. The key role to be played by administrators as change agents is discussed in the last section, which also provides suggestions for improving our methods of selecting administrators.

Chapter Eight analyzes trends in the characteristics of new students entering American higher education by summarizing the results of eighteen annual surveys conducted by the Cooperative Institutional Research Program. The survey results not only confirm the widely discussed decline in students' academic skills but also reveal major changes in their educational plans, career plans, and personal values. Students' increasing interest in business and other high-paying professional careers has been accompanied by increasing materialism and greater concern for attaining personal power and status. Declining student interest in the liberal arts and in virtually all of the human service occupations (such as teaching, social work, and the clergy) has been accompanied by declining altruism and declining social concern. These trends are seen as analogues to the different conceptions of excellence discussed in previous chapters. The reputational and resources views, for example, by emphasizing the enhancement of reputation and the acquisition of resources, represent values that parallel the increased student interest in money, power, and status. The talent development view, on the other hand, by focusing institutional resources and energies on helping students develop their talents to the fullest, promotes values that more closely parallel concern for others and for the society. The chapter concludes by discussing the significance of these alternative values for the larger society and for the excellence of the American higher education system.

In many respects this book can be viewed as a critique of the values that underlie much of our current educational practice and that give rise to our traditional conceptions of excellence in higher education. In many respects these values, once articulated, are not especially flattering. But beyond providing just a critique, I have also tried to articulate an alternative conception of excellence based on values that are not only more positive but also more compatible with our educational mission and purpose. Moreover, I have tried to suggest a number of practical steps that institutions can take to implement this alternative view. If any significant fraction of our institutions is successful in implementing this alternative—the talent development approach—both the excellence and equity of our higher education system will be enhanced.

Acknowledgments

Many people contributed to the production of this book. In the early planning stages, I was especially fortunate in having an opportunity to interview six leading scholars and educators—Howard Bowen, Arthur Chickering, Russell Edgerton, Patricia Graham, Joseph Katz, and David Riesman—to sound out their views on some of the issues I was grappling with. Although I realize that they may not agree with everything I have to say, their candor and their generosity with their time are much appreciated.

During the past two years I have had an opportunity to test out and refine my ideas through a number of speeches, workshops, and seminars conducted on a variety of college and university campuses and at the annual meetings of various educational and scholarly associations. The feedback received on these occasions has been invaluable in helping me clarify and sharpen my views, and I am grateful to the many faculty members, administrators, students, and association officials who took the trouble to ask questions and offer their views on what I had to say.

My thinking about these issues has also been facilitated greatly by my association during the past year with the Study Group on the Conditions of Excellence in American Higher Education. I particularly want to express my appreciation to my study group colleagues—Herman Blake, Howard Bowen, Zelda Gamson, Harold Hodgkinson, Barbara Lee, and Kenneth Mortimer—and to our very talented staff: Cliff Adelman, Barbara Hetrick, and Dennis Jones. Our final report, *Involvement in Learning: Realizing the Potential of American Higher Education,* was a joint effort, with each of us sharing responsibility for different writing tasks. The reader may find occasional similarities between parts of our report and sections of Chapter Six in this book. I shared an early draft of that chapter with the study group during our early deliberations, and I am flattered that they chose to incorporate some of the ideas in our final report.

When I finally decided to sit down and write this book, many colleagues at the University of California at Los Angeles and the Higher Education Research Institute willingly pitched in to help. Kenneth (Casey) Green was always ready to offer advice, assistance, and constructive criticism. William Korn has been a real gem in running a number of complicated data analyses, usually on very short notice. Paul Astin prepared a very useful summary of the research evidence on the underprepared student. Ayako Kadogawa, John Somers, Harrison Togiai, and Marilynn Schalit somehow managed to transcribe my (often inaudible) tapes. Mary Jane Maier not only transcribed tapes but was also able to keep track of the long list of references and the bits and pieces of chapters as they were completed. Laura Kent, the world's best editor, provided amazingly fast turnaround on some pretty rough drafts.

Various parts of this book utilize, in somewhat altered form, material that has appeared in earlier publications. The section of Chapter One on the benefits of higher education is based in part on the article "Differing Views of Institutional Quality: Implications for College Admissions Counselors" (*Journal of College Admissions*, Winter 1984, *102*, 3-10). Some parts of Chapters Two and Three borrow heavily from the article "Excellence and Equity: Achievable Goals for American Education" (*The National Forum: Phi Kappa Phi Journal*, Spring 1984, pp. 24-29). An earlier version of Chapter Six appeared in "Student Involvement: A Developmental Theory for Higher Education" (*Journal of College Student Personnel*, July 1984, *25* (4), 297-308). And portions of Chapter Eight were taken from "Students in the 1980s: Democracy and Values" (*AAHE Bulletin*, May 1984, *36* (7), 11-14).

The Ford Foundation was generous enough to provide me with a travel and study grant that greatly facilitated the writing of this book. I especially want to thank Fred Crossland, who was at the foundation when the grant was made, for encouraging me to complete this work.

Finally, I want to thank my wife and colleague, Lena, for putting up with the disorganization and craziness that usually accompany one of my writing projects and especially for the wise advice and counsel she has offered on many aspects of this book.

Los Angeles, California   Alexander W. Astin
March 1985

Contents

The Author

Alexander W. Astin is professor of higher education at the University of California, Los Angeles; director of the Higher Education Research Institute at UCLA; and director of the Cooperative Institutional Research Program. Previously he was director of research for the American Council on Education (1965–1973) and the National Merit Scholarship Corporation (1960–1963). Astin has received awards for outstanding research from the American Personnel and Guidance Association (1965), the National Association of Student Personnel Administrators (1976), the American College Personnel Association (1978), and the American College Testing Program–American Educational Research Association (1983). He has also been a fellow at the Center for Advanced Study in the Behavioral Sciences (1967–1968) and a recipient of several honorary degrees. Astin's work has appeared in more than one hundred articles and fifteen books, including *Minorities in American Higher Educa-*

tion (1982), *Maximizing Leadership Effectiveness* (1980, with R. A. Scherrei), *Four Critical Years* (1977), and *Preventing Students from Dropping Out* (1975).

Astin, an amateur jazz pianist and photographer by avocation, lives in Los Angeles with his wife, psychologist Helen S. Astin.

Achieving Educational Excellence

A Critical Assessment
of Priorities and Practices
in Higher Education

Chapter One

How Educational Excellence Is Determined

This book is about educational quality: what it means, how it is measured, how it can be improved. The book also tries to show that our traditional beliefs about excellence or quality in American higher education do not serve us well. Not only do these beliefs interfere with our attempts to achieve greater equality of opportunity, but—ironically—they also frustrate our attempts to upgrade the quality of the system.

In this chapter I shall first describe the American system of higher education from several different perspectives, with particular emphasis on its hierarchical nature. Basically, this hierarchy is a set of shared beliefs that constitute the basis for our conventional notions about excellence. Next I shall discuss the purposes of higher education by examining several models of the American system. I will argue that our definitions of excellence in higher education should be consistent with its pur-

1

poses. The chapter concludes with a consideration of the benefits of higher education and of how these benefits relate to concepts of excellence and equity.

General Characteristics

The terms most often used to describe American higher education are *large, diverse, complex,* and *decentralized.* That the system is indeed large is obvious: It comprises more than 3,000 institutions, 600,000 faculty members, and twelve million students. It is also a very open system in the sense that it enrolls a higher proportion of the population than does any other higher education system in the world (about 6 percent).

That the system is both diverse and complex is attested by the wide variety of institutional types that it encompasses: community colleges, research universities, liberal arts colleges, technical schools, Bible colleges, music and art institutes, and so on. Institutions also vary dramatically with respect to enrollment size (from fewer than 100 students to more than 60,000), control (federal, state, denominational, private-nonsectarian), program offerings, admissions policies, and course requirements.

That this massive system is decentralized is also clear: Fewer than a dozen of its institutions are federally controlled. About half of the remainder are controlled by state or local governments, and the remaining half are private institutions controlled either by religious denominations or by lay boards of trustees. Even in the public sector, many institutions have independent boards that protect them to some extent from political control or interference.

The complexity, diversity, and decentralized nature of American higher education might tempt one to conclude that the system is disorganized and chaotic. On the contrary, the institutions that make it up are remarkably homogeneous in several important respects. For example, most of them offer some form of a liberal arts curriculum for their undergraduates. Most college professors, regardless of where they teach, have received the same kind of academic preparation and utilize similar approaches to teaching, testing, and grading. And most institutions have a similar administrative structure, with a chief executive officer; vice-presidents or vice-chancellors for academic, student, and fiscal affairs; deans; department heads; admissions officers; registrars; and financial aid officers.

Moreover, American higher education is characterized by one feature that, paradoxically, makes it more of a system than perhaps any other higher education system in the world: the awarding of course credits and degrees. The credit system is, in effect, the glue that binds this congeries of institutions. Thus, a student who successfully completes a course in one institution can, in theory, transfer the credit received for that course to almost any other institution in the system. Similarly, nearly all four-year institutions award the baccalaureate, which constitutes the main prerequisite for admission to most graduate and professional programs. The credit and degree system not only gives great flexibility to the system but also makes it possible for students to "stop out" of college or to transfer from one college to another with relative impunity.

This is not to suggest that the system is monolithic or that it is free of ambiguities and contradictions. Indeed, one of my favorite class exercises is to ask my doctoral students at the University of California at Los Angeles to select ten words or phrases that describe the American system of higher education. They regularly come up with a wildly heterogeneous—and even contradictory—set of descriptors such as the following:

> selective vs. open
> stable vs. dynamic
> permissive vs. strict
> elite vs. mass
> progressive vs. conservative
> rich vs. poor
> flexible vs. rigid
> independent vs. tool of society
> humanistic vs. indifferent
> organized vs. anarchic
> liberal arts oriented vs. professionally oriented
> meritocratic vs. egalitarian

resistant to change vs. innovative
business-oriented vs. antibusiness
exciting vs. dull
experimental vs. cautious
efficient vs. inefficient
collegial vs. bureaucratic
accountable vs. autonomous

When asked to justify these apparent contradictions, students typically reply that their descriptions were based on the few institutions with which they have had direct personal experience; they were not attempting to characterize the system as a whole. A major point of this book, to be developed in more detail in subsequent chapters, is that most educators and even most scholars of higher education tend to view the postsecondary educational system in the United States from an *institutional* rather than a *systems* perspective. I will try to show that an institutional perspective, while useful for some purposes, can lead to the adoption of policies and practices that—whatever their immediate benefit to a particular institution—weaken the system as a whole.

A Hierarchy of Institutions

While American higher education can be accurately described as large, complex, diverse, and decentralized, these descriptors do not tell us much about the internal organization of the system. At first glance, one might conclude that the system has no internal structure or organization, given its highly decentralized governance structure. After spending some twenty-five years studying the system, however, I am convinced that most of the three thousand institutions are organized into a highly refined status hierarchy. What is especially interesting about this hierarchy is that it has no formal organizational properties (such as public versus private) but rather exists as part of our belief system. More important from a practical perspective, this widely shared belief system has profound implications for almost every aspect of institutional functioning: admissions policies, faculty recruitment, fund raising, curriculum, certification, and governance. It also has important implications for government policy, business and industry, and equality of opportunity. Finally, our acceptance of the hierarchical arrangement of institutions greatly influences our definitions of excellence and quality in American higher education. Veysey (1980), for example, argues that this "informal pecking order" serves as a substitute for "state-controlled decisions concerning quality" (p. 21).

Like most status hierarchies, our system comprises a few well-known elite institutions, a larger group of institutions with modest reputations, and a very large group of institutions that are virtually unknown outside their geographic region. Included at the top of the hierarchy are most of the major research universities and a number of elite private colleges. At the next level are the lesser-known research universities and a substantial number of liberal arts colleges. At the bottom are most of the community and junior colleges, a number of state colleges, and a sizable number of small private colleges.

If you doubt the existence of this hierarchy, let me suggest a simple parlor game that I sometimes play with my graduate students or even with dinner guests: Ask a group of friends or acquaintances to list what they regard as the ten or fifteen best or highest-quality institutions in the country. Almost everyone's list will include such institutions as Harvard, Yale, and Stanford. Considering that people have more than three thousand institutions to choose from, this agreement is indeed remarkable. Next, ask them to list the five or ten best institutions in your particular state or metropolitan area. Again, you will find a remarkable consensus.

Note here that the terms *best* and *highest quality* are synonymous with *most prestigious*. This usage is deliberate on my part: I wish to emphasize that lay persons and academics alike are inclined to equate prestige with quality. (This phenomenon is treated at greater length in Chapter Two.)

In what ways do institutions at the top differ from those further down? To answer this question, one must first identify each institution's standing on the prestige ladder. Although an institution's prestige or reputation can be assessed in several ways (see Chapter Two), a large body of research shows that the best single index is the institution's selectivity (Astin and Henson, 1977), defined as the average score of its entering freshmen on the College Entrance Examination Board's Scholastic Aptitude Test (SAT). This average is derived from the composite (verbal plus mathematical) SAT scores or, in the case of institutions that use the American College Test (ACT), from scores converted to SAT equivalents (Astin, Christian, and Henson, 1978). Table 1 divides institutions into nine levels of selectivity. The institutions at the top have scores of 1300 or higher; those at the lowest level have scores below 775. Each of the seven intervals in between covers seventy-five selectivity points. This arrangement reveals a classic pyramid: Only a few institutions occupy the top levels, and the numbers increase as one moves downward. It would be a simple matter, of course, to make the lowest level in the hierarchy the largest one by combining the two bottom levels. Note that the three levels at the bottom include more than twenty times as many institutions as the three levels at the top.

The types of institutions found at each level are predictable. Note that those at the very top are all private universities and four-year colleges. This group includes such institutions as Harvard University, Yale University, Princeton University, Brown University, the Massachusetts Institute of Technology, Swarthmore College, and the California Institute of Technology. There are no public two-year colleges in the top three selectivity groups and only four (less than half of 1 percent of the total) in the top five. As a matter of fact, more than 95 percent of the community colleges are at the bottom three levels. By contrast, more than two thirds of the public universities are located at the middle selectivity levels. The public four-year colleges rank somewhat lower in the hierarchy: Close to three in four are located at the lowest three selectivity levels, and 15 percent are at the very bottom. No universities, either public or private, are located at the lowest level of the hierarchy.

Among private institutions, the two-year or junior colleges follow the pattern for the public community colleges, being

Table 1. Distribution of Institutional Types by Selectivity Level.

Selectivity Level (Mean SAT Composite[a] for Entering Freshmen)	Total	Public Sector			Private Sector		
		University	Four-Year College	Two-Year College	University	Four-Year College	Two-Year College
1300 or higher	14	0	0	0	6	8	0
1225–1299	20	0	2	0	8	10	0
1150–1224	47	1	5	0	11	30	0
1075–1149	78	7	11	1	9	50	0
1000–1074	215	29	32	3	15	135	1
925–999	310	32	53	28	10	181	6
850–924	673	18	144	116	2	358	35
775–849	1,106	7	94	669	1	133	202
below 775	227	0	61	80	0	66	20
Total	2,690	94	402	897	62	971	264

[a]ACT scores have been converted to SAT equivalents (see Astin, Christian, and Henson, 1978).

Source: Higher Education Research Institute and National Center for Education Statistics.

concentrated at the lowest selectivity levels. Private universities
vary widely in selectivity, although the proportion occupying
the upper levels of the hierarchy is larger than that of any other
type of institution. The private four-year colleges are the most
heterogeneous of all, spanning the entire range of selectivity.
Even though more than half of the institutions in the top two
groups are private four-year colleges, there are also sixty-six
such institutions at the lowest level. In summary, these data suggest that the traditional division of institutions into two-year
colleges, four-year colleges, and universities to some extent rep-
licates the hierarchical arrangement based on selectivity. That is,
universities tend to rank relatively high, two-year colleges fall at
the lowest levels of the hierarchy, and four-year colleges generally rank in between. There is, nevertheless, considerable variation *within* each of these types; and so one cannot know an
institution's position in the hierarchy simply by knowing whether it is a two-year college, four-year college, or university.

What kinds of students enter institutions at different levels of the hierarchy? Data to answer this question were derived
from the 1983 annual freshman survey conducted by the Cooperative Institutional Research Program (CIRP) of the University
of California at Los Angeles and the American Council on Education (Astin and others, 1983). In the CIRP study four variables were selected to represent the student's academic preparation and socioeconomic status: average grade in high school,
parental income, father's education, and mother's education. As
the first column of Table 2 indicates, the higher an institution's
position in the hierarchy, the larger the proportion of freshmen
with A averages who enter the institution. This finding is perhaps to be expected, since freshmen's admission test scores are
used to compute selectivity level and since students' test scores
tend to be closely related to their high school grades. Nonetheless, the one-to-one correspondence between selectivity level
and grade level is remarkable, as is the magnitude of the differences. Thus, for every A student who enters a college at the
lowest selectivity level, almost eight such students enter colleges
in the top selectivity group.

Students' socioeconomic levels are also associated with

Table 2. Entering Freshmen (1983) and Financial Characteristics of Institutions at Different Selectivity Levels.

| | Characteristics of 1983 Freshmen | | | | | Characteristics of Institutions | | |
| | | Parental Income | | Parents with College Degrees | | | | |
Selectivity Level (Mean SAT Composite[a] for Entering Freshmen)	A or A– Average in High School (%)	$50,000 or More (%)	Less Than $15,000 (%)	Father (%)	Mother (%)	Total Per-Student[b] Educational Expenditures[c] (1981–82)	Average Faculty Salary (1982–83)	Tuition and Fees (1982–83)
1300 or higher	79.2	47.1	6.8	83.7	72.3	$11,243	$34,056	$6,406
1225–1299	75.2	39.1	8.0	73.9	57.3	8,944	32,275	6,158
1150–1224	58.6	39.4	7.1	69.8	52.3	9,037	27,915	5,166
1075–1149	39.8	24.8	12.5	56.1	42.0	5,624	29,414	2,673
1000–1074	33.1	22.5	13.2	51.7	34.9	5,095	27,031	2,120
925–999	22.3	17.0	15.7	42.0	27.4	4,183	25,769	1,537
850–924	13.6	10.5	22.8	30.6	20.0	3,816	24,853	1,065
775–849	12.7	10.4	25.7	26.9	18.5	3,474	23,073	546
below 775	10.0	7.2	40.1	21.1	19.6	3,676	21,979	640
All Institutions	20.7	15.2	16.0	36.8	25.5	4,418	25,350	1,291

[a] ACT scores have been converted to SAT equivalents (see Astin, Christian, and Henson, 1978).

[b] Part-time students are counted as one-third full-time. Graduate and professional students are counted as three undergraduates.

[c] Includes expenditures for instruction, academic support, student services, administration, and physical plant.

Source: Unpublished data, Cooperative Institutional Research Program, Higher Education Research Institute, and National Center for Education Statistics, 1984.

their institution's position in the hierarchy. Of those freshmen entering institutions at the top level, nearly half come from families with annual incomes of $50,000 or more, and less than 10 percent come from families with incomes below $15,000 per year. Among students entering institutions at the very bottom of the hierarchy, the pattern is reversed: less than 10 percent come from families with incomes of $50,000, whereas two in five come from families with incomes of less than $15,000. Similarly, students entering institutions at the top of the hierarchy have much more highly educated parents than do students entering institutions at the bottom.

Clearly, the poorest students and those from the least educated families are not well represented in the "best" institutions and are disproportionately concentrated in the least selective institutions. Such a pattern has important implications for educational equity, a concept treated in considerable detail in Chapters Two and Four.

Our final comparison involves the financial characteristics of institutions at different levels of the hierarchy: specifically their total educational expenditures per student, average faculty salary, and tuition and fee charges. As Table 2 shows, each of these measures turns out to be closely correlated with an institution's position in the hierarchy, and once again the differences are substantial. Compared with institutions at the bottom, those at the top selectivity level spend more than three times as much per student on their educational programs, pay their faculty members more than half again as much, and charge ten times as much in tuition and fees. This last difference is partly attributable to the concentration of private institutions at the top of the hierarchy; private institutions, of course, tend to charge much larger fees than do public institutions. Nonetheless, there are substantial numbers of private institutions at the bottom levels. Moreover, tuition and fee charges at both public and private institutions follow the hierarchical ordering.

These comparisons make it clear that an institution's position in the academic hierarchy is closely related to important characteristics of its students and its finances. Specifically, the most prestigious institutions attract the best-prepared students from the most affluent and highly educated families, spend the most on their educational programs, pay their faculties the highest salaries, and charge the highest tuition and fees. In contrast, institutions at the bottom of the hierarchy enroll low-achieving students from the poorest and least educated families, spend the least on their educational programs, pay their faculties the lowest salaries, and charge the lowest tuition and fees. The magnitude of these differences underscores the fact that the institutional hierarchy is more than just an interesting sociological phenomenon; it has important implications for the kinds of students and financial resources that an institution is able to attract. (Chapter Two discusses other characteristics associated with the academic hierarchy.)

Although the institutional hierarchy in the private sector developed more or less by historical accident, the public hierarchy in many states has evolved as part of a conscious plan. Perhaps the prototype is the state of California, whose *Master Plan for Higher Education* (California State Department of Education, 1960) specifically mandates a hierarchical structure, with the nine-campus University of California at the top, the nineteen-institution state college and university system in the middle, and the more than one hundred community colleges at the bottom. The relative exclusiveness of these three sectors is officially reflected in differential admissions policies: Access to the University of California is limited to the top one-eighth of high school graduates, admission to the state college and university system is limited to the top one-third, and the community college system is open to all.

What are some of the consequences of this institutional hierarchy? Since, as already noted, institutions at the top of the hierarchy are regarded as the best, institutions lower down have a natural tendency to imitate them. Riesman (1956) described the situation as a kind of snakelike procession, in that each institution follows the path taken by the head. That this procession is seen in terms of differential quality is indicated by Riesman's terminology: He refers to institutions at the head of the procession as "distinguished," "famous," "centers of decisive influence." Institutions next in line are "quite good," those further behind are "run-of-the-mill," and the remainder form the "tail end of the procession."

As Riesman's observations suggest, the institutional hierarchy tends to promote conformity, a fact that may explain why American higher education, despite its apparent diversity, is in fact highly homogeneous with respect to such critical matters as admissions policies, curriculum, the training and evaluation of faculty, and administrative structure. Howard Bowen (1977) has commented that most campuses even look remarkably alike. Hodgkinson (1971) has observed that "institutions of higher education respond to stimuli in very similar ways. This is partly what makes them often rather dull" (p. 277). This homogeneity has also been lamented by social critic Paul Goodman (1962, pp. 7-8). After referring to the several thousand academic institutions in the United States as "centers of lively and promising youth," Goodman goes on to say: "Yet one could not name ten that strongly stand for anything peculiar to themselves, peculiarly wise, radical, experimental, or even peculiarly dangerous, stupid, or licentious. It is astounding! That there should be so many self-governing communities, yet so much conformity to the national norm. How is it possible?" Perhaps the best answer to Goodman's question lies in the hierarchical structure and the "snakelike procession" it fosters.

The institutional hierarchy also provides a means whereby people can acquire an academic pedigree. It is a common practice both inside and outside academia to introduce or identify persons by the institution from which they received their postsecondary degrees. This pedigree seems to follow people for the rest of their lives, even after they have been away from formal education for many decades. As a matter of fact, the prestige of the institution awarding the degree affects the practical value of that degree in getting a job. (This fringe benefit is discussed more thoroughly later in the chapter.)

Another consequence of the institutional hierarchy is that it tends to breed a great deal of competition among institutions: not only for such resources as money, faculty members, and students but also for a higher place in the hierarchy as revealed in reputational surveys. (The relationship between reputation and resources is discussed in much more detail in Chapter Two.)

Many educators see the hierarchy as essential to the preservation of quality in what they view as a very open higher education system. The British scholar Eric Ashby (1971, pp. 101–102), for example, believes that only those institutions at the apex of the hierarchy can provide an appropriate education for the brightest students: "The highly gifted student needs informal instruction, intimate contact with other first-class minds, opportunities to learn the discipline of dissent from men who have themselves changed patterns of thought: in a word (it is one which has become a five-letter word of reproach) this sort of student needs to be treated as elite."

Given that institutions at the top of the hierarchy are regarded as the best, it is not surprising that those at the bottom of the hierarchy are often treated with something not far from contempt. For example, the historian Frederick Rudolph raises questions about the viability of one large group of institutions at the bottom of the hierarchy, the community colleges. He wonders, in effect, if such institutions ought to be considered part of the higher education system: "In its rejection of national norms, cosmopolitan values, academic credentials, traditional standards, and professionalism, as well as in its embrace of the local, parochial, anti-intellectual, and familial, the community college, for all of its great service as an educational institution, may have placed itself beyond consideration, except in a limited sense, as a college" (Rudolph, 1962, pp. 485–486).

It is interesting to speculate on why American higher education has taken this particular hierarchical shape. To some extent, the system mirrors the larger society. Many nonacademic institutions in the United States are competitive and hierarchical. We Americans seem preoccupied with being the best, whether in sports, automobile manufacture, military weaponry, television shows, or morality. And in higher education, as in society as a whole, the competition frequently focuses on the acquisition of material resources and the enhancement of image or reputation. Indeed, in many sectors of U.S. society there is a tendency to measure excellence or worth in material terms. (We shall return to this point in Chapter Two.)

Purposes of Higher Education

Is it reasonable to equate an institution's excellence or worth with its position in the academic hierarchy? To answer this question, we must first consider the *purposes* of the American higher education system, since any index of an institution's quality or excellence should be consistent with its purposes.

The traditional activities of American higher education are teaching, research, and public service. What purposes or functions do these activities serve? As the list of contradictory descriptors generated by my graduate students makes clear, higher education can be viewed as serving many different purposes. Scholars of higher education have described academic institutions in a variety of ways, from "social service stations" (Wolff, 1969) to instruments for preserving the class system (Touraine, 1974), to holding pens for keeping young people out of the labor market (Rudolph, 1962), to places providing jobs for scholars (Jencks and Riesman, 1968). But most attempts to define the purposes of American higher education are epitomized by two antithetical models. For simplicity, let us label these the industrial production model and the talent development model.

Industrial Production Model. During the 1970s and early 1980s, American higher education experienced pressures created by declining resources and the threat of declining enrollments. Partly in response to these pressures, colleges and universities began experimenting with techniques borrowed from the corporate world. In addition to trying out computerized management information systems, program budgeting, and management by objectives, they hired management consultants and sought chief executive officers who were "good managers." At the same time, some higher education planners and policy makers began to view American higher education as "producing" both knowledge and trained manpower. There was also much talk of making higher education more "accountable." Thorstein Veblen's 1918 prophecy seemed to be coming true: "Principles and standards of organization, control, and achievement, that have been accepted as an habitual matter of course in the conduct of business, will, by force of habit, in good part reassert themselves as indispensable and conclusive in the affairs of learning" (1957, p. 64).

How appropriately does the industrial production model portray the purposes of higher education? Like most analogues, it is seriously flawed and basically fallacious. To begin with, manufacturing is a physical process: Raw materials are fabricated into parts that are put together in an assembly line. The finished product is a direct result of the manufacturing process. Superficially, higher education may appear to produce knowledge and educated graduates in the same fashion. The graduates of institutions have been influenced in certain important ways by their educational experiences in college. But their talents, skills, and abilities at the time of graduation have also been influenced by heredity, by early family and school influences, and —even during the college years—by environmental factors outside the institution. Students, in other words, are fully functioning organisms before they get to college. The purpose of college is presumably to *enhance* the student's functioning. Many people, I might add, can learn college-level material without even attending college.

A similar argument can be made about the production of knowledge in the form of scholarly research: Just because a scholar happens to be employed by a particular institution, it does not follow that the institution can take full credit for that scholar's contribution to knowledge. The scholar might have produced just as much or even more good scholarship working in a different college or university, a research institute, a private corporation, or a federal agency. Furthermore, the scholar probably already had much of the potential needed to produce the knowledge when he or she was hired by the institution.

An equally serious problem with the industrial production model concerns the assessment of quality or excellence. A fundamental purpose of any business or industry is to make a profit. Consequently, its quality or excellence must ultimately be evaluated in terms of its profitability, not its productivity. A firm may produce large quantities of goods or services but still be a total failure if it fails to show a profit. Conversely, a firm that turns a good profit can be considered of high quality even if it produces no goods or services.

What is the analog to profit in the field of education? It is unfortunate that many policy makers and even some educators are inclined to assess institutions in terms of their balance sheets rather than the quality of their teaching, research, and public service. And the interest in students is all too often in their sheer numbers (and the income those numbers bring) rather than in the quality of their learning. The analog to profit, it would seem, is not whether the institution makes or loses money but rather the quality of the education it provides and its success in facilitating faculty productivity. Thus, learning and knowledge constitute the profit of higher education.

Talent Development Model. During my twenty-five years of research on American higher education, I have been increasingly attracted to what I shall term the talent development model of higher education. Under this model, the major purpose of any institution of higher education is to develop the talents of its faculty and students to their maximum potential. In economic terms, then, higher education's purpose would be to develop the "human capital" of the society. The verb *develop* seems more appropriate than the verb *produce* (which figures so heavily in the industrial model) because it assumes that students and faculty possess certain skills and abilities before they have any contact with the institution. The institution thus represents an intervention in the life of these individuals that is designed to improve and strengthen their talents. And hence an institution's quality or excellence is assessed in terms of its ability to achieve those aims.

The closest analog outside the field of education is medicine rather than business. Elsewhere (Astin, 1977) I have suggested that students may be likened to patients, educational assessment and placement to medical diagnosis, and teaching to treatment. The object of any medical practice is, of course, to improve the condition of the patient. In the same way, education strives to improve the condition (develop the talent) of its students and faculty members. This analogy—like that of the industrial production model—has inherent limitations: Students are not ill, and the treatments in education are usually psychological rather than physical in nature. Even so, the similarities between medicine and education are far greater than the similarities between business and education, and so the analogy is appropriate.

Scholars and educators who have written about the purposes of higher education would probably be more inclined to support the talent development model than any other single model. For example, Adam Ulan (1972) says that "the goal of undergraduate education . . . must be to try to make *every* student know well—to understand thoroughly—something" (p. 31). Similarly, Jose Ortega y Gasset (1944) states that "the mission of the university . . . [is] to teach the ordinary student how to be a cultured person and a member of a profession" (p. 85). Irving Louis Horowitz (1968) sees talent development in a broader sense: "the American college . . . has as its fundamental purpose the enlightenment of the whole person and seeks to provide intellectual and ethical preparation for worldly enterprise" (pp. 138–139). Nevitt Sanford (1968) expands on this general idea: "One model badly in need of representation is that of education for the development of the whole person, not just of those peculiar skills which assure his admission to graduate school. For our own sons and daughters, we want a college that will help them become persons of character as well as of intellect" (p. 177).

Educational Equity. While talent development is certainly a fundamental and legitimate purpose of American higher education, simply endorsing this goal does not address the question of *whose* talent gets developed. Here we come to the issue of educational equity. In this book I shall argue that the achievement of equity, like the development of talent, is one of the fundamental purposes of American higher education. Equity will be defined, in part, as the provision of higher education opportunities to all persons who are capable of benefiting from them.

Equality of opportunity in higher education has traditionally been defined in terms of access (Green, 1982). That is, we are inclined to believe that the goal of equality has been attained when opportunities are made available to all who desire them and when no person is denied access to higher education because of race, gender, income, or social status. Clearly, this definition of equity has fundamental implications for the goal of talent development: The system obviously cannot develop the talent of individuals whom it excludes. Consequently, in evaluating various approaches to defining and measuring quality or excellence, I shall give preference to those that maximize the number of people availing themselves of the opportunity for higher education.

But is access by itself sufficient to ensure equality of opportunity? Given the great diversity in the faculties, facilities, and other resources of American colleges and universities, it seems necessary to expand the concept of equality of opportunity to take into account the relative quality or excellence of the opportunities provided. Thus, in reviewing various approaches to defining and measuring quality, I shall give preference to those approaches that offer the "best" opportunities to all students regardless of race, gender, income, or social status.

Benefits of Higher Education

In this chapter and throughout the rest of the book, I shall assume that the validity of any measure of excellence or quality must be assessed in light of the purposes of goals of higher education. In the preceding section I argued that higher education's ultimate social purposes are to develop student and faculty talent and to expand opportunities. But what about the benefits to the *individual*? What do individual students and faculty members get from their institutions? Three different kinds of benefits or outcomes can be distinguished: educational benefits, fringe benefits, and existential benefits. Let us consider each of these in order.

Educational Benefits. From the perspective of the student, educational benefits refer to changes in the student—in his or her intellectual capacities and skills, values, attitudes, interests, habits, mental health, and so forth—that are attributable to the college experience. Obviously, educational benefits are closely related to the talent development model. There is a close correspondence between individual and societal goals: If the higher education system succeeds in developing student and faculty talent to its maximum potential, then both the individual and society benefit. Under these conditions, excellence should be defined to reflect an institution's ability to confer significant educational benefits on its students and faculty.

Scholars of higher education have devoted more effort to studying educational benefits for students than to any other type of benefit (Astin, 1977; Bowen, 1977; Feldman and Newcomb, 1969). In these studies the basic approach is to assess the talents, skills, and attitudes of students when they first enter college and then to repeat these assessments later on, in order to ascertain the extent to which these student characteristics have changed or improved. Generally such studies show that the undergraduate experience does indeed confer significant educational benefits on most students, although the benefits vary somewhat by type of institution. (The specific results of these studies will be discussed in subsequent chapters.)

From the perspective of the faculty member, educational benefits include improvements in teaching skills or in research and scholarly skills that result from working for a particular institution. Thus, they correspond closely to what some educators call "faculty development" (Astin and others, 1974). Despite their obvious importance both to faculty members and to institutions, educational benefits to faculty members have received little attention in the scholarly literature.

Fringe Benefits. From the student's perspective, the fringe benefits of attending a given college include those post-college outcomes that are related not to the student's personal attributes but rather to the institutional credential that the student receives. Some writers call this the "sheepskin effect." Having a bachelor's degree from certain colleges confers vocational and social advantages that may have nothing to do with the graduate's personal characteristics or qualifications. In fact, many graduate and professional schools, as well as many em-

ployers, regard the candidate's undergraduate institution as one of the most important considerations in admissions or hiring. That is, a baccalaureate from one institution may constitute a much better entree to later educational or vocational opportunities than the same degree from another institution, regardless of the candidate's real talent or potential and regardless of what educational benefits may have accrued to the candidate as a result of attending that college.

Curiously enough, even though less research has been done on fringe benefits than on educational and existential benefits, we probably know as much about the factors that determine fringe benefits as we do about those that determine the other two types of outcomes, perhaps even more. The reason is that *the fringe benefits of attending a particular college or graduate or professional school are directly related to the position of that institution in the academic hierarchy* (Henson, 1980). This situation has obvious implications for equity: Opportunities for fringe benefits are *not* equally distributed in U.S. higher education. Specifically, since students from the poorest and least educated families are concentrated in institutions at the bottom of the hierarchy, relatively few such students are afforded an equal opportunity to capitalize on the fringe benefits associated with attending a prestigious institution.

The importance of fringe benefits varies tremendously from field to field. In most cases the prestige of the undergraduate college is much more important if the student aspires to attend a graduate or professional school than if that student plans to become, say, a nurse or a schoolteacher. The significance of institutional prestige also varies greatly at the graduate level. Among lawyers, for example, graduation from a prestigious law school opens more employment doors than attending a nonprestigious one. Among physicians, however, the prestige of the medical school probably makes less difference to later employment opportunities.

Fringe benefits are particularly significant to faculty members. In the case of new doctorate-recipients, the hiring institution places heavy emphasis on the prestige of the department that awarded the doctorate. Indeed, some research universities are reluctant to hire anyone who did not receive the doctorate from one of the institutions at the top of the institutional hierarchy (see Chapter Two).

Fringe benefits are also important to employed faculty members. Thus, faculty members employed by an institution at the top of the hierarchy probably find it easier to get grants from government agencies and private foundations, in part because they have contact with many highly visible scholar-colleagues who can facilitate the obtaining of funds. Further, faculty members employed by a highly prestigious institution probably have more employment opportunities elsewhere than do those working in a relatively unknown institution. It is important to note here that if faculty members' research skills benefit from their association with faculty colleagues in a prestigious institution, such an effect would be regarded as an educational benefit rather than a fringe benefit. Fringe benefits are those advantages that derive simply from association with a prestigious institution, not from any improvements in research skills that are attributable to that association.

Existential Benefits. From the student's perspective, existential benefits refer to the quality of the undergraduate experience itself, independent of any changes in competence (educational benefits) or any sheepskin effect (fringe benefits). Thus, they derive from the subjective satisfaction associated with peer contacts, extracurricular and academic involvement, recreational activities, and virtually any other experience connected with college attendance. Existential benefits are, in effect, the sum total of the student's subjective experiences while attending college. Such experiences may, of course, yield educational benefits (learning, changes in values, and so forth). But the main point here is that these experiences have value to students in and of themselves.

Educators frequently overlook the fact that the four or more years involved in a college education represent a sizable portion of the student's total lifespan. For the student, then, existential outcomes are important in themselves, not merely for what they will mean later. Research on student development (Astin, 1977) suggests that existential benefits are more dependent than either fringe or educational benefits on the character-istics of the institutional environment. In other words, institu-tions can probably exert more direct control over the existential benefits for students than over the other two types of benefits.

Existential benefits can also accrue to faculty members. Obviously, the quality of the work environment and the per-sonal satisfaction that a faculty member derives from working at a particular institution are important. Unfortunately, this area of research has been neglected; so little is known about what types of college environments confer the greatest existen-tial benefits on faculty members.

Different groups place different values on the three types of benefits. To educators, parents, policy makers, and legisla-tors, educational and fringe benefits are usually of greatest con-cern. Students, on the other hand, tend to emphasize the exis-tential benefits. Many students are more interested in their actual experiences during the undergraduate years than in the longer-term effects of these experiences on their personal devel-opment and their later careers.

The belief system that supports the institutional hierar-chy in American higher education is inclined to assume that educational benefits are proportional to fringe benefits. That is, it is widely believed that students learn more and develop their intellectual capacities more fully in an elite or highly selective institution than in a nonselective or unknown institution. Lon-gitudinal studies of student development, however, generally fail to support this belief. Thus, highly selective institutions do not appear to confer more educational benefits on their stu-dents than do moderately selective or even nonselective institu-tions (Astin, 1968b).

Throughout this book, the primary emphasis is on educa-tional benefits. The main reason for this emphasis is that edu-cational benefits relate directly to the talent development model of higher education and represent long-lasting effects. I shall also give some attention to existential benefits. But I shall say little about fringe benefits. This last decision is predicated on two considerations. First, much is already known about fringe benefits—they are directly proportional to an institution's position in the academic hierarchy. Second, fringe benefits do not appear to be closely related either to educational or to existential benefits.

Plan for the Book

In the remaining chapters I shall examine traditional ways of defining and measuring institutional excellence and suggest alternative approaches that give promise of simultaneously enhancing excellence and equity. Chapter Two summarizes four traditional views of excellence: the reputational, resources, outcomes, and content conceptions. Chapter Three reviews the talent development model, which appears to offer a better means not only for promoting educational equity but also for enhancing the overall excellence of the system. Chapter Four considers in depth the issue of educational equity, first by reviewing the many inequities in the system and then by identifying some of the policies and practices that tend to perpetuate these inequities. Chapter Five analyzes the relationship between higher education and precollegiate education, emphasizing how the hierarchical nature of the higher education system affects both the status of schools and departments of education and the selection and training of teachers and administrators for the lower schools.

Chapter Six outlines a preliminary theory, the theory of student involvement, which may be helpful in strengthening the effectiveness of our institutions and promoting the development of students' talent. Chapter Seven presents a series of proposals for specific changes in the theory and practice of higher education that are designed to (1) promote a closer correspondence between purposes and practices, (2) make the system more equitable, and (3) enhance the system's overall excellence. The book concludes (Chapter Eight) with an analysis of recent trends in the aspirations and values of students entering the higher education system. Recent value changes are seen as paralleling the values inherent in different definitions of excellence.

Chapter Two

Why Traditional Views
of Excellence
Are Counterproductive

A major theme of this book is that policy and practice in American higher education are strongly influenced by our traditional conceptions of excellence. In this chapter, I shall consider four such conceptions: the reputational view, the resources view, the outcomes view, and the content view. The advantages and disadvantages of each view will be assessed by means of three criteria: (1) Is it consistent with higher education's basic purposes? (2) Does its use promote excellence in the system as a whole? (3) Does its use promote the cause of educational equity?

Some academics, espousing what I have earlier labeled the nihilist view of excellence (Astin, 1982), argue that *no* conception of excellence is valid. These critics maintain that the quality of, say, undergraduate education simply cannot be defined or measured because the educational activities of institutions are too complex and varied, because different institutions have different objectives, because the outcomes of an undergraduate education are too subtle, because methodological problems are insurmountable, and so on.

What the nihilist view fails to recognize is that judgments about the quality of colleges and their programs are made every day. These judgments are not mere intellectual exercises; rather, they form the basis for important decisions. Students deciding where to attend college, prospective professors deciding where to apply for a job, officials of federal agencies or philanthropic foundations deciding where to award grants, and state budget officers deciding how to allocate resources among various institutions within a system—all these people are making quality assessments. Even within individual institutions, faculty members, administrators, and trustees apply judgments about quality when they set admissions policies, establish course and degree requirements, hire faculty and staff members, and develop the library and physical plant. In short, the nihilist view that quality in higher education cannot be defined or assessed is simply unrealistic. The real issues are how these assessments are made and whether they are adequate.

Let us now consider the four traditional conceptions of excellence in higher education.

Excellence as Reputation

In Chapter One, I suggested that the hierarchy in American higher education is a psychological phenomenon. There exists in the minds of educators and of many lay persons a shared set of beliefs (a folklore, if you will) about which are the best or most excellent institutions. This folklore, which forms the basis for the institutional hierarchy in American higher education, is also the source of the reputational view of excellence. In other words, the reputational view and the hierarchy are one and the same. According to the reputational view, excellence is whatever people think it is.

How does this reputational folklore get translated from a shared set of beliefs into something more concrete? Most commonly, this conversion is effected by means of reputational surveys. Opinion surveys are, of course, a popular American pastime. People are constantly being asked to give their opinions about everything from television shows to athletic teams and political candidates. In the case of higher education institutions, the usual procedure is to identify some population of knowledgeable experts (college faculty, for example) and to ask a sample from this population for their opinions about the relative excellence or quality of various institutions. What is remarkable about these surveys is the very high rate of agreement among respondents. Because of this consensus, one can get a reliable estimate of an institution's *perceived* excellence by surveying a relatively small sample of respondents. Indeed, one can also get fairly accurate reputational ratings from people in fields other than education. If you doubt this, just ask a group of your friends to list what they consider to be the ten or fifteen best institutions in the United States; the lists will be consistent not only with one another but also with the lists generated when a group of professional educators is surveyed. This fact underscores my point that the folklore about excellence in American higher education is widely shared by people from many walks of life.

Graduate School Ratings. Reputational ratings of colleges and universities have a long history in the United States. Indeed, Webster (1981) found more than one thousand references to quality ratings in higher education before 1925! In recent years the greatest attention has focused on ratings of graduate and professional schools. The most common practice is to ask representative samples of faculty members in the graduate or professional field being rated (chemistry departments, law schools, or whatever) to rate institutions in terms of their quality or excellence in that field. Each institution is rated on a multipoint scale, which uses such terms as *distinguished, strong, good, adequate, marginal,* and *not sufficient for doctoral training.* Respondents' ratings of each department or school are then averaged. By comparing these averages across institutions, one arrives at a ranking.

Perhaps the most widely publicized and discussed reputational ratings of this type are those that have been done periodically for Ph.D.-granting departments: by Cartter in 1966, by Roose and Andersen in 1970, and by Jones, Lindzey, and Coggeshall in 1982. An examination of these various ratings suggests the following conclusions:

1. Regardless of when the ratings are done, virtually the same institutions always show up at the top, and in more or less the same order. Thus, in the recent National Academy of Sciences (NAS) ratings, the fifteen top-ranked institutions were as follows (in descending order of quality): Massachusetts Institute of Technology, Harvard University, the University of California at Berkeley, Stanford University, California Institute of Technology, Yale University, the University of Chicago, Princeton University, the University of California at Los Angeles, the University of Michigan, Columbia University, Cornell University, the University of Wisconsin, the University of Illinois, and the University of Pennsylvania. In earlier decades, these same instructions appeared at the top of the reputational rankings in most fields.

2. The reliabilities of these ratings are extremely high, averaging around .98 (with 1.00 representing perfect reliability). It would thus appear that faculty members agree on which graduate or professional schools in their fields are the most excellent.

3. Although most of these reputational surveys ask the respondents to rate departments on more than one characteristic (for example, "quality of graduate faculty," "effectiveness of doctoral program"), the correlations between these ratings are extremely high ($r = .95$ or higher); this fact suggests that the folklore about the institutional hierarchy creates a halo effect. That is, an institution's overall position in the hierarchy influences the raters' judgment about each particular departmental characteristic being rated.

4. The reputational ratings are strongly and positively influenced by the raters' self-reported familiarity with the institution. Thus, in the NAS ratings, the raters' average familiarity with the institutions correlated .98 and .95, respectively, with the mean overall ratings of faculty quality and of program effectiveness. Moreover, the ratings of these two characteristics correlated .99. Again, a halo effect seems to be operating in that

a lack of familiarity with the institution is the equivalent of a low rating.

5. Reputational ratings of graduate programs are strongly influenced by the *size* of both the program and the institution. For the thirty-two different departments rated in the NAS survey, the median correlation between the mean quality rating and the number of doctorates awarded by the department during the preceding five years was .82. And the mean rating averaged across all departments correlated .62 with the number of departments rated.

6. Though the ratings given to different departments within a particular institution may differ slightly, the similarities are much more striking than the differences. At the Higher Education Research Institute, we recently conducted a factor analysis of the ratings of different departments. The results reveal a single "overall-quality" dimension that accounts for most of the variance among ratings. The fields that are most representative of the overall reputation of the institution, and their correlations with the overall-quality factor, are mathematics (.91), physics (.91), zoology (.90), political science (.89), and English (.89). The fields that are least representative are geography (.50), linguistics (.52), art history (.67), and physiology (.68).

7. Ratings are extremely consistent over time: Overall quality ratings conducted during the past three decades produce a median intercorrelation of .93. Thus, the folklore that underlies institutional reputations seems to be highly stable and resistant to change. (This issue is discussed in more detail later in this section.)

8. Multivariate studies suggest that one can get a good estimate of an institution's reputation without resorting to expensive surveys (Lawrence and Green, 1980). For example, by using a simple weighted combination of three institutional characteristics—undergraduate selectivity, per-student expenditures, and the number of doctorate-granting departments—one can arrive at a reasonably accurate estimate ($r = .83$) of an institution's overall quality as assessed in the NAS survey. Adding a fourth characteristic—the number of doctoral degrees awarded by the institution—raises the multiple correlation to over .90. Similarly, Morgan, Kearney, and Regeus (1976) obtained a mul-

tiple correlation of .91 between Cartter's quality ratings (1966) and four institutional characteristics: library size, per-student revenues, student-faculty ratios, and faculty salaries.

A particular institution's ranking among the top-rated institutions depends partly on how the ranking is done. For example, using the latest NAS ratings of the quality of graduate programs, one can change considerably the relative positions of the top twenty universities by modifying the method used to average the ratings. Table 3 shows the results of four different methods of computing the relative scores on which the ranking is based. In the first column, the ranking is based on the mean rating across all programs rated. Thus, the mean ratings for the universities of Minnesota, Wisconsin, and Washington and the universities of California at Los Angeles and at Berkeley are based on all thirty-two graduate programs that were included in the survey. By contrast, the means for the California Institute of Technology and Carnegie-Mellon University were based on only eleven and twelve programs, respectively.

The last three columns of Table 3 show the institutions that had the most programs with ratings above 4.5, 5.0, and 5.5, respectively. Using the lowest cutting score (4.50) substantially improves the rankings of several of the large public universities: the University of California at Los Angeles jumps from ninth to third place, and the University of Michigan jumps from tenth to fifth. Conversely, the technologically oriented private universities take a precipitous drop: The Massachusetts Institute of Technology drops from first place to fourteenth, and the California Institute of Technology and Carnegie-Mellon University are eliminated entirely from the top twenty. This pattern is to some extent reversed as the cutting point rises to 5.00 and 5.50. The cutting point of 5.50 (last column) does not differentiate very well after the first few institutions: Each of the last five institutions has only one program above that cutting score, and each of the next four institutions has only two programs above that score. Among other things, these results dramatize the effects of institutional size and complexity. Simply counting the number of institutions with highly rated programs clearly favors the larger and more complex universities.

Despite the considerable reshuffling of ranks demonstrated

Table 3. Four Methods of Reporting Reputational Ratings of Graduate Programs: Effects on Ranking of Top Twenty Universities.

Rank	Mean Rating Across All Programs Rated	Number of Programs with Ratings Above		
		4.50	*5.00*	*5.50*
1	MIT (5.67)	UC–Berkeley (30)	UC–Berkeley (26)	UC–Berkeley (15)
2	Harvard (5.40)	Stanford (27)	Yale (19)	MIT (13)
3	UC–Berkeley (5.39)	UCLA (26)	Harvard (18)	Harvard (12)
4	Stanford (5.18)	Yale (24)	Stanford (18)	Yale (10)
5	Cal Tech (5.17)	Michigan (23)	MIT (15)	Stanford (10)
6	Yale (5.06)	Chicago (22)	Chicago (15)	Chicago (7)
7	Chicago (5.04)	Cornell (22)	Wisconsin (14)	Princeton (7)
8	Princeton (5.02)	Columbia (21)	UCLA (13)	Cal Tech (5)
9	UCLA (4.83)	Harvard (21)	Princeton (13)	Wisconsin (4)
10	Michigan (4.79)	Princeton (21)	Michigan (11)	Michigan (4)
11	Columbia (4.79)	Wisconsin (20)	Columbia (11)	Columbia (2)
12	Cornell (4.78)	Illinois (19)	Cornell (10)	Illinois (2)
13	Wisconsin (4.66)	Pennsylvania (18)	Illinois (9)	Minnesota (2)
14	Illinois (4.66)	MIT (17)	Pennsylvania (9)	NYU (2)
15	Pennsylvania (4.62)	Texas–Austin (14)	Cal Tech (7)	Cornell (1)
16	Texas–Austin (4.44)	Washington (14)	Minnesota (5)	Texas–Austin (1)
17	Carnegie–Mellon (4.38)	N. Carolina (12)	Texas–Austin (5)	Carnegie–Mellon (1)
18	Washington (4.33)	Northwestern (10)	UC–San Diego (5)	Virginia (1)
19	UC–San Diego (4.32)	Indiana U. (10)	NYU (4)	U. Pittsburgh (1)
20	Brown (4.28)	Minnesota (10)	Washington (4)	—

Note: Program ratings are based on ratings of the quality of the faculty, done on a six-point scale: distinguished (6), strong (5), good (4), adequate (3), marginal (2), insufficient (1).

Only universities with at least ten graduate programs are included. If all universities were included, Rockefeller University (with five programs) would be ranked second in the overall mean rating, tied for twentieth in the number of programs above 5.00, and ranked eleventh in the number of programs above 5.50; the University of California–San Francisco (with three programs) would be ranked ninth in the overall mean rating.

in Table 3, the composition of all four top-twenty lists is about the same. This consistency is remarkable, considering that 228 universities were included in the ratings. Thus, of the twenty top-ranked institutions in the first column, all but three (Brown, Carnegie-Mellon, and UC–San Diego) are included in the second column, all but two (Brown and Carnegie-Mellon) in the third column, and all but four (Brown, Pennsylvania, UCLA, and Washington) in the last column. Further, the halo effects that operate in such ratings are dramatized by the fact that all but two of the top-twenty institutions in mean overall quality rating (first column of Table 3) are also among the twenty top-ranked institutions in terms of raters' familiarity with the institutions. And the rankings of the top twenty on both dimensions—familiarity and overall quality—are nearly identical. The converse is true at the lower end of the rankings. Thus, of the twenty universities which were the least familiar to the raters, thirteen are also among the bottom twenty in terms of the overall quality of the faculty.

In short, while the relative position of top-ranked institutions can be altered considerably by using different methods to calculate the ratings, virtually the same institutions appear at the top of the list no matter what computational method is used. How stable are these ratings of graduate programs? In a comprehensive analysis of the various ratings of graduate programs that have been done since Hughes's original study (1925) was conducted some sixty years ago, Webster (1983) notes that, of the twenty universities that were top-ranked in Hughes's survey, sixteen are among the top twenty in the 1982 NAS survey of graduate programs. Similarly, of the twenty-five top-ranked institutions in Cartter's 1966 survey, all but two are also among the twenty-five top-ranked institutions in the 1982 NAS survey. And fourteen of these twenty-three overlapping institutions are within three ranks of each other, even though almost two decades separate the two surveys. Clearly, the top of the institutional hierarchy in American higher education changes very little over time.

Undergraduate Ratings. Reputational ratings of undergraduate programs are much rarer than ratings of graduate and professional schools, probably because of the much larger number of undergraduate institutions. The results of those undergraduate ratings that have been done, however, are strikingly similar to the results of graduate and professional ratings, with some interesting exceptions.

The most recent and comprehensive rating was carried out in 1980 (Astin and Solmon, 1981; Solmon and Astin, 1981). Faculty members in six representative liberal arts fields—biology, chemistry, economics, English, history, and sociology—were asked to rate undergraduate departments in their fields according to six criteria: overall quality of undergraduate education, scholarly and professional accomplishment of faculty, faculty commitment to undergraduate teaching, innovativeness of curriculum and pedagogy, preparation of students for graduate or professional school, and preparation of students for employment after college.

A factor analysis of these ratings showed that, in reality, only two dimensions of quality were being rated. The first of these, labeled "scholarly excellence of faculty," was most closely associated with scholarly and professional accomplishment of faculty, but three of the other six rating criteria were also closely associated with this factor: preparation of students for graduate or professional school, preparation of students for employment after college, and overall quality of undergraduate education. The strong association between this last rating criterion and this particular factor suggests that academicians' judgments of the overall quality of an undergraduate department are heavily influenced by their perceptions of the scholarly accomplishments of the faculty in that department.

The second dimension of quality, labeled "commitment to teaching," was associated most closely with faculty commitment to undergraduate teaching and, to a lesser extent, with innovativeness of curriculum and pedagogy.

Further analyses indicated that differences in quality ratings from one academic field to another were trivial. In other words, the same undergraduate institutions tended to appear at the top of the lists in all six fields. Perhaps, if the ratings had covered a larger number of disciplines, some fields would not have followed this pattern. Be that as it may, the similarities across the six representative disciplines suggest that the halo effect operates just as strongly for undergraduate as for graduate ratings.

What types of institutions are viewed as having high-quality undergraduate programs? Their most striking characteristic is their high selectivity (the median correlation of selectivity with mean ratings of the overall quality of undergraduate education across the six fields was .73), a finding that confirms the validity of selectivity as an index of an institution's position in the hierarchy. Institutional size is also strongly related to ratings of overall quality, but the relationships are complex. If the institution is highly selective, the relationship is positive; if nonselective, negative (Snyder, 1983). Apparently, large enrollment size is an asset for a selective institution, but a drawback for a nonselective institution.

Indeed, one can accurately estimate the overall quality rating received by an undergraduate institution using a weighted combination of selectivity and size. The median multiple correlation between overall quality and these two variables (weighted appropriately) is .91 across the six fields.

What do these findings tell us about undergraduate reputational ratings? One clue comes from their very high reliability (see, for example, Cartter, 1966). Why is it that academicians from all parts of the nation hold such similar views about departments in hundreds of undergraduate institutions across the country? Clearly, very few of these faculty raters are familiar with more than a handful of undergraduate institutions. The most plausible explanation is that academicians share a folklore that closely resembles the folklore governing bright students' choices of institutions. (When students act on these choices, of course, they generate what I have called selectivity.) While most academics are probably aware of the relative size of various institutions, they are unlikely to have any direct knowledge of institutional selectivity. But they are tuned into the folklore about the hierarchy of institutions, which corresponds very closely to institutional selectivity. Thus, a faculty rater may regard both Harvard University and Swarthmore College as high-quality institutions but may, in his ratings, give a slight edge to Harvard, simply because of its much larger size ("more of a good thing"). Larger institutions are, of course, much more likely to have graduate programs than are small institutions. The same faculty rater may regard two nonselective institutions—say, a state college and a small sectarian liberal arts college—as equally mediocre because of low selectivity but may give a higher rating of *undergraduate* quality to the private college simply because of its small size. This line of reasoning is consistent with the fact that, in the academic hierarchy, highly selective and relatively large institutions (such as Ivy League schools) are at the top, whereas large but nonselective institutions (community colleges, for example) are at the bottom.

Commitment to undergraduate teaching is also closely related to selectivity (the median correlation across the six fields was .60) and even more closely related to size ($-.72$), though in this case the size relationship is straightforward, unlike the complex relation between overall quality and size. The smaller the institution, the better the rating, regardless of selectivity. Nonetheless, selectivity remains a key consideration. Of the twenty institutions rated highest on commitment to undergraduate teaching, shown in Table 4, fifteen are among the twenty most selective institutions in the country. There is no good reason to think that the faculties of these liberal arts colleges are any more committed to undergraduate teaching than are the faculties of the next-highest-rated group of liberal arts colleges. The only apparent difference is that the latter are slightly less selective than the institutions listed in Table 4.

Table 4 shows the twenty institutions ranked at the top with respect to overall undergraduate quality. Notice that, in addition to a number of small, highly selective liberal arts colleges, this list includes a number of research universities and that their ranking is almost identical to their ranking with respect to the judged quality of their graduate education (Table 3). When the raters are judging faculty commitment to undergraduate teaching rather than overall quality of the undergraduate program, however, all of the research universities disappear from the list and are replaced by much smaller, highly selective

Table 4. Reputational Ratings of Undergraduate Quality:
Top-Twenty Institutions on Two Criteria.
(Mean Ratings Across Six Disciplines)

Rank	Overall Quality of Undergraduate Education	Faculty Commitment to Undergraduate Teaching
1	Cal Tech[a]	Reed
2	MIT[b]	Swarthmore
3	Harvard	Oberlin
4	Chicago	Harvey Mudd
5	Stanford	Carleton
6	Princeton	Haverford
7	Yale	Wesleyan
8	Harvey Mudd[c]	Grinnell
9	Oberlin	Bryn Mawr
10	Swarthmore	Smith
11	UC–Berkeley	Mount Holyoke
12	Reed	Amherst
13	Haverford	Wellesley
14	Dartmouth	Bennington
15	Cornell	Williams
16	Johns Hopkins	Colby
17	Bryn Mawr	Middlebury
18	Carleton	Dartmouth
19	Columbia	Pomona College
20	Wesleyan	Bowdoin College

Note: The six disciplines are biology, chemistry, economics, English, history, and sociology.

[a] Based on only two fields (biology and chemistry).

[b] Based on only three fields (biology, chemistry, and economics).

[c] Based on only one field (chemistry).

Source: Unpublished data, Higher Education Research Institute.

liberal arts colleges. Apparently, academics believe that faculty members in highly selective liberal arts colleges are more committed to teaching undergraduates than are faculty members in major research universities. This belief has a real basis in fact, as is evidenced by a recent survey (Green and others, 1983), which found that undergraduates enrolled in liberal arts colleges are much more likely than those enrolled in universities to report frequent contacts with faculty and less likely to complain that faculty members neglect their teaching responsibilities.

The high degree of overlap between undergraduate and

graduate quality ratings can be demonstrated from another perspective. Ten research universities were highly rated on at least one of the six criteria of undergraduate quality in at least four of the six fields. (Six of the ten actually received high ratings in all six fields.) All ten of these universities are also included among the top twenty with respect to the overall quality of their graduate programs (Table 3, first column). As a matter of fact, none of them ranks lower than thirteenth in the graduate program ratings. Moreover, the only reason why two of the top thirteen in overall graduate ratings are not among the top-rated undergraduate institutions in at least four of the six disciplines rated is that they do not offer majors in all those disciplines. One of these institutions, the Massachusetts Institute of Technology, is among the top-rated undergraduate institutions in all three departments where it offers majors (economics, chemistry, and biology). The other institution, the California Institute of Technology, was also top-rated in both the fields where it offers a major (biology and chemistry).

Are undergraduate quality ratings as stable over time as ratings of graduate programs? There are no comparable surveys of undergraduate quality that go as far back as the Hughes (1925) rating of graduate programs, but indirect evidence suggests that the reputations of undergraduate institutions do remain stable. For example, my estimates of selectivity (Astin, 1965), based on data collected in 1961, show that thirteen of the twenty-five most selective institutions were undergraduate liberal arts colleges. All but two of these institutions were also among the eighteen undergraduate colleges receiving the highest ratings in the 1980 survey (Solmon and Astin, 1981). One of the two, Harvey Mudd College, failed to make the list simply because only one of its departments (chemistry) was ranked in the Solmon-Astin survey. And Harvey Mudd's was the top-ranked undergraduate chemistry department. The other institution that failed to make the list of top undergraduate programs was the Webb Institute of Naval Architecture, a highly specialized institution enrolling fewer than 100 students that does not offer degrees in any of the six fields covered by the Solmon-Astin survey. In other words, one could have predicted the undergraduate colleges that would turn out to have top-ranked undergraduate programs in 1980 simply by knowing their selectivity rank nearly twenty years earlier. Again we have strong evidence here that reputational rankings are highly stable over relatively long periods.

This analysis of reputational ratings at the undergraduate and graduate levels leads to the following conclusions. First, reputational ratings of the overall quality of graduate and undergraduate programs produce very similar listings of top-ranked institutions. Moreover, both these lists are very stable over a relatively long time. These findings underscore the fact that beliefs about the institutional hierarchy in American higher education affect our perceptions of both graduate and undergraduate programs and are highly resistant to change.

Second, institutions whose programs or departments are highly rated in one field tend to receive high ratings in other fields. The differences in reputations by field or program are less impressive than the similarities. This finding suggests the existence of a halo effect in reputational ratings of quality.

And third, at the graduate level, an institution's reputation tends to be constant, regardless of the specific quality being rated (excellence of faculty, excellence of graduate program, and so on). At the undergraduate level as well, ratings of different qualities tend to merge into a single overall quality dimension with one exception: Faculty commitment to undergraduate teaching is judged somewhat independently of overall quality. Institutions whose undergraduate programs are perceived to be outstanding in this regard are highly selective but *small* rather than large. In other words, large size is an asset for graduate ratings and for all undergraduate ratings except faculty commitment to teaching, for which large size appears to be a drawback. Selectivity, however, is a strong positive correlate of all types of quality ratings.

Excellence as Resources

The reputational view of institutional excellence is frequently criticized on the grounds that it is too subjective. Educators and policy makers who want more objective indicators are inclined to embrace the resources conception. For instance, resource measures are the ones most favored by institutional accrediting agencies.

The four basic types of resources in higher education are the staff, physical facilities, students, and money. The first three types can, of course, be acquired with money, particularly physical facilities, which can be directly purchased. Thus, for simplicity, it is reasonable to consider three different types of resources: personnel, students, and financial resources. Faculty members constitute the principal personnel resource, and the quality of the faculty is assessed by measures such as the proportion with doctorates, publication rates, and other indications of scholarly visibility. Student quality is typically assessed in terms of performance on standardized tests (the selectivity measure discussed earlier). Physical plants are evaluated in terms of the number and quality of classrooms, library resources, laboratories, residential facilities, and so on. Fiscal resources are assessed by a variety of measures, including endowment, per-student expenditures, student-faculty ratios, average class size, and faculty salaries.

Many of these resource measures have become popular indicators of institutional excellence. Research universities, for example, commonly gauge the quality of their faculty members in terms of how many have been elected to membership in the National Academy of Sciences or have won Guggenheim Fellowships, Nobel Prizes, and other awards given in recognition of outstanding scientific or scholarly contributions. Almost all baccalaureate-granting institutions are interested in raising their selectivity levels and in enrolling larger numbers of National Merit Scholars and other highly able students. And, of course, all institutions continually seek additional financial resources. The *Chronicle of Higher Education* annually publishes detailed information on institutional endowments on a college-by-college basis.

U.S. higher education institutions vary remarkably on almost all resource measures. For example, the proportion of faculty members with doctorates ranges from less than 40 percent to more than 90 percent. Average faculty salaries range from about $15,000 to more than $40,000. At the most selective institutions, students in the *lowest* 5 percent in academic ability have higher test scores than the *highest* 5 percent of students in the least selective institutions (Astin, 1971). A few institutions enroll several hundred Merit Scholars; most institutions enroll none.

The variations in financial resources are just as remarkable. Perhaps the single best measure of an institution's financial position is the amount of money it spends on its educational program. For the purpose of this discussion, I have identified six different categories of expenditure: instruction, academic support (includes libraries, audiovisual services, and academic computing), student services, administration, physical plant, and research. With the exception of research, these categories account for what are commonly referred to as educational expenditures.

Table 5 shows the per-student expenditures for each of these measures by institutional selectivity level. For each measure, expenditures increase at each step up in selectivity. The institutions at the top level spend twice as much on student services as do the institutions at the bottom; three times as much on instruction, administration, and physical plant; and nearly four times as much on academic support. By far the largest discrepancy appears with respect to research funds: The most selective institutions outspend the least selective ones by better than fifty to one.

As might be expected, resource measures are strongly correlated with reputational ratings. Thus, per-student educational expenditures correlate .65 with the overall NAS rating of graduate programs and .62 with undergraduate quality rankings. Resource measures are also strongly correlated with each other: Selectivity correlates .65 with per-student educational expenditures, .64 with per-student endowment, and .55 with research expenditures. The correlations among resource measures are even greater when computed separately for different types of institutions (research universities, liberal arts colleges, and so forth).

As these strong intercorrelations suggest, the reputational and resources conceptions of excellence tend to be mutually reinforcing. That is, if the reputational folklore views a particu-

Table 5. **Per-Student Expenditures of Institutions at Different Selectivity Levels.**

Selectivity Level (Mean SAT Composite[a] for Entering Freshmen)	Number of Institutions	Instruction	Academic Support	Student Services	Administration	Physical Plant	Research
1300 or higher	14	$5,865	$1,303	$625	$1,666	$1,783	$4,637
1225–1299	20	4,663	1,178	667	1,174	1,262	3,112
1150–1224	47	4,471	1,016	541	1,711	1,299	1,816
1075–1149	78	3,008	628	346	833	808	1,447
1000–1074	215	2,797	580	335	696	688	1,043
925–999	310	2,271	464	316	567	564	494
850–924	673	2,017	403	304	563	527	223
775–849	1,106	1,813	318	324	548	469	86
below 775	227	1,807	360	338	626	545	84
All Institutions	2,690	2,343	472	338	655	611	585

[a] ACT scores have been converted to SAT equivalents (see Astin, Christian, and Henson, 1978).

Source: Higher Education Research Institute and National Center for Education Statistics.

lar institution as being excellent, this view gets reinforced by the fact that the institution also has highly able students, a highly paid and prestigious faculty, large endowments, and other financial resources.

The process of selective admissions represents another way in which resources enhance reputation, and vice versa. Institutions that occupy high positions in the hierarchy naturally attract relatively large numbers of student applicants. Through selective admissions, whereby only those applicants with high test scores and outstanding high school records are admitted, the institution comes to be regarded as a kind of exclusive club, and membership becomes a badge of honor. This process feeds on itself: As the institution's admissions policies become more selective, its reputation is enhanced, and ever larger numbers of students seek admission to the club. In the minds of many educators and lay persons, selective admissions policies themselves are directly associated with excellence. An "excellent" institution, in their view, is one that "maintains high standards," and high standards in turn mean highly selective admissions policies. Indeed, about the only substantive recommendation concerning higher education made by the National Commission on Excellence in Education in its final report, *A Nation at Risk,* is that colleges and universities raise their admissions standards.

The tendency of educators to equate academic excellence with high admissions standards is widespread. For example, in *Meeting the Need for Quality: Action in the South,* the Southern Regional Education Board (1983) recommends that "states and institutions . . . raise admissions standards to improve quality." As evidence of some progress in this direction, the report notes that "the University of Texas at Austin now requires a minimum SAT score of 1100 for applicants who are not in the upper 25 percent of their high school class."

The supposedly close connection between selective admissions policies and excellence, as revealed in an institution's reputation or resources, helps to explain some of the terms usually heard in discussions of excellence. College faculty members and administrators are fond of such phrases as *academic excellence* and *academic standards.* Just as stringent admissions standards are regarded as necessary to *maintaining academic standards,* so open admissions policies are seen as a *threat to academic excellence.* The resources view of excellence is fundamental to such beliefs, in that the excellence or quality of the institution is identified with the excellence or quality of the *people* it admits.

No discussion of the resources view of excellence would be complete without some consideration of institutional size. As we have already seen, size is a major factor in quality ratings of both graduate and undergraduate programs. Other things being equal, faculty members in most graduate fields and certainly the administrators of most research universities are growth-oriented. To a certain extent this orientation reflects a national belief that bigger is better. Of course, bigness carries certain advantages. It means larger libraries, nationally known athletic teams, a greater variety of curricular options, and departments large enough to reach the critical mass believed by many scholars to be essential for effective research and scholarly study. Growth in size also tends to elevate the institution's position in the hierarchy (provided, of course, that it is at least moderately selective). Finally, the formula funding that has historically supported public institutions provides a natural incentive for growth, since increases in revenues normally outpace increases in the costs associated with growth.

The importance that institutions place on growth and on the acquisition of resources—in the form of bright students, prestigious faculty, and money—cannot be overestimated. These values are illustrated in the following biographical note about a university president who was one of the major speakers at the 1983 annual meeting program of the Middle States Association of Colleges and Schools (1983, p. 3), one of the regional accrediting associations: "Under his guidance the university's endowment has more than doubled, its percentage of yield has been the highest in the nation; SAT scores of its entering freshmen have increased by 120 points. . . . Its annual fund raising has increased more than 300 percent; numerous new programs have been introduced; several distinguished persons have joined its teaching faculty; and the net financial worth of its board has increased by more than three billion."

The symbiotic relationship between the reputational and resources views of excellence should also be borne in mind. That is, college faculties and administrators realize that recruiting more nationally visible faculty scholars and more National Merit Scholars and other highly able students will enhance the reputation of their institution. At the same time, an institution that can strengthen its reputation probably improves its ability to attract faculty members, students, and money. This close interplay between reputation and resources explains why measures based on the two conceptions are so strongly correlated.

One major appeal of the resources view lies in its consistency with today's dominant values. We live in a highly acquisitive society, in which the quality of life and the worth of the individual are often equated with material possessions. The various news media devote substantial time and space to discussions of the economy, most political candidates these days stress economic issues in their campaigning, and publications such as the *Chronicle of Higher Education* regularly print articles and statistical summaries related to the public and private funding of higher education. Little wonder, then, that so many persons equate quality in higher education with institutional resources.

Excellence as Outcomes

An increasingly popular approach to assessing the quality of undergraduate institutions is to focus on outcomes. Proponents of the outcomes view argue that the ultimate test of an institution's quality lies neither in its reputation nor in its resources but rather in the quality of its products. Some of the earliest work taking this approach looked at such results as the proportion of an institution's baccalaureate-recipients who are listed in *Who's Who,* the proportion who win graduate fellowships (Knapp and Greenbaum, 1953), and the proportion who go on to get doctorates (Knapp and Goodrich, 1952). Other outcome measures that have been used from time to time include the persistence rates of an institution's undergraduates, the lifetime earnings of its alumni (Solmon, 1975), and alumni's ratings of their undergraduate experience (Wise, Hengstler, and Braskamp, 1981).

The outcomes view has a special appeal to faculty members and administrators because most outcomes measures, like most resource measures, turn out to be highly related to reputational measures and, ultimately, to an institution's position in the hierarchy. Thus, institutions at the top of the hierarchy—which tend to have good reputations, selective admissions, large endowments, and highly paid faculties—also tend to have low attrition rates and to produce large proportions of alumni who earn doctorates, make good salaries, and get listed in *Who's Who*. Again, the close relationship of these three types of measures probably gives added validity, in the eyes of many academics, to the three traditional views of excellence discussed so far (reputational, resources, outcomes).

One of the most ambitious applications of the outcomes approach is New York's ten-year plan for the development of postsecondary education (University of the State of New York, 1982). Under the goal of "Excellence," the plan calls for improving institutional performance with respect to several output measures: retention, student achievement, employment of graduates, and entry of graduates into graduate and professional schools (pp. 11–12).

First, a word of clarification: Many educators, and particularly some of the regional accrediting associations, interpret the term *outcome* as anonymous with institutional impact. Marcus, Leone, and Goldberg (1983), for example, argue that "the strongest indicator of student learning is the relative future success of program graduates" (p. 50). But in this discussion, the term *outcome* simply refers to some performance measure: retention rates, alumni achievements, and so on. No causal connection between the outcome and the institutional environment can be inferred.

A simple example will serve to illustrate this point. If the graduates of, say, Harvard make more money than the graduates of some nonselective college at the bottom of the hierarchy, is it reasonable to attribute this difference to the differential environments of the two institutions? Clearly, students who enroll at Harvard tend to be more academically able and to come from more affluent and educated backgrounds than do students entering a nonselective institution. Given these initial differences in student characteristics, we would expect Harvard graduates to end up with higher earnings than would the graduates of the other institution, even if the college environments had identical effects. Just because institutions differ on some outcome measure like alumni earnings or retention rates, it does not follow that these differences were caused by the different environments of the institutions.

The same ambiguity arises in talking about faculty outcomes. Let us again take the example of Harvard versus a nonselective college. If faculty members at Harvard have higher publication rates than faculty members at the nonselective college, is it legitimate to assume that this difference is caused by the differential environments of the two institutions? Clearly, Harvard has both the resources and the desire to recruit faculty members who will publish a great deal. Therefore, the higher publication rates of its faculty cannot automatically be attributed to the environment at Harvard. In short, one cannot conclude that differential institutional environments cause differential faculty outcomes simply by looking at the outcomes.

Before leaving this discussion, I should note that outcome measures are the most common means of assessing the quality of elementary and secondary schools. Most public school districts in the country regularly administer standardized achievement tests to their students, and the mean scores of these tests are often published in the local newspaper on a school-by-school basis. These outcome measures are then used to make judgments about the comparative quality of the schools. Presumably, the schools whose students make the highest average scores are the best and, conversely, the schools whose students make the lowest average scores are the worst. Whether the high-scoring schools can actually take credit for the good performance of their students, and the low-scoring schools can be blamed for their students' relatively poor performance, is another question. Given that the performance levels of students may already be different when they first enter the different schools, it stands to reason that their performance levels will differ after they have been in the school for a while, even if the different schools have exactly the same effect on achievement. The problems that arise in interpreting outcome measures are discussed in more detail later in this chapter.

Excellence as Content

The final traditional conception of institutional excellence may be termed the content view, which defines the quality or excellence of an institution in terms of what it teaches. Despite the supposed diversity of American higher education, our notions of what constitutes excellent content are remarkably homogeneous. They are epitomized by Horowitz's statement (1968) that "the American college is, in the main, defined and circumscribed by the phrase 'liberal arts' " (pp. 138–139). Believing that the highest-quality education is one that exposes undergraduates to the liberal arts and sciences, most institutions have adopted some kind of core curriculum that comprises a predetermined set of courses or distributional requirements covering the traditional disciplinary categories of the arts, humanities, social sciences, and natural sciences. The core liberal arts curriculum has many variants. (For an illuminating discussion of these variants, see Levine, 1978.)

Do institutions at various positions in the hierarchy emphasize different aspects of the curriculum? To explore this issue, the Higher Education Research Institute tabulated separately, by institutional selectivity level, the proportions of bachelor's degrees awarded in various fields in 1981–82. As Table 6 shows, institutions at different levels in the hierarchy do differ markedly in the kinds of degrees awarded. Basically, the most selective institutions award a disproportionate share of degrees in engineering, physical sciences and mathematics, and biological sciences. These institutions also award relatively large proportions of degrees in English, history, political science, and other social sciences. The institutions at the highest selectivity level award slightly smaller proportions of degrees in these latter fields than do institutions at the next-highest selectivity level, a finding that is probably explained by the concentration of technological institutions, which award relatively few degrees

Table 6. Baccalaureate Degree Fields by Selectivity Level, 1981–82.

Selectivity Level (Mean SAT Composite[a] for Entering Freshmen)	Number of Institutions	Percentage of 1981–82 Bachelor's Degrees Awarded in										
		Engineering	Physical Science and Math	Biological Science	English	History and Political Science	Other Social Science	Arts and Humanities	Education	Business	Other Professional Fields	All Other Fields
1300 or more	13	27.0	13.8	8.2	4.4	11.8	14.5	11.1	0.2	1.6	0.5	6.8
1225–1299	20	19.3	10.7	8.2	7.2	14.0	17.7	11.3	0.1	4.9	1.1	5.5
1150–1224	47	14.7	7.4	6.4	7.0	13.2	18.2	11.3	0.8	6.2	1.4	13.4
1075–1149	77	9.3	6.9	7.7	5.0	8.8	18.3	14.8	2.9	13.5	2.0	10.8
1000–1074	210	7.3	5.0	5.7	3.7	6.4	13.4	13.5	7.4	20.0	5.3	12.3
925–999	277	4.3	3.5	4.6	2.7	4.2	10.4	10.1	12.5	25.2	7.2	15.5
850–924	513	4.4	2.4	3.1	2.2	2.6	8.2	22.2	12.8	22.3	5.5	14.2
775–849	236	2.1	2.8	3.5	2.1	2.6	8.8	12.0	20.6	26.5	4.9	14.1
Below 775	127	4.1	3.6	4.1	1.8	3.4	9.3	7.5	20.3	27.2	3.7	15.1
All Institutions	1,520	5.4	3.7	4.3	2.8	4.3	10.5	15.0	12.7	22.2	5.1	13.8

Note: Percentages may not sum to exactly 100.00 across rows because of rounding errors.

[a] ACT scores have been converted to SAT equivalents (see Astin, Christian, and Henson, 1978).

Source: National Center for Education Statistics and the Higher Education Research Institute.

in English and the social sciences, at the top level. The pattern for the least selective institutions is very different. They award a disproportionately large number of degrees in professional fields, especially education and business, and relatively few in engineering and the liberal arts.

Thus, the most prestigious institutions emphasize the traditional liberal arts, especially the sciences. The only exceptions are the technologically oriented universities such as the California Institute of Technology and the Massachusetts Institute of Technology, which award very large proportions of degrees in engineering. As a matter of fact, engineering is the only professional (that is, non-liberal-arts) field associated with a high position in the institutional hierarchy. One possible explanation for this association is that such institutions receive large amounts of federal research support and that their admissions policies have traditionally been among the most selective in the country. Otherwise, the most selective institutions would appear to offer very few opportunities for degrees in professional fields, especially in education: Less than 1 percent of the baccalaureates conferred by the eighty most selective institutions (those in the top-three selectivity groups) are awarded in the field of education! (The implications of this are discussed more fully in Chapter Five.) Indeed, for both education and business, one finds an almost perfect inverse hierarchical pattern: The more selective the institution, the fewer undergraduate degrees it awards in these fields.

The curricular offerings at some American colleges and universities have changed markedly over the years, and the institutional hierarchy probably had a great deal to do with these changes. During the immediate post–World War II period, the U.S. higher education system included a substantial number of institutions whose curricula differed considerably from the liberal arts pattern: teachers colleges, agricultural and mechanical colleges, and institutions emphasizing art, music, religion, and other specialized or technical fields. During the late 1950s and early 1960s, however, many of these institutions began to broaden their curricular offerings and to introduce components of the liberal arts. Perhaps the most dramatic change occurred in the teachers colleges. Back in the 1950s there were more than 200 teachers colleges in the United States; today there are practically none. Most of them have become so-called state universities with traditional undergraduate liberal arts requirements. Even some of the more elite technological universities "liberalized" their curricula, and at least two noted technological institutions—Rice and Carnegie—changed into general-purpose universities and dropped "Institute of Technology" from their names.

As for the teachers colleges, most of them—unhappy with their relatively low position in their state's institutional hierarchy—turned away from teacher training, recruited young Ph.D.s from the more prestigious graduate schools, and established large undergraduate liberal arts programs and graduate programs. As state universities, they have continued to cut back on their teacher-training programs and to concentrate their resources on the development of large liberal arts and graduate programs, in an effort to dissociate themselves from the teachers college image.

The content view of excellence has important implications for teaching theory, method, and practice. I shall defer a discussion of this issue until Chapter Six.

Evaluation of Traditional Conceptions

As indicated at the beginning of the chapter, I shall now evaluate each of the four traditional conceptions of excellence— the reputational, resources, outcomes, and content views—in terms of three criteria: (1) Are they consistent with the purposes of the institution; that is, do they reflect what we really mean by excellence? (2) Does their use promote excellence in the system as a whole? (3) Does their use promote the cause of educational equity? Let us consider each of these questions in turn.

Are They Consistent with Institutional Purposes? In Chapter One, I argued that the principal purpose of academic institutions is to develop talent. How well do the traditional concepts of excellence reflect this fundamental institutional purpose? Can we assume that an institution that is excellent in conventional terms is also excellent in its capacity to develop student and faculty talent? The reputational view presents the biggest stumbling block here: Just because people *believe* that an institution is excellent, it does not necessarily follow that the institution is any more effective in developing talent than a less prestigious institution. A more plausible case can be made for the resources view: It is reasonable to assume that a student will be able to develop his or her talent more fully in an environment having a lot of other bright students, excellent physical facilities, and a prestigious and highly paid faculty. Similarly, it is reasonable to assume that a faculty member's scholarly productivity will be enhanced if he or she associates with other highly productive scholars and has access to large libraries, good laboratory facilities, and outstanding graduate students. Such reasoning constitutes the rationale for "centers of excellence," which are believed to foster not only the academic development of the student but also the productivity of faculty. Unfortunately, this belief receives little support from the few studies that have tested the center-of-excellence concept. Institutions with highly able students, large libraries, highly paid faculty, and large per-student expenditures do not seem to foster any greater degree of intellectual development than do institutions without such resources (Astin, 1968b). Economist Howard Bowen, who has reviewed much of this literature (Bowen, 1977, 1980, 1981a), notes that the wide-ranging variation in the amounts of money institutions invest in their educational programs is not associated with any differences in educational payoffs. Bowen (1981a) concludes: "This apparent randomness [in educational expenditures per student] is tolerated . . . because no one knows with any certainty the relationship between money spent and true educational outcomes" (p. 27).

On the other hand, institutional selectivity—the dominant factor in an institution's prestige and resources—does appear to have a significant influence on the noncognitive aspects of student development. In particular, attending a selective institution seems to foster greater political liberalism and hedonism and to weaken students' conventional religious beliefs. This may well be a peer-group effect, given that the highly selective institutions enroll larger proportions of politically liberal and nonreligious students than does almost any other type of institution (Astin and others, 1983). Selectivity also appears to enhance student retention, but the effect is entirely attributable to the much lower retention rates of (relatively nonselective) community colleges. In other words, once the effect of community colleges on student persistence is discounted, selectivity bears no consistent relationship to retention.

Size—another important factor in institutional prestige and resources—also has some significant effects, most notably on students' involvement in campus life (Astin, 1977). Involvement, in turn, appears to be a critical factor in developing students' talent (see Chapter Six). Students attending small institutions are much more likely than those attending large ones to interact with the faculty, to get involved in campus government, to participate in athletics, to become involved in honors programs, and to be verbally assertive in the classroom. The only exception to this general pattern is that students at large institutions are more likely than those at small institutions to get involved in demonstrations. (Possibly this represents a greater sense of alienation among students at larger institutions.) Large institutions also tend to have either neutral or negative effects on student satisfaction, with one exception: Students at large institutions tend to be more satisfied than students at small institutions with the "variety of courses offered." These findings suggest an important fact about large institutions: Even though they may offer more courses and a greater variety of organizations and extracurricular activities, the probability that a given student will get involved in such activities is lower at large institutions. In short, the evidence does not support the notion that large institutions are more excellent in the educational sense.

So far I have been talking about educational benefits. What about existential benefits? Do institutional resources have any significant effect on students' actual experiences in college? The environments of highly selective colleges, compared with less selective ones, tend to be highly competitive academically. In addition, their students are more likely to be highly independent and to engage more frequently in hedonistic behavior. The administrative policies of selective institutions tend to be permissive with respect to almost all aspects of student conduct except cheating, which is treated somewhat more severely in selective institutions than it is in nonselective ones. Relatively nonselective colleges, on the other hand, tend to give greater emphasis to cohesiveness among students, intercollegiate athletics, and religious activity (Astin, 1968a). Clearly, the existential outcomes experienced by students attending selective institutions differ from those of students attending nonselective institutions. Except for greater academic competitiveness, however, the existential benefits the selective schools confer seem in no way more excellent than those conferred by nonselective institutions.

As for institutional size, students attending large institutions typically see their schools as showing relatively little concern for the student. In addition, these students say that they are unlikely to know their instructors well, that both instructors and students are less personally involved in classroom activities, and that the environment is relatively permissive, emphasizes students' social life, and encourages snobbishness. By way of contrast, students attending smaller institutions are usually on more familiar terms both with faculty members and with other students and see both faculty members and students as being more involved in the classroom experience (Pace, 1984). If anything, then, smaller institutions would seem to confer more excellent existential benefits than larger ones (Snyder, 1983).

And what of the outcomes and content views of excellence? Are these conceptions of excellence consistent with institutional purposes? As mentioned earlier, one is not justified in assuming that any given college outcome (whether it be high retention rates, high earnings after graduation, or whatever) is attributable to the institutional environment. Indeed, studies of Ph.D. productivity show that some of the institutions with high Ph.D. outputs (that is, relatively large proportions of graduates who go on to earn doctorates) should actually have higher outputs than they do, considering the abilities and interests of the students they admit (Astin, 1962). In other words, a high or low output cannot, by itself, be taken as an indication of an institution's educational effectiveness. Rather, such output measures can only be interpreted in light of some kind of input measure that reflects the potentials that students bring with them to college. The necessity for interpreting output measures in this way is underscored by the extreme diversity of student bodies entering different types of higher education institutions (Astin and others, 1983).

As for the content approach, there is remarkably little empirical evidence that the liberal arts experience is superior to other types of curricular experiences. Indeed, little research has been done to test this assumption, partly because of the wide variations both in definitions of what constitutes a liberal arts education and in the pedagogical techniques used to deliver the liberal arts curriculum to the student. The content approach to excellence does, however, have important implications for the particular pedagogical techniques that are used. (This issue will be discussed in more detail in Chapter Six.)

Is the faculty member's talent developed more effectively in an institution that is excellent in conventional terms? Again, well-designed studies of this issue are virtually nonexistent, though some evidence suggests that research productivity can be enhanced by employment at an elite research university, but not necessarily at an elite small college (Davis and Astin, 1984).

In summary, institutions that are deemed excellent in terms of reputation, resources, outcomes, or curricular content are not necessarily effective in developing student and faculty talent. In fact, the only resource measure consistently related to educational benefits for students is institutional size, and it turns out to have a largely negative effect on student development.

Do They Promote Excellence in the Whole System? As already noted, one consequence of the hierarchical arrangement of institutions in the U.S. higher education system is that it breeds a good deal of institutional conformity, in the form of imitation of the model represented by the elite institutions: outstanding reputation, prestigious faculty members, highly select student body, large endowments, substantial research grant funds, and a liberal arts curriculum. Does the pursuit of excellence in these terms tend to enhance the overall excellence of the system?

Let us first consider the reputational conception of excellence. Because it is basically normative, the reputational view, by definition, limits the amount of excellence that is possible within the higher education system. In any competitive system —whether it involves athletic teams, television shows, or educational institutions—there must be winners and losers. Only a limited number of institutions can be considered excellent; all others are necessarily relegated to lower positions. And if one institution manages to improve its rank, then some other institution must be displaced.

Moreover, the top-ranked institutions account for only a small fraction (perhaps 5-10 percent at most) of all institutions. In national ratings, then, at least half of all institutions—including most community colleges, many state colleges, and a great many small private colleges—get the same (low) rating, primarily because most raters are simply unfamiliar with all but a few institutions. Since familiarity is virtually synonymous with quality in the reputational approach, most institutions get the lowest possible rating.

Similar problems arise with the resources view of excellence: Resources such as highly able students, highly qualified faculties, and money are finite. Thus, in a highly competitive and meritocratic educational system, the distribution of these resources tends to be highly skewed, with the few "top" institutions monopolizing a disproportionate share and the many "mediocre" institutions making do with whatever is left. Competition among institutions for the most finite resources—faculty and student talent—may serve to redistribute these resources, but it cannot increase the total pool available to the educational system as a whole. We are, in other words, playing a zero-sum game when it comes to student and faculty resources. Finally—and this is a subtle but very critical point—resource-based conceptions of excellence tend to focus institutional energies on the sheer accumulation or acquisition of resources rather than on the effective *use* of these resources to further the educational development of the student and to promote faculty development. Paradoxically, in the pursuit of resources, institutions *expend resources without generating more resources, thereby depleting the total pool.* While it might be argued that the combined effort of institutions to acquire financial resources enlarges the total pool, this is not the case when it comes to student and faculty talent. Thus, in their efforts to recruit highly able students and faculty members, institutions are, in effect, squandering resources. If these financial resources were redeployed to strengthen the *educational* programs of institutions, the overall excellence of the system might be significantly enhanced.

In a recent editorial in *Science,* Rice University president Norman Hackerman (1984, p. 577) poignantly observes how the pursuit of reputation and resources has distracted us from our primary educational mission: "Although we are properly impressed by fine ideas and impressive new salients into our ignorance, we are often bemused by a less rational view of such things as ranking—'number one' and other such competitive trappings that develop in a vain desire to simplify evaluation of a complex system. This leads to an exhausting attempt by each field, each institution, each individual, to be number one. I have no interest in stifling ambition but intend rather to suggest that the process of educating individuals, because of the relative anonymity associated with it, has not maintained its proper preeminent position."

And what about the outcomes view? Does focusing on educational outcomes as an index of excellence tend to promote the overall excellence of the system? It can, provided the outcomes are seen in proper perspective. If the emphasis on outcomes leads an institution to strengthen its educational programs, then the system's excellence is enhanced. On the other hand, if the institution tries to improve outcomes merely by acquiring more resources (brighter students, more productive faculty members), the excellence of the system as a whole remains unchanged. Once again, we are engaged in a zero-sum game: High-achieving faculty members and students are simply recruited from one institution to another. That acquiring more and better inputs is the simplest and surest way to enhance outputs is illustrated by research into Ph.D. productivity (Astin, 1961, 1962), which shows that most of the differences in the Ph.D. outputs of institutions are attributable to differences in their student inputs. Similarly, the Graduate Record Examination scores of college seniors are much more dependent on their SAT scores as freshmen than on any aspect of the institutional environment (Astin, 1968b). Whether or not the intervening educational program plays any role in the process of enhancing outputs is another question.

The limitations of the resources and outcomes views of excellence can be further illustrated with an analogy from the corporate world. Is it legitimate to conclude that a given company is excellent just because it produces a lot of products (high output) or because it spends a lot of money to produce these products (high resources)? Obviously not. In business, the cost of running a company and the products produced by the company can be evaluated only in terms of whether the company makes a profit.

The business of academia, as I said in discussing the industrial production model in Chapter One, is not profit but talent development, or, more simply, education. And educational effectiveness must be judged in terms of talent development, not outputs or expenditures. As Bowen (1980) notes, there is a kind of unwritten law in academia that institutions somehow spend whatever financial resources they manage to acquire: Some institutions that spend very little seem to have highly effective educational programs, while some that expend much more money appear to have relatively ineffective programs.

In short, the pursuit of excellence—if that means no more than seeking to enhance an institution's reputation or to accumulate resources—can do little to improve the overall excellence of the system in terms of its capacity to develop student and faculty talent. Indeed, obeisance to the reputational and resources conceptions of excellence is counterproductive, in that it wastes the limited financial resources available to invest in the educational program.

As to the content view of excellence, educators make very compelling theoretical arguments in favor of a liberal arts education. But given the extreme variation in the way this particular curricular model is implemented, and given the paucity of evaluative research comparing the liberal arts with other models, it is difficult to reach any firm conclusions about how the liberal arts model relates to the overall excellence of the system. (In Chapter Six, I will give several examples of how adherence to the content approach in teaching may actually detract from effective teaching.)

Do They Promote Equity? Does adherence to traditional conceptions of excellence promote the aim of educational equity? If one accepts the resources view, there is a clear-cut conflict between excellence and equity, since the expansion of educational opportunities to more members of society (the pursuit of equity) necessarily requires that finite resources be distributed among a larger number of individuals, thereby diluting the average investment in any given individual and reducing overall excellence. Conversely, without an increase in the total resource pool, the only way to enhance quality (the pursuit of excellence) is to redistribute resources selectively from one group to another, thereby reducing equity. Since resources are never infinite, the twin goals of equity and excellence are inherently in conflict when we embrace a resource conception of excellence.

Similar problems arise with the reputational view. In our decentralized, diverse, and competitive higher education system, institutions inevitably will differ substantially in their reputations. Only a limited number of colleges and universities will emerge at the top of the reputational pecking order, and since the top-ranked institutions tend to attract a disproportionate share of applicants, many persons must be denied entry through the process of selective admissions. In reputational terms, these rejected applicants are denied an equal opportunity because they are not permitted to avail themselves of the most excellent opportunities. And even if an institution succeeds in enhancing its reputation (becomes more excellent), it subsequently tends to become more selective (less equitable).

Adherence to the outcomes view of excellence is also not likely to promote the cause of equity, primarily because the eas-

iest way to enhance outputs is to enhance inputs. To put it another way, if an institution wants to produce better-performing
graduates, it simply imposes more stringent admissions policies
at the point of entry. As already suggested, the process of selective admissions does not promote the cause of educational
equity, since it denies many people entry into the system.

The relationship between equity and the content view of
excellence, as reflected in the liberal arts model that dominates
American higher education, is unclear. Some critics argue that
the courses in Western civilization that characterize core curricula in liberal arts institutions are less appropriate for poor
and minority youth than they are for white, middle-class youth.
Again, this is an untested proposition that cries out for better
research. When it comes to pedagogy, however, the content approach may represent a serious obstacle to equity because it
tends to favor the assertive, well-prepared student. (See Chapter Six for a fuller discussion of this issue.)

Summary

In this chapter we have examined four traditional conceptions of institutional excellence: the reputational, resources,
outcomes, and content views. The first three of these produce
very similar rankings of institutions, primarily because they all
ultimately derive from the institutional hierarchy in American
higher education. The two most widely held views—those based
on reputation and resources—are mutually reinforcing in the
sense that enhanced reputation can bring an institution additional resources, and additional resources (particularly of highly
able students and nationally visible faculty members) can enhance an institution's reputation.

Both the reputational and resources views failed to meet
all three of my evaluative criteria. Neither view is necessarily
consistent with the institution's primary purposes: to develop
student and faculty talent. Furthermore, adherence to either
view offers little possibility of enhancing the overall quality of
the higher education system in the United States. Indeed, the
resources conception may, paradoxically, deplete the total

amount of resources available for institutions to invest in their educational programs. Finally, neither the reputational nor the resources view contributes to increasing equal opportunities in higher education.

Although the outcomes view suffers from some of the same problems as the reputational and resources views, it does offer some possibility of improving the quality of institutions, provided that it is applied with the intention of strengthening the institution's educational and faculty development programs. The content conception of excellence, which is not so widespread as the three other approaches, is difficult to evaluate because of the lack of research evidence.

Chapter Three

Excellence
as the Development
of Human Talent

In the previous chapter, I observed that the traditional views of excellence in higher education—the reputational and resources views, in particular—are not necessarily consistent with the purposes of higher education discussed in Chapter One. If talent development is indeed the principal raison d'être of our system of higher education, why not define the excellence of an institution in terms of its ability to develop the talents of its students and faculty members? In this chapter I shall examine in detail the talent development view of excellence, applying the same three evaluative criteria as were used to assess the traditional views.

The talent development view of excellence emphasizes the educational impact of the institution on its students and faculty members. Its basic premise is that true excellence lies in the institution's ability to affect its students and faculty favorably, to enhance their intellectual and scholarly development, and to make a positive difference in their lives. The most excellent institutions are, in this view, those that have the greatest impact—"add the most value," as economists would say—on the student's knowledge and personal development and on the faculty member's scholarly and pedagogical ability and productivity.

In its simplest terms the talent development conception of excellence focuses on changes in the student from the beginning to the end of an educational program. These changes can cover a wide range of cognitive and affective attributes. For the faculty member, the desired changes occur along such dimensions as teaching ability, mentoring ability, and scholarly ability and productivity. In recognition of the central role of colleges and universities as educational institutions, however, the ensuing discussion centers primarily on the student.

How does one judge whether or not an institution is excellent in carrying out its talent development function? Assessing an institution's reputation or its resources is a relatively simple matter. Assessing its success in developing the talents of its students is a more difficult task, one that requires information on changes or improvements in students' performance over time. Under the talent development model, students enrolling in the institution for the first time would be tested across a wide range of talent dimensions to determine their entering levels of competence. After they had completed appropriate courses or programs of study, the same or similar tests would be readministered to measure their growth.

Unfortunately, very few institutions currently have programs of student assessment that generate such longitudinal information. To be sure, they engage in a wide variety of assessment activities, but rarely can these be used in the way described above. For example, most institutions collect information on students' entering levels of competence by examining their high school records and their scores on standardized college admission tests. New students may also be asked to take certain other tests for purposes of course placement and academic counseling. Once enrolled in courses, they are again assessed by means of quizzes, midterm examinations, and final examinations. A few institutions now administer comprehensive junior-level exams to determine whether undergraduates are qualified to begin upper-division courses, and some require that students pass competence tests on such skills as writing before they can receive the bachelor's degree. And, of course, seniors aspiring to advanced study must also take a series of examinations in connection with their applications to graduate or professional schools.

It is virtually impossible, however, to link any two of these assessments, because they are simply not comparable. Course grades are not comparable to admission or placement tests, upper-division competence examinations are not comparable to course grades or admission test scores, and graduate or professional school admission tests are not comparable to any of the others. Moreover, each of these assessments is done primarily for purposes of *screening* and *credentialing*: Admission tests are used to screen applicants, course examinations are used to award grades for credit toward graduation, competence tests are used to determine eligibility for upper-division work or for the bachelor's degree, and graduate and professional school entrance exams are again used to screen applicants. While these uses are perfectly legitimate, the results of such evaluations tell us little about the effectiveness of the institution's talent development activities.

Assessments of faculty members present similar difficulties. Their competence is judged when they apply for faculty positions, and their performance is examined for purposes of promotion and tenure decisions, but these assessments cannot tell us much about the extent to which a faculty member has *improved* his or her competence and performance over time. Again, the assessments are primarily used to screen and sort.

Despite our adherence to the resources and reputational conceptions of excellence, most of us, if we took the time to stop and think about it, would probably embrace the talent development view of institutional excellence. Why, then, is this approach not more widely used? The answer lies partly with our assessment procedures: They simply do not produce the kinds of information required to make valid judgments about an institution's educational effectiveness.

That many authorities accept the talent view of excellence in theory can be illustrated by a few quotations from national educational associations and prominent scholars of higher education. One of the most consistent supporters of this view is the American Association of State Colleges and Universities, a membership organization for more than three hundred public colleges and universities that award approximately one-third of all U.S. bachelor's degrees. In *Quality and Effectiveness in Undergraduate Higher Education* the Association observes: "The customary measures of quality in most colleges and universities fail to deal with the impact of the institution on its students. However, if it is assumed that the teaching-learning function is the heart of the educational process, then the impact of the institution upon its students becomes critically important" (1971, pp. 3-4).

Similarly, the Southern Association of Colleges and Schools, one of the regional accrediting associations, recently issued the following statement: "The ultimate measure of the effectiveness of an educational institution . . . is . . . the success of its students in acquiring knowledge, competencies, and skills in learning their meaningful application; in forming attitudes and in gaining values and perspectives; and in developing the capacity for further learning" (1982, p. 12).

In a series of interviews with prominent educators and scholars, I asked for a definition of excellence. Virtually all of them touched on the talent development view in their answers. For instance, Howard Bowen said that excellence means "helping people become cultivated persons." According to Russell Edgerton, excellent institutions "convert students from being passive learners to active learners. . . . It's the engagement factor, I guess, that is the key to potency." And Arthur Chickering defined an excellent institution as one "that enables, provokes, and encourages significant learning for students." Elsewhere Chickering has articulated the same idea in more detail: "The principal justification for the existence of a college or university does not rest on its capacity simply to provide credentials, but on its capacity to create educational environments, teaching practices, and evaluative procedures that result in solid learning for the students to be served"(1983, p. 11).

Why is it that most people, when given a chance to think about the meaning of excellence in higher education, espouse a talent development view, even though they tend to rely on traditional reputational and resource conceptions when it comes to *measuring* institutional excellence? And why are most of us inclined to accept the validity of the institutional hierarchy even when we know that it is not necessarily based on the institutions' relative effectiveness in developing talent? These are complex questions and require complex answers.

As already suggested, one reason for this apparent contradiction relates to the information available about institutions: Freshmen test scores, faculty publication rates, and figures on institutional finances are much more readily available than information on changes in students over time. But this is not the whole answer. The values of the larger society are also a factor. American society has traditionally placed considerable value on wealth, size, and fame. Indeed, these three values tend to be mutually reinforcing. Thus, in American higher education, the most famous institutions tend to be the largest and to have the most wealth and power. The fact that these qualities are relatively easy to measure also reinforces these values. And if these values are challenged on the grounds that they do not necessarily signify excellence in talent development, one can simply respond by saying that, given their substantial resources, these institutions are "obviously" more effective at their talent development mission. Such views are not likely to be altered by a few highly technical research studies directed primarily at a professional audience (see, for example, Astin, 1968b; Bowen, 1977; Feldman and Newcomb, 1969).

Multidimensionality of Talent Development

One question that arises in connection with the talent development approach is which talents an academic institution should strive to develop. I will not try to answer this question in any comprehensive way, given that many educational associations and institutions have long struggled with it. About the only indisputable conclusion to emerge from these efforts is the following: Higher education is in the business of developing *multiple* talents, and no unidimensional definition of talent adequately reflects the institution's educational mission.

Education associations and individual educators have said a good deal about the issue of multidimensionality. For example, the American Association of State Colleges and Universities (1976, unpaginated brochure) has declared: "Colleges and universities have a responsibility to educate the whole student, not just serve vocational and scholarly interests. This becomes more evident as the complexities of the postindustrial society increase and as the influences of international events draw the world into a global community. Decisions, judgments, and perceptions are not as clear as they once were; and the consequences of actions are more far-reaching. To function at the highest level possible, students will require knowledge, insight, and a foundation of values which have withstood the tests of history."

Several of the higher education scholars I interviewed also mentioned the multidimensional nature of educational excellence:

> If a college or university gives someone a diploma, that person needs to have met some quite rigorous requirements having to do with the ability to express themselves in any one of various symbolic ways: language, mathematics, and so on. We need to be able to demonstrate that they could engage in something called critical thinking. [Patricia Graham]
>
> [By excellence] I mean significant gains in various kinds of critical thinking skills, areas of interpersonal competence, increased clarity of purpose, increased willingness to invest yourself in something larger than yourself. . . . [Institutions should] help persons learn better how to take charge of their own learning and development so that they come out . . . knowing how to continue their own lifelong learning in a systematic and

thoughtful way, how to define some objectives, how to get resources and use them, how to use authority wisely, what kinds of inquiry methods are appropriate to what problems, then how to evaluate what they've learned. [Arthur Chickering]

[Excellence means] a depth of cultivation, which is not just intelligence, not gamesmanlike quickness (which is often passed off as excellence) but intellectuality, depth, profundity . . . a common culture in which people are familiar with the Bible, with great works of the Western tradition, [have] some ethnographic sense of other cultures, some worldly knowledge of this country, some skills in writing, in organizing a paper, some sense of style, [know] the difference between junk and elegance, [have] some knowledge of quantitative and technical matters, possession of a craft, knowledge of a musical instrument and of a sport. [David Riesman]

[Excellence] means [being] knowledgeable, moral, interested in aesthetics, socially responsible . . . a phrase I use a lot is a nation of educated people. By that I mean broadly cultivated individuals. . . . It just means more than having some kind of professional competence. [Howard Bowen]

In an earlier book, Bowen (1977) argues that student development should be assessed in terms of the following diverse traits: verbal skills, quantitative skills, substantive knowledge, rationality, intellectual tolerance, esthetic sensitivity, creativeness, intellectual integrity, and wisdom.

As these statements make clear, student development is a multidimensional matter, and no single measure of talent is adequate to reflect the excellence of any institution. Nevertheless, the great majority of institutions see certain talents as especially relevant to their educational objectives: verbal and communication skills (reading, writing, listening, speaking), some basic mathematical and computational competence, a working knowledge of Western civilization and culture, and critical thinking abilities. In recent years, many institutions have added computer literacy to their lists of relevant talents. And most institutions that offer majors would include on the list knowledge of a specialized subject matter corresponding to the student's major field of study.

Affective development is also regarded as important by many institutions. This includes the development of such personal characteristics as emotional maturity, tolerance, empathy, and leadership ability. Longitudinal research on college students, it might be added, has tended to concentrate on these affective qualities (Astin, 1977; Chickering, 1969; Feldman and Newcomb, 1969).

While the task of measuring talent development along so many dimensions may seem horrendous, instruments for assessing a wide range of student talents, particularly in the cognitive domain, are available (Ewell, 1984). Some testing organizations have recently developed test batteries to assess the more generic outcomes of a liberal education such as critical thinking, communication skills, and the like. Among the more promising of these efforts are the Behavioral Event Interview of the McBer Company (Winter, McClelland, and Stewart, 1981), the American College Testing Program's COMP Battery (Forrest and Steele, 1982), and the Academic Competencies in General Education Battery developed at the Educational Testing Service (Warren, 1978). The talent development approach does not require the use of any particular assessment method. Objective tests, essays, oral examinations, performance examinations, and various other techniques may be appropriate, depending on the content and objectives of the course or program in question. Note that the testing is done not so much to select or screen as to measure improvement over time in the performance of individual students.

At first glance, courses in the creative and performing arts might not seem to lend themselves to this type of assessment. On the contrary, since assessment in these fields is intense and frequent, the issue becomes how to design and use assessments so that the development of the student's talent can be charted adequately. For example, the creative products or performances of the student (paintings, musical compositions, musical or dance performances, short stories) could be assessed before the particular course or program and then compared with similar products or performances produced during or after the course or program. Any improvement in the judged quality of these products or performances would presumably represent that part of the student's talent which was "developed" by the course or program.

Talent Development and Public Policy

Each of the many talents on which undergraduate programs are focused may be visualized as a continuum from low performance to high performance. Somewhere near the high end is a point, call it C, which is defined as the level of proficiency required for receiving the bachelor's degree, as indicated, for example, by some minimum score on the test used to measure this particular talent. One purpose of an institution's educational program is to move students up to the level of proficiency designated by point C. To represent the different points at which entering students fall on the continuum, let us imagine Student A near the low end and Student B near the middle. Both students have a considerable distance to travel (a lot to learn) before they reach point C, but A has a longer way to go than B. Depending on the institution's admissions standards, A may be an average student and B a superior student deserving advanced placement. On the other hand, B may be the average student and A a student admitted under some special action program. In either case, A will probably require more time and resources than B to reach the designated proficiency level.

Two other facts are clear from considering this continuum. First, the goal of most educational programs is to enable students not just to meet minimum performance standards but to exceed them by as much as possible. Thus, if A and B equally develop their talent—communication skills, for example —during their undergraduate years, B will still surpass A, even if both achieve the minimum standards. B's "extra" competence is not necessarily superfluous: it may come in very handy, depending on what B plans to do after college. The second point is that both A and B could gain significantly in communication skills and still not reach the level required for the awarding of the baccalaureate. Under these conditions, it would *not* be appropriate to argue that the investment in these students was wasted, since the increment in skills might still prove very useful to them in later life. These facts illustrate an important principle about performance standards: They are necessarily arbitrary, since they impose a dichotomous cutting point on what is fundamentally a continuum.

But the most important lesson to be learned is that if an institution maximizes the talent development of its students, it will also maximize (*a*) the number of students who manage to attain minimum performance levels and (*b*) the "margin of safety" by which students surpass those performance levels. In other words, the talent development view of excellence is entirely compatible with the maintenance of academic standards.

One of the most appealing aspects of the talent development conception of excellence is that it provides a framework for discussing large-scale educational policy objectives. To illustrate one such application of the concept, let me take the continuum I have been discussing and show the entire population of college freshmen (Figure 1). Distribution 1a is normal in shape, but there is no necessary reason why the actual distribution of talent in the population could not assume some other shape. If distribution 1a represents the scores of all entering freshmen, note that only a very few are performing at the Ph.D. level, while a substantial number are at or below the borderline literacy level. (The cross-hatched areas of the distribution above and below these two points are arbitrary and illustrative only.)

Now if the purpose of the higher education system is to develop talent, this goal can be specified in terms of desired changes in the characteristics of the distribution. An almost infinite number of such changes is possible: Figures 1b, 1c, and 1d represent only three basic kinds of changes. The dotted line in each case shows the desired shape of the distribution after four years of college, and the solid line repeats distribution 1a (students' performance at matriculation). The first of these hypothetical changes in the performance distribution (Figure 1b) involves an upward shift in students' *mean* performance only.

Figure 1. Hypothetical Distribution of Talent in the Population of
Entering College Students and Three Possible Outputs of
the Higher Education System Expressed in Terms of Changes
in the Shape of the Distribution.

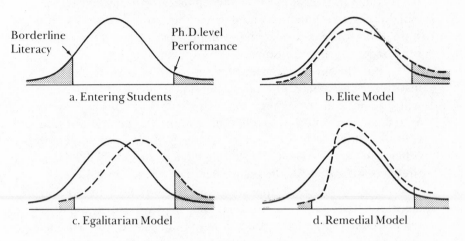

Source: Adapted from Astin, 1973b, p. 118.

The entire distribution has simply shifted to the right; the shape of the distribution remains unchanged. Given that all seniors appear to benefit equally, a policy that produces the distribution in 1b may be referred to as a democratic or egalitarian policy.

In Figure 1c the proportion of students performing at or near the Ph.D. level has increased substantially, while the performance of those at the lowest end of the distribution remains almost unchanged. The type of policy producing this distribution can be characterized as elitist, in the sense that it emphasizes increasing the proportion of students who perform very well but pays little attention to the students at the low end of the continuum.

The outcomes of a third policy are shown in Figure 1d. It is concerned primarily with minimizing the proportion of low performers by improving the performance of those who start out at the low end of the continuum. Here the number of persons performing at or near borderline literacy is greatly reduced, but the number performing at the Ph.D. level changes only slightly. Because it aims primarily at eradicating illiteracy, such a policy can be labeled remedial.

Our higher education policies in the past have tended to be a mixture of elitist and egalitarian plans, with a smattering of remedial plans. A selective admissions policy is clearly elitist, whereas an open admissions policy tends to be egalitarian. Special programs for disadvantaged students are remedial in the sense that they invest disproportionately in educating those students performing least well. The value of the talent development model is that it permits policy makers to specify, in concrete terms, just what their objectives are. Those objectives will vary, of course, depending on the institution, the state or region of the country, and many other factors.

This view of talent development raises a number of other intriguing questions. For example:

- What types of educational programs are most likely to produce the largest gains at various points on the continuum?
- What are the relative costs of these programs?
- What individual and societal benefits are associated with increments at various points on the talent continuum?
- Do investments at the low end have significant payoffs in terms of lower unemployment, less crime, and reduced reliance on welfare programs?
- Do investments at the high end of the scale pay off significantly in increased scientific and technical advances?
- Are there points of diminishing returns with respect to investments at various positions on the continuum?
- How much of an increase or a decrease in talent occurs among students who do not attend college (the maturation effect)?

Considering the obvious bearing of these questions on our higher education policies, it is unfortunate that they have received so little attention from researchers. One possible reason for this paucity of research is the lack of good longitudinal information on talent development. Without systematic data on how much people's talent levels change, it is very difficult to obtain reliable answers to these important policy questions.

This way of looking at talent development also dramatizes the importance of the admissions process. Let us assume for a moment that the distributions shown in Figure 1 are based not just on entering college freshmen but on the entire population of high school graduates. Clearly, the higher education system cannot hope to develop the talent of individuals who do not enter the system. These same individuals, it must be pointed out, are part not only of the population but of the nation's talent reservoir. If our public institutions are to modify their policies regarding who is encouraged or permitted to attend a postsecondary institution, then policy makers might appropriately use this model to assess the likely consequences of such modifications: that is, to gauge their probable impact on the development of the total talent reservoir within the states.

A similar model could be applied in assessing policy with respect to talent development among faculty. If the research and teaching talent of faculty members were assessed when they were first hired and then reassessed after they had been employed at the institution for some specified period, the extent to which the institution had developed these talents could be determined. With this information, one could evaluate the relative effectiveness of various kinds of institutional environment in developing faculty members' abilities. Such knowledge would be invaluable in developing policy with respect to the knowledge production function of institutions.

Evaluation

Let me now evaluate the talent development conception of excellence by applying the same criteria I used to assess the four traditional conceptions. First, is it consistent with the institution's purposes? If one accepts the idea that developing talent is the primary purpose of higher education, then the talent development view of excellence is by definition consistent with that purpose: Those institutions that are most successful in developing the talents of their students and faculty members are

to be regarded as excellent. We must recognize, however, that because talent is multidimensional, no single yardstick of institutional excellence (in the talent development sense) is appropriate. Different institutions may be excellent in developing very different types of talent.

Second, does its use promote excellence in the system as a whole? By focusing on the improvement of student performance, the talent development view would seem to foster excellence by emphasizing the need to employ existing resources in such a way as to maximize student learning. Equally important, a given college's capacity for excellence, in talent development terms, is not constrained by the degree of excellence attained by other colleges. Thus, unlike the reputational and resources views, which define excellence in comparative terms, the talent development view permits institutions to attain high levels of excellence without regard to what other institutions accomplish. Of course, institutional comparisons can be made using the talent development model, but such comparisons would still focus on the degree to which student performance improves in the individual colleges and universities. It seems reasonable to assume that interinstitutional competition to determine who was most effective at developing talent would be a more effective way to improve our nation's talent pool than competition to see who can amass the most resources or attain the best reputation.

Let us assume that an institution wants to implement the talent development approach and so sets out to assess its students longitudinally. The resulting data can be used for several educational purposes beyond simply assessing the degree of change. For example, the initial pretest scores not only give both students and faculty valuable information about the students' special strengths and weaknesses but also can be used for academic advising and career counseling. Similarly, posttest results (data collected following the completion of appropriate courses or programs of study) constitute critical feedback on the nature and extent of student growth, useful to students, professors, and administrators alike. Years of research on human learning suggest that a knowledge of results greatly enhances the effectiveness of the teaching-learning process and thus benefits both students and professors (Gagne, 1977).

Finally, does the talent development concept promote educational equity? Since excellence in this model depends on improving student performance, the education of high achievers is not necessarily given higher priority than the education of middle or low achievers. Rather, equal efforts are made to encourage student learning at all levels. No student is denied the opportunity for further education simply because he or she performs at a lower level than some other student. According to the talent development view, any educational investment pays off as long as the student continues to show progress. In short, the talent development conception of quality promotes the cause of equity to a much greater extent than does any traditional approach.

Assessing Talent Development

Implementing a talent development approach on any campus first requires that we consider a number of practical issues concerning the assessment procedures to be used. While Chapter Seven includes specific suggestions about assessment, it may be useful here to consider briefly some of the more general questions. How, for example, are the students' entering and exiting levels of proficiency to be determined? Should we strive to develop a series of national examinations that everyone would use, or should each institution develop its own? The advantages of national examinations are that (*a*) they can be used to generate norms with which individual institutions can compare themselves, and (*b*) their technical quality tends to be superior to that of locally devised measures. The major advantages of assessments developed locally are that (*a*) they are more likely to reflect the specific curricular emphases and pedagogical style of the institution, and (*b*) they are easier to change. In all likelihood, most institutions would be better off using a mix of national and local assessment procedures.

A related question concerns those performance standards required for certification purposes and the associated system of rewards. Since the talent development approach emphasizes growth or improvement in performance, should students be rewarded simply on the basis of how much they improve, regardless of whether or not they are able to reach the minimum standards required for receiving a degree? My feeling here is that (a) absolute levels of performance can and should be defined and maintained in order to protect the integrity of the degree, and (b) improving one's talent or competence is its own reward and thus does not require special recognition. As a matter of fact, maximizing one's talent development is the surest way to maximize one's chances of reaching or surpassing minimum standards of performance.

A final question concerning the efficacy of the talent development approach to excellence is the matter of costs. In reviewing the first draft of the manuscript for this book, JB Hefferlin stated, "I would define 'excellence' in higher education as *efficient* talent development in that I don't believe an institution or system of institutions can be excellent if it squanders resources ineffectively and inefficiently on talent development." There is no question that costs have to be considered. Among institutions that are equally successful in carrying out their talent development missions, those that are able to accomplish that mission most economically would probably be judged as the most excellent. However, I might add here that cost considerations should be just as important in assessing the reputational and resource approaches to excellence, even though they are frequently ignored by those pursuing these traditional approaches. It is not an uncommon practice for major research universities, for example, to lure a single faculty star with a salary and perquisites that could easily support three or four new assistant professors. And increasing numbers of ambitious institutions are now expending substantial sums of money on "merit" scholarships to attract highly able students, many of whom have little or no financial need.

Role of Values

If the talent development view really represents a significant improvement over traditional conceptions of educational excellence, then why (you may ask) has it not been followed all along? I have already mentioned the problems connected with assessing talent development, but there are several other reasons.

We live in a society that is both competitive and acquisitive, a society where success and personal worth are often measured in terms of possessions and fame. Thus, most Americans accept uncritically the resources conception of excellence: that the best institutions are those with the most resources and that an institution can best increase its quality by acquiring more highly trained faculty members, better-prepared students, better facilities, and more money. Educators put so much energy into competing for these limited resources that acquiring them takes precedence over using them effectively. As a consequence, a casual visit to almost any college or university will demonstrate that educational practitioners frequently ignore some of the fundamental principles of learning and human development. (See Chapter Six for a fuller discussion of this issue.) I believe that if educators focus their attention on the talent development question—if they ask how much students are actually learning—they will be forced to apply some of this neglected knowledge to current institutional policies and practices, with the ultimate aim of improving the quality of the student's learning experience.

The reputational view emphasizes what others *think* of you, the resource view emphasizes what you *have*, and the talent development view emphasizes what you *do*. On a more subtle level, the talent development model of excellence implies a set of institutional values that is very different from the values underlying the resources and reputational concepts. The dominant value of the resources view would seem to be acquisitiveness or, to put it less charitably, greed. The dominant values of the reputational view would seem to be vanity and self-aggrandizement. And, as has been pointed out, these two views are mutually reinforcing: Administrators see resources—bright students, nationally visible faculties, research grants, and other financial resources—as a way of enhancing institutional prestige. At the same time, they see the enhancement of an institution's reputation as way of attracting more resources.

Inherent in the talent development view is a very different value system, one in which student growth and development are the central institutional concerns. When an institution manifests this philosophy by collecting and disseminating before-and-after data on the learning and personal development of its students, that institution is making a concrete commitment to its talent development mission. At the same time it is also saying that its educational programs are open to critical scrutiny and self-examination.

Summing Up

In this chapter I have suggested that the talent development view of excellence is superior to traditional notions that emphasize the enhancement of institutional reputation through the amassing of resources. In contrast, the talent development view emphasizes the intellectual and personal development of individual students as a fundamental institutional purpose. According to the talent development view, a high-quality institution is one that facilitates maximum growth among its students and faculty and that can document that growth through appropriate assessment procedures.

Unlike the reputational and research approaches, the talent development approach to excellence does not limit educational opportunity by identifying only a limited number of colleges and universities as the best. Moreover, under the talent development approach, an educational investment in students at any ability level is justified as long as it pays off in continued intellectual growth and development. The reputational and resources approaches, on the other hand, tend to limit the educational opportunities of less-well-prepared students by restricting entry to the "best" colleges and universities.

But merely embracing the talent development view does not resolve all questions of equity or resource use. We know very little about the causal relationship between resource investments and talent development. How much talent development results from a given investment of financial resources? Do equal investments produce equivalent gains in performance for students at differing levels of achievement? And even if it could be shown that given investments have given payoffs at all points along the talent spectrum, virtually nothing is known about how talent development is related to individual and social benefits. Here is an area where more research is urgently needed.

The notion that colleges and universities should focus more on their talent development function implies a definition of excellence that deviates considerably from traditional definitions. A high-quality institution knows what is happening to its students educationally and can make appropriate adjustments in its programs or policies when the data so indicate. In other words, excellence is equated here with a continuing process of critical self-examination focusing on the institution's contribution to the student's intellectual and personal development.

Chapter Four

Expanding
the Quantity and Quality
of Educational Opportunities

"Our kind of society demands the maximum development of individual potentialities *at every level of ability*.... We are now
talking about an approach to excellence and a conception of
excellence that will bring a whole society to the peak of performance" (Gardner, 1961, pp. 74, 132–133).

Although equity in higher education did not become a
topic of national debate until the late 1960s, equal educational
opportunity is by no means a new idea. Indeed, more than two
thousand years ago, Aristotle said, "The system of education in
a state must ... be one and the same for all, and the provision
of this system must be a matter of a public action" (quoted in
Walzer, 1983, p. 202). But the antiquity of the idea does not
mean that it has gained universal acceptance or that proposals
to expand educational opportunities at the postsecondary level

have not met with strong opposition. In 1952, before the post-war expansion of higher education in the United States, the Commission on the Financing of Higher Education asserted, "If it is democratic to admit to our colleges great numbers of students who lack intellectual interests and to attune the educational system to their subintellectual needs and capacities, there has been an excess of democracy in the conduct of American higher education" (Hofstadter and Hardy, 1952).

This chapter reviews a number of issues related to educational equity: the meaning of equity, the distribution of educational opportunities, the use of tests in admissions and tracking, the supposed conflict between excellence and equity, and the education of underprepared students.

What Is Equity?

Equality of opportunity in higher education, as I observed in Chapter One, has traditionally been defined in terms of access. Policy makers have tended to believe that the goal of educational equity is attained when no person is denied access to the higher education system because of race, gender, income, or social status. This definition is, however, inadequate. Given the great diversity in the faculties, facilities, and other resources of American colleges and universities, any adequate definition of the term must also take into consideration the quality of the opportunity itself. In other words, guaranteeing that opportunities are available for all does not ensure equity unless the opportunities themselves are of equal quality.

The American system of higher education has come closer than any other system in the world to achieving the objective of making some kind of postsecondary educational opportunity available to all citizens. The pioneers in this effort were the great state universities of the Midwest, which have long had a policy of open admissions. In such states as Minnesota, Ohio, and Illinois, the major state university was accessible to just about all of the state's high school graduates. But at the national level, by far the greatest responsibility for expanding access has been shouldered by the community colleges. These institutions, most of which have open admissions policies, now enroll about one in three of the first-time full-time freshmen entering college each fall (Astin and others, 1983).

How does one go about evaluating the quality of the opportunities offered? In approaching this problem, one must recognize that each of the 3,000 higher education institutions in the United States represents a different opportunity. It seems logical to regard the excellence of the institution as a yardstick for judging the quality of the opportunity it represents. Therefore, the relative quality of two or more opportunities (institutions) can be assessed by comparing their relative excellence. But how does one determine an institution's excellence? Its resources constitute one possible measure, and its reputation is another. As Chapter Two suggested, however, resources and reputations may not be the most valid indicators of institutional excellence or of the quality of the opportunities offered; in fact, talent development may be the best guide. To put it another way, one can argue that opportunities are equal when outcomes are equal.

Let me illustrate this view with a concrete example. If a student applies to institutions A and B and is rejected by A but accepted by B, the question of whether that student has been denied an equal educational opportunity comes down to a question of whether the student could expect the same outcomes at the two institutions. The term *outcomes* is used here in its broadest sense to include existential and fringe benefits as well as educational (talent development) outcomes. Clearly, if the student could expect more favorable outcomes at institution A, then that student has been denied an equal educational opportunity.

The term *equal outcomes* as I am using it here must be distinguished from equal outcomes with reference to differences between students. Some observers argue that true equality will be achieved only when all students are able to reach the same level of proficiency or graduate from college with the same job opportunities open to them. I have chosen to reject this particular interpretation, simply because it is unrealistic: Students differ widely in their abilities, motivation, and preparation, and

one cannot expect all of them to attain the same level of proficiency, even under the most ideal educational circumstances.
The real issue, then, is whether certain types of students are
being denied access to educational opportunities that would
confer greater benefits than the opportunities that are available
to them.

But the institutions that confer the greatest benefits may
not be able to accept all applicants. How does one deal with
this problem? Here it would seem that the admissions process
plays the key role. If all applicants are on an equal footing (as,
for example, with a lottery system), then their opportunities
are equal (they all have the same chance of being admitted). But
if certain applicants are given preference over others (because of
test scores, high school grades, or athletic talents, for example),
then their opportunities are no longer equal.

Equality of opportunity does not guarantee excellence.
Students can have equal access to equally bad opportunities. In
the ideal society, the educational system would be characterized by both excellence and equality. Such a system would enable the society to develop the talents of all its citizens to their
maximum potential. As Gardner (1961) puts it, "Equality of
opportunity . . . [means that] every individual should be en-
abled to achieve the best that is in him" (p. 135).

To sum up, equality of access relates to the number of
available places: Are there opportunities available for everyone
who wants a postsecondary education, and are they affordable?
Equality of opportunity, on the other hand, requires not only
that the supply of available spaces be adequate to meet the demand but also that students have equal access to the best opportunities (for them), regardless of race, gender, income, social
class, or other personal qualities.

Distribution of Opportunities

How equitably are higher education opportunities distributed among various types of students? Do all students—regardless of race, gender, social class, and so forth—have an equal
chance to avail themselves of the best opportunities? As we

have already seen, students from the more affluent and better-educated families tend to be disproportionately represented in institutions at the top of the hierarchy, while students from poor and less-educated families tend to be concentrated in institutions at the bottom of the hierarchy. Given that every measure of institutional resources is also strongly correlated with the hierarchy, it seems clear that opportunities—in terms of institutional reputation and resources—are not equitably distributed among students of different social classes. Clearly, upper-class students have access to "better" opportunities. Even though reputational and resource measures may not be valid indices of excellence when it comes to educational benefits, one should bear in mind that the fringe benefits of attending college are strongly correlated with an institution's reputation. Thus, students from upper socioeconomic levels have greater access than those from lower levels to the institutions most likely to confer the greatest fringe benefits.

Why this strong association between socioeconomic class and hierarchical position? The explanation would seem to lie in the close relationship between social class, on the one hand, and high school grades and admission test scores, on the other. Since grades and scores are the principal criteria for admission to selective institutions, students from more affluent families are more likely to be accepted at the most elite institutions. However, social class seems to play a role apart from its effect on grades and scores. That is, even after the student's high school grades and admission test scores are taken into account, the student's socioeconomic class is still significantly related to the selectivity of the institution in which he or she enrolls (Karabel and Astin, 1975). In other words, given students of comparable academic preparation and ability, those from better-educated and more affluent families are more likely to enroll in highly selective colleges than are those from poorer and less-educated families.

One can only speculate on the reasons for this relationship. For one thing, the more prestigious institutions cost more, and so it is not surprising that poorer students attend the less elite (less costly) institutions, even if their grades and test scores qualify them for admission to the more elite ones. Even though financial aid is designed to neutralize such economic barriers, evidence suggests that poorer students continue to believe that they cannot afford to attend elite institutions (Astin, Christian, and Henson, 1978). Another possible explanation is that better-educated and more affluent parents are more likely to encourage their children to attend prestigious institutions. Indeed, in some very well-to-do families, attendance at a particular college is a family tradition, and the children grow up with the expectation of attending that college.

Ethnicity. The Civil Rights Movement of the 1960s aroused growing national concern over minority representation in higher education. A number of studies have been conducted to determine how educational opportunities are distributed among various minority groups, the most recent being that of the Commission on the Higher Education of Minorities (1981). After examining the educational pipeline beginning in secondary school and ending at the doctorate and professional levels, the commission reached the following general conclusions:

1. The four largest disadvantaged minority groups in the United States—blacks, Chicanos, Puerto Ricans, and American Indians—are underrepresented, relative to whites, at each level of degree attainment: high school completion, baccalaureate attainment, and advanced-degree attainment. The higher the level, the greater the degree of underrepresentation.

2. The most serious leakage in the pipeline occurs at the secondary school level: disadvantaged minority students, especially hispanics, are much less likely than whites to graduate from high school. But minorities also have higher-than-average attrition rates at the undergraduate and graduate levels.

3. Minorities are underrepresented in all fields of study except the social sciences and education. At the graduate level, they are most underrepresented in the natural sciences and engineering. To achieve proportionate representation at the doctoral level in these fields, the number of minority students would have to be increased anywhere from four to seven times, depending on the specific field. Proportionate representation in law and medicine could be achieved by doubling the number of minority degree-recipients.

4. Although minority representation in higher education increased dramatically between the mid 1960s and the mid 1970s, it has since leveled off or declined slightly.

The commission also noted that minorities tend to be concentrated in certain types of higher education institutions. Table 7 shows the distribution of various ethnic groups among different types of public and private institutions. Note that

Table 7. Percentages of Various Racial/Ethnic Groups
in Institutions of Different Types.

Type of Institution	All Students	Whites	Blacks	His-panics	Asians	American Indians
Private						
Two-year college	1.6	1.5	2.9	2.3	0.5	1.5
Four-year college	13.6	13.8	13.1	15.3	8.1	6.1
University	5.9	6.2	4.2	3.5	6.8	2.3
Public						
Two-year college	36.5	35.1	40.7	46.8	43.8	53.9
Four-year college	24.3	23.9	29.6	21.3	23.3	23.5
University	18.0	19.5	9.5	10.8	17.5	12.7
Total	100.0	100.0	100.0	100.0	100.0	100.0

Source: Unpublished data, Higher Education General Information Survey, 1982.

blacks, hispanics, and American Indians are disproportionately represented in two-year colleges, especially in the public sector. At the same time, they are underrepresented in both public and private universities. Asians, it should be noted, do not follow this general pattern: Although they are overrepresented in public two-year colleges, they are underrepresented in private two-year colleges, only slightly underrepresented in public universities, and overrepresented in private universities. The greatest degree of underrepresentation occurs among hispanics and American Indians in the private universities, and among blacks and hispanics in the public universities. As a matter of fact, in the public universities, whites are better represented than blacks by a ratio of two to one.

In light of the fact that public higher education is supposed to serve all of a state's citizens, the commission expressed considerable concern about the maldistribution of minorities across the various types of public institutions and decided to explore this question further. Using the typology of universities developed by the Carnegie Commission on Higher Education (1973), the Commission on the Higher Education of Minorities identified the "flagship" public university in each state. If more than one university in a state received the highest Carnegie classification, all such institutions were used. Most states had only one flagship university, and only one (California) had more than two.

The representation of blacks, hispanics, and American Indians in each flagship university was determined by comparing the institution's undergraduate minority enrollment with the total minority enrollment in all colleges and universities within the state. Of the sixty-five flagship universities, fifty-six had significant underenrollments of blacks, forty-eight had significant hispanic underenrollments, and forty-six had significant underenrollments of American Indians. Moreover, the degree of underenrollment was greatest in those states with the largest minority populations. To attain proportionate representation of the underrepresented minorities in the flagship universities in New York, Texas, and California, and in most of the southern states, the numbers would have to increased by between 200 and 600 percent!

This underrepresentation of minorities in the most prestigious public universities is especially significant given the fringe benefits usually associated with attending such institutions. Among other things, the flagship universities in most states serve as conduits to positions of power and influence within state government and private industry. That is, access to the state's major public university promises career benefits not generally available to students attending other public institutions within the state.

The overrepresentation of minorities in the community colleges has important implications for certain types of educational benefits: in particular, the student's chances of persisting to the bachelor's degree. As mentioned earlier, the likelihood of a student's attaining the baccalaureate is reduced significantly if the student begins postsecondary education in a community college (Astin, 1975, 1977, 1982; Breneman and Nelson, 1981). Perhaps the most plausible explanation for this finding is that the environment of the typical community college has a relatively weak capacity to promote student involvement (see Chapter Six) because of the lack of residential facilities, the large population of relatively underprepared students, and the substantial numbers of part-time students and part-time faculty members.

These problems in involvement have particular implications for hispanics and, to a lesser extent, for American Indians. Both of these groups are heavily concentrated in community colleges, primarily because they live in states such as California that have hierarchies with large community college systems. On the basis of interviews with minority students and academicians, the Commission on the Higher Education of Minorities (1981) concluded that attending community colleges creates special problems for hispanics, who come from a culture that emphasizes family loyalty. Since hispanics from poor families are expected to contribute to the family's support, many young hispanics take a light course load at the local community college, live at home, and even hold down full-time jobs.

In short, attending a community college—though convenient—exacts a heavy toll. More often than not, the student fails to get sufficiently involved in the academic experience. Going to campus for an hour or so each day and then returning home or to the job represents radically less involvement than, say, leaving home, living on campus, and taking a full course load. Given such a low degree of involvement, the probability of dropping out is substantial.

Family Income. How equally are higher education opportunities allocated among American college students from different income groups? Earlier we observed a strong positive correlation between college selectivity and the income of the student's parents, with the poorer students disproportionately enrolled in the least selective institutions. Table 8 shows the distribution

Table 8. Trends in Enrollments of Low-Income Freshmen, 1966–1983,
by Institutional Type.

	Percentage of Entering Freshmen from Lowest Quintile in Parental Income	
Type of Institution	1966	1983
Public two-year colleges	23.6	22.2
Public four-year colleges	28.4	19.7
Public universities	16.8	12.0
(Most selective public universities)[a]	(NA)	(8.2)
All institutions (public and private)	20.0	20.0

[a]The mean SAT (verbal + math) scores of entrants are 1100 or higher (24 institutions).

Sources: Astin, Panos, and Creager, 1966; Astin and others, 1983.

of low-income students among various types of public institutions in 1966 and 1983. (The bottom 20 percent of the income distribution was arbitrarily chosen to represent low income.) In the 1983–84 crop of college freshmen, low-income students are disproportionately concentrated in the community colleges and, to a lesser extent, in the public four-year colleges (many of which used to be teachers colleges). Conversely, they are substantially underrepresented in the public universities, especially in the most selective ones. To achieve proportionate representation in the most selective public universities, the numbers of low-income students would have to be more than doubled.

Since the proportion of low-income students attending two-year colleges has declined slightly since 1966 (from 23.6 to 22.2 percent), it is tempting to conclude that public systems are moving toward greater equity. But this conclusion is unwarranted. The percentages have declined at all three types of institutions, especially at four-year colleges and universities. How could this happen? The answer lies in the tremendous increase in the undergraduate population since 1966, an increase that has been concentrated in the community colleges. The real question of equity would seem to depend on the gaps between the various types of institutions. Thus, the difference between universities and two-year colleges, with respect to their enrollment of low-income students, has grown from less than 7 percent in 1966 to more than 10 percent in 1983. In short, public four-year colleges and universities seem to have become increasingly inaccessible to low-income students since the 1960s.

Distribution of Resources. To give a more comprehensive picture of the distribution of higher education opportunities in relation to ethnicity and family income, Table 9 combines data from the 1983 entering freshman population with four resource measures: institutional selectivity, and per-student expenditures for instruction, the library, and the physical plant. It shows, for example, that American higher education spends an average of $2,024 for instructional purposes on each white student. And the average selectivity score of those institutions attended by white students is 917 (the sum of the verbal and mathematical scores on the Scholastic Aptitude Test). To put this figure in proper perspective, one should keep in mind that the middle 50 percent of institutions fall between 820 and 940 on this selectivity scale.

The data in Table 9 lead to one conclusion: Minority students and students from poor families tend to enroll at institutions with fewer resources than do white students and students from well-to-do families. As far as the first two fiscal resource measures are concerned, hispanics appear to be at the greatest disadvantage. When it comes to college selectivity, blacks are at the greatest disadvantage, a finding consistent with the fact that blacks tend to make lower scores on standardized tests and to earn lower high school grades (the two measures most often used as criteria for admission to the more selective institutions) than do hispanics and American Indians.

Disparities in institutional resources appear to be even greater when it comes to parental income. Per-student instructional expenditures for students at the highest income level are $600 greater than are those for students at the lowest income levels. Similarly, the most affluent students attend institutions that are substantially more selective (by about 125 SAT points) than those that the poorest students attend. Clearly, in American higher education, "them that has, gets."

That expenditures for hispanics are so low is attributable chiefly to the heavy concentration of this ethnic group in com-

Table 9. Distribution of Four Resource Measures by
Ethnicity and Parental Income of Students.

Student Characteristics	Per-Student Expenditures		Per-Student Value of Physical Plant and Facilities[c]	Selectivity Score[d]
	Instruction	Library		
Ethnicity[a]				
White	$2024	$168	$13,144	917
Black	1942	150	11,197	847
Hispanic	1807	141	8,029	889
American Indian	2099	165	12,496	877
Parental Income[b]				
Less than $8,000	$2017	$160	$15,254	865
$ 8,000- 9,000	1991	157	16,598	872
$ 10,000-12,499	2031	163	17,002	880
$ 12,500-14,999	2074	165	16,513	884
$ 15,000-19,999	2102	167	17,215	891
$ 20,000-24,999	2094	163	16,777	899
$ 25,000-29,999	2114	167	17,907	909
$ 30,000-34,999	2147	174	17,380	919
$ 35,000-39,999	2204	182	18,592	924
$ 40,000-49,999	2278	194	20,699	931
$ 50,000-99,999	2434	225	22,763	961
$100,000 or more	2633	268	25,406	997

[a]Includes all enrolled students in 1982-83 (part-time students counted as one-third full-time).

[b]Based only on full-time freshmen entering in Fall 1983.

[c]Fiscal resources as of 1981-82.

[d]Selectivity is the mean SAT (verbal plus mathematical) score of the entering freshmen at an institution (ACT scores have been converted to SAT equivalents). The value shown in this column is the mean selectivity of the institutions attended by all students in a particular group.

Sources: Unpublished data from the Higher Education General Information Survey of 1982, *The American Freshman* (Astin and others, 1983), and the Higher Education Research Institute.

munity colleges, which generally have more meager financial resources than do four-year colleges and universities. And, as already noted, the overrepresentation of hispanics and American Indians in community colleges is due chiefly to the concentration of these ethnic groups in states that have large community college systems and that practice selective admissions in the public four-year colleges and universities.

In view of the earlier discussions of various quality measures (Chapters Two and Three), it would be desirable at this point to show the distribution of minorities and low-income students among institutions classified according to their ability to develop talent. Unfortunately, such information is simply not available. But information is available on one institutional characteristic that is significantly related to talent development: residential facilities. A substantial body of research (see Chapter Six) shows that living in on-campus residential facilities (as opposed to living at home or in an apartment) increases the likelihood that the student will complete the baccalaureate and contributes to other aspects of student development. Two-thirds of the students enrolling at public four-year colleges and universities live in dormitories during their freshman year, compared with less than one-fourth of the freshmen enrolling at community colleges (Astin and others, 1983). At the more selective flagship universities, 80 percent of the freshmen live in dormitories. The figures are similar for private institutions: the proportions of freshmen living on campus are 84.5 percent in private universities, 79.2 percent in four-year colleges, and 66.1 percent in two-year colleges. As a matter of fact, at the most selective private colleges and universities, more than 95 percent of the freshmen live in residence halls. Given the distribution of minority and low-income students among various types of institutions (Tables 7 and 8), it is clear that the "opportunity" to live in a residence hall is not equally allocated among American college students by ethnicity and income level.

Selectivity, Testing, and Tracking

So far, I have reiterated the point that American institutions differ widely in selectivity and that these differences correspond closely to the hierarchical ordering of institutions that constitutes such an important part of our belief system in higher education. The American higher education system is, in effect, a de facto tracking system whereby students are sorted into different institutions on the basis of their differing levels of academic preparation. Standardized college admission tests provide one of the major vehicles for this sorting process (indeed, selectivity is defined in terms of students' scores on these tests), and high school grades provide the other.

The main reason that minorities and poor students suffer a competitive disadvantage in gaining access to the most selective institutions is that they tend to score much lower on college admission tests and to earn lower high school grades than do white students. Test scores, it might be added, are a more serious handicap than high school grades, even though high school grades are usually a better indication of the student's ability to do college-level work (Astin, 1971). The differences between whites and disadvantaged minority groups with respect to college admission test scores are indeed substantial. For example, using the composite (verbal plus mathematical) score on the SAT as a basis for comparison, we find that blacks score about 250 points below whites and that hispanics, Puerto Ricans, and American Indians score between 100 and 125 points below whites (Astin, 1982, Table 17). Minorities also tend to earn lower grades in high school than whites do, but the differences are not as great as is the case with test scores (Astin, Fuller, and Green, 1978).

Student Self-Selection. One particularly interesting feature of the selective admissions process in American higher education is that most of the selecting is done not by the institutions but rather by the students. There is, in other words, a great deal of self-selection. If one were to take the entire pool of applicants to one of the more selective and prestigious institutions and simply draw lots to determine who should be admitted, the resulting class of entering freshmen would not be radically different, in terms of test scores and high school grades, from the class actually selected under normal circumstances (Astin, 1971). This is not to say that the applicant pool would not change if the admissions policies were changed. I am simply saying that, under current conditions, differences in institutional selectivity result more from student self-selection than from the selection decisions of the institutions themselves.

Why is self-selection such an important factor in institutional selectivity? The answer here would seem to lie primarily in the folklore about the hierarchy of institutions. Most college-bound students probably know and believe in the folklore discussed in Chapters One and Two. Their parents, schoolteachers, and guidance counselors share these beliefs. As a consequence, students are urged to apply to institutions whose selectivity is compatible with their test scores and high school grades. Students with relatively low test scores and poor grades are almost never encouraged to apply to elite or prestigious institutions, and those with top test scores and grades are discouraged from applying to community colleges and other nonselective institutions. Basically, guiding students in their choice of colleges seems to involve matching students to colleges where they have some significant chance of being accepted and where the overall ability of entering freshmen does not fall below their own. In short, differences in institutional selectivity are highly dependent on the folklore about institutional excellence. Standardized testing and grading are simply quantitative mechanisms for perpetuating this folklore. As Schudson (1972) observes, "The College Board, as the testing agency which serves these high status institutions, has been the most visible device for sorting students into the different strata of higher education" (p. 61). Schudson goes on to say: "The use of the tests . . . has relatively little to do with instruction or the search for truth" (p. 65). Rather, he believes that tests are used because of a perceived need to "identify, select, and appraise the best-qualified individual competitors for membership and preferment within a meritocratic hierarchy" (Friedenberg, 1970, p. 33; quoted in Schudson, 1972, p. 65).

To say that American higher education has evolved into a kind of de facto tracking system is not to imply that this system is part of a rational plan. Indeed, it is not even a pure tracking system, given that lower-ranking institutions do not reject those few top students who apply for admission. Quite the contrary. Institutions at almost every level of the hierarchy seek the best-prepared applicants they can find, and many institutions use their own scholarship resources to lure such students. It is now a common practice, for example, for relatively nonselective colleges to "sponsor" National Merit Scholars by agreeing to provide a scholarship to any National Merit finalist who agrees to enroll. This is a good example of the monolithic value structure that characterizes the American higher education system: Institutions further down in the hierarchy seek to imitate those at the top by becoming more selective and acquiring more resources.

Testing to Predict, Sort, and Screen. Why do institutions place such a high value on enrolling students with good grades and high test scores? If one were to ask a typical faculty member why these criteria are used in deciding which students to admit and which to reject, the most likely response would be "Because they predict grades in college." Forgetting for the moment that college grades leave something to be desired as a measure of student learning—a point discussed later in this chapter—let us consider the educational implications of this argument. (For simplicity, the following discussion focuses on the use of standardized admission tests.) People with high scores on admission tests are preferred over those with low scores on the grounds that they will subsequently earn higher grades in college. Although the predictive relationship between admission test scores and college grades is more modest than such statements imply, the more crucial point is that predicting an applicant's subsequent performance has little, if anything, to do with the institution's talent development mission. This is not to say that standardized test scores do not reflect the applicant's level of preparation or that they should not be used to place a newly admitted student in appropriate college courses. The problem comes when such devices are used to deny applicants entry to the institution.

Let us examine the prediction argument in the light of the institution's talent development mission. Suppose that a college is admitting all the wrong students, so that the ones who are enrolling learn absolutely nothing from their college experience. In other words, the institution is failing utterly to develop the talents of the students it admits. Even in this extreme case, the admission tests would still predict students' grades. All that prediction requires is that the relative ranking of students on the admission instrument (tests or high school grades) corresponds to their relative ranking in terms of college grades. If both rankings are similar, then a "significant correlation" is obtained. Even if their talents had not developed at all, students would still vary in their performance on final examinations simply because they varied in their performance at the time of college entry.

To take an even more extreme example: If one could administer a college admission test to a group of high school seniors, put them in a state of suspended animation for four years, then revive them and give them a set of final examinations, the college admission test would still have "validity" in predicting their performance on the final examinations.

I have tried out this argument on several of my faculty colleagues, and their usual response is to insist that the college gradepoint average does reflect what the student has learned in college. Although little research has been done on this question, the evidence that does exist fails to support their assertion. In one very interesting study, Harris (1970) used tests to show how misleading college grades can be. The study examined gains in scores on a standardized test administered before and after exposure to various courses. Not surprisingly, these gains were related to the types of courses the students took. Thus, the tests appeared to be measuring the amount of learning that had actually occurred in various courses. However, the test score gains of students who had received failing or near-failing grades were comparable to the gains of students who had received high grades. In other words, course grades did not really reflect the amount of learning that was occurring among students. These results suggest that standardized testing, when carried out to measure talent development (that is, on a pretest-posttest basis), may offer a much better means of assessing student progress than gradepoint average does. (This matter is discussed in more detail in Chapter Seven.)

One of the major drawbacks of the typical college grading system is that it reflects a student's relative—rather than absolute—level of performance. Much the same criticism can be leveled at standardized tests. Typically these tests are reported not in raw score form but in standardized form; that is, the score indicates the student's relative performance compared with that of other students. Such a scoring approach greatly limits the usefulness of these tests in measuring gains in performance (talent development), since it is very difficult to evaluate the significance of any change in a relative score.

Why do higher education institutions rely so heavily on measuring devices that reflect relative rather than absolute performance and that are, as a result, poorly suited to their talent development mission? To answer this question, one must consider the purpose of testing in higher education. In most cases, testing is done not so much for educational reasons (to fulfill the institution's talent development function) as to sort and screen students. Undergraduate admission testing is used to decide who should be admitted and who should be rejected. Competence testing at the junior and senior levels—an increasingly common practice—is used to decide who should be admitted to the upper division and who should receive the baccalaureate. Course grades are awarded to determine who should receive credit for courses and to compute the gradepoint average, which is then used by employers and by graduate and professional schools for selection purposes. Testing at the graduate and professional levels is used, again, to decide who should be admitted and who should be rejected. Both the normative scoring of tests and the relativistic nature of letter grades lend themselves well to such purposes: These scores and grades represent a convenient way of comparing students with each other and of identifying the "best" and the "worst" students for sorting and screening purposes.

Reasons for Selective Admissions. Perhaps the main reason that institutions practice selective admissions—and base this practice on test scores and grades—lies in their unquestioning faith in the validity of traditional criteria of excellence. Take the resources conception, for example. In Chapter Two, I pointed out that well-prepared students (as measured by standardized test scores and high school grades) are considered a valuable institutional resource. Selective admissions is a process whereby an institution acquires as many such students as it can. The same is true of the reputational conception. Most institutions believe they can enhance their reputations by enrolling as many bright students as possible. Indeed, many colleges and universities regularly monitor the test scores of their entering freshmen and count the number of Merit Scholars they enroll, as "proof" of their quality or excellence. And so it is with the outcomes conception as well. The easiest way to ensure a high-performing group of graduates is to make sure that entering students are well-prepared. In short, the three most popular views of institutional excellence—the resources, reputational, and outcomes conceptions—are well served by adherence to a selective admissions policy.

Reinforcement for the practice of selective admissions comes from other directions as well. Most professors support selective admissions because they find well-prepared students are easier to identify with and easier to teach than underprepared students. Indeed, within a given classroom, professors probably favor their most advanced students (see Chapter Six). Alumni, administrators, trustees, and students themselves tend to support selective admissions because they know that a good input of highly motivated and talented students almost guarantees that the institution will have a good reputation and will produce a good many distinguished and possibly wealthy alumni. And the secondary schools, especially the more selective ones, support the tracking system that results from selective admissions in higher education because they see it as a way to motivate their students ("Study hard so you can get into a 'good' college").

A selective admissions policy is also justified on the grounds that any relaxation of admissions standards would lower academic standards. But just what does this mean? I think that two very different meanings can be extracted from this statement. First, the phrase *academic standards* can be interpreted as a referring to the level of performance the student must demonstrate in order to be awarded certain grades or to receive the bachelor's degree. When the term is used in this sense, the concern about lowering admissions standards is ac-

tually a concern that the final performance standards will also
be lowered. But changed admissions standards do not lead inevitably to changed performance standards. Performance standards can be defined and maintained independently of admissions standards. The problem would seem to be a failure to
recognize that if an institution enrolls more underprepared students (students who, at college entry, perform less well than do
normally admitted students) but at the same time maintains the
same performance standards, one or more of the following
changes must occur: The underprepared students must be given
more time to reach performance standards; a greater share of institutional resources must be deployed to deal effectively with
the underprepared students; or the institution's dropout and
failure rates must increase. In other words, the lowering of admissions standards does not necessarily require any alteration in
performance standards at the exit point.

The second interpretation of lowering academic standards
involves the talent development mission of the institution. Here
the concern is that if larger numbers of underprepared students
are admitted, the institution's academic program will become
less demanding and will thereby lose its potency in developing
student talent. Presumably, in attempting to gear its program to
the underprepared students, the institution will slight its better-
prepared students, giving them a watered-down education that
will fail to develop their talent to the maximum. In essence, this
concern derives from a problem that all institutions, regardless
of their admissions policies, confront: how to deal effectively
with students who enter college differing significantly in their
academic preparation. Even the most selective institutions face
this difficulty, particularly with respect to specific academic
skills such as writing ability. Good diagnostic assessment and appropriate guidance and course placement are among the techniques most commonly used to deal with these differences.
When such diagnosis and placement is done thoroughly and
thoughtfully, there is no reason why students at all levels of performance cannot be exposed to rigorous courses that challenge
them to develop their talents.

Selectivity and Equity in the Public Research University.
In the case of the major public research universities, the practice

of selective admissions raises grave questions relating to equal opportunity. As mentioned earlier, these institutions generally offer higher-quality educational opportunities—in terms of fringe benefits and residential facilities—than do other public institutions, particularly the community colleges. And because most public research universities practice selective admissions, minority and low-income students are, in essence, denied equal access to these higher-quality opportunities. American higher education has sometimes been accused of racism, but the basic problem for minorities is not institutional racism. The basic problem is that the higher education system favors the best-prepared students. And, for a variety of social and economic reasons (some of which unquestionably derive from past racism), most minority students receive relatively poor preparation in the lower schools.

It should be remembered that the better-prepared students are not denied access to the community colleges (as would be the case if we had a true tracking system); rather, they have a free choice among all types of institutions. California, which is perhaps the prototype for states with a hierarchically structured public system of higher education, makes this favoritism toward the better-prepared student explicit in its *Master Plan for Higher Education* (California State Department of Education, 1960): The "quality of an institution and that of a system of higher education are determined to a considerable extent by the abilities of those it admits and retains as students" (p. 66). The hierarchical nature of the public higher education system is also made explicit: "The state colleges and the university . . . have the heavy obligation to the state to restrict the privilege of entering and remaining to those who are well above average in the college-age group. . . . The junior colleges relieve them of the burden of doing remedial work" (p. 66).

Like most other institutions, the public research universities have vigorously sought to acquire the resources and reputations that are the tokens of excellence in the traditional sense. Selective admissions is just one aspect of this acquisitive process. While their diligence and fervor in the pursuit of excellence (in traditional terms) are easy to understand, one may reasonably ask whether the public university's mandate is not somewhat broader. Surely, the public university has a responsibility to provide high-quality education to the general public. Surely, as part of a public system of higher education, it is also responsible for assuring that its "superior" programs are available to the state's minority and low-income students.

Although precise numerical goals with respect to the enrollment of minority and low-income students cannot realistically be set, most public universities have implicitly acknowledged their responsibilities in this area by introducing special admissions programs, remedial and support services for underprepared students, and the like. Indeed, several major research universities in the Midwest have a long-standing policy of open admissions. At the same time, virtually every state has acknowledged its commitment to expanding opportunities by providing all their high school graduates with access to some type of public institution. As we have seen, however, not all these opportunities are "equal."

Equity and Excellence

The more I consider the twin issues of excellence and equity, the more I am convinced that there is something inherently contradictory about a higher education system where quality and opportunity are in conflict rather than in harmony. To offer only "low-quality" opportunities to some students betokens mediocrity. To pursue quality in a way that limits opportunity betokens elitism. It seems to me that the apparent conflict between excellence and equity has its roots in the reputational and resources views of excellence. If only a few institutions can be regarded as excellent (the reputational view), then most students will be forced to attend "mediocre" institutions. And if excellence depends mainly on resources, then the expansion of opportunities requires that finite resources be distributed more thinly, thereby diluting the overall quality of the system. Taking the talent development view of excellence, however, one sees that institutional reputation is largely irrelevant and that the connection between resources and excellence (in the talent development sense) is tenuous at best.

It is naive to say that resources have no bearing on excellence. Clearly, institutions need resources to create excellent programs, and some resources such as residential facilities are known to have beneficial effects on talent development. My basic point is that: Within certain generous limits, variations in available resources are probably less important than variations in resource utilization. Earlier in the book I argued that excellence, in the talent development sense, is probably best achieved by focusing resources on the student's personal and educational development, and in Chapter Six I will propose that this can best be accomplished by using resources to stimulate and intensify student involvement.

In my interviews with leading educators I also tried to learn their views on the relationship between excellence and equity. Several of them expressed the conviction that the two goals are complementary rather than contradictory. For instance, Arthur Chickering said, "It's nice to have an educational system that functions in a way that's reasonably congruent with the constitution of its country. . . . To act as though you can have an educational system that is only reserved for a select portion of the population runs counter to all of the basic values on which this country was built. . . . I don't think it makes much sense to talk about a higher educational system which is only accessible to a select portion of the population."

Similarly, Joseph Katz asserted: "I think that it is false populism to play one against the other [excellence and equity]. . . . Only a simple-minded understanding of democracy leaves out the possibility for excellence." And Patricia Graham defined the following role for higher education: "Equity, from my point of view, means that you maximize the talent and temperament that is available in society, not simply reinforce the advantage which young people bring to college. My other catch phrase is that [higher] education should maximize talent, not reinforce advantage."

Several educators, however, raised questions about the feasibility of pursuing both excellence and equity. Thus, Howard Bowen felt that "the cost would be very great. I worry about those ghetto kids, the people in the rural backwaters. . . . Equity requires diversity in the providers, but I fear that equity, as I have defined it, costs so much . . . that for the foreseeable future, equity is unattainable with quality." Russell Edgerton also believed that the simultaneous pursuit of excellence and equity is "very, very difficult. The caste system tends to rule, and as we provide opportunities for the so-called disadvantaged of society to reach some level of performance at a given set of institutions, society keeps changing the rules of the game, so it's no longer 'Did you get into college?' or 'Did you graduate?' but 'Where did you graduate from?' . . . It's a vanishing Holy Grail. It's the way this society is constructed." Although Bowen and Edgerton reach the same conclusion, their reasons are very different. Bowen believes that the costs of providing a high-quality education for everyone are simply too great, whereas Edgerton believes that, because of the nature of society, the hierarchical structure of the higher education system would be difficult to change.

The push for greater excellence in American education—as exemplified in the National Commission on Excellence's recent report, *A Nation at Risk*—has been applauded by most educators. But some observers are concerned that the renewed emphasis on excellence may come at the expense of opportunity or equity. Gregory Anrig, the president of the Educational Testing Service, gave voice to this concern in a recent speech: "The drive for excellence and higher standards can easily cause a setback in equality of educational opportunity. . . . History will not judge us well if educational reform in the 1980s reaches its goal in improved achievement at the expense of the gains in equity earned so slowly and painfully over the past twenty years" (Anrig, 1984, p. 11).

Similar concerns are expressed by Robert McCabe, president of Miami-Dade Community College: "Many who are concerned with improving the quality of postsecondary education offer a simplistic solution to the problem, and that is to reverse the gains in access and limit admission to those demonstrating high ability on completion of high school. While raising admission criteria might be appropriate for certain universities, such a policy applied to all higher education would have a devastating, negative impact on this county. The American economy needs more, rather than fewer, well-educated individuals" (McCabe, 1982, p. 1). McCabe goes on to argue that open-door institutions can achieve excellence by paying closer attention to individual differences among students, by giving students more latitude in the time they take to complete programs, by maintaining adequate exit standards, by doing better economic and institutional planning, and by making greater use of communications technology.

Perhaps the best evidence that a mass system of education can also be of high quality comes from the elementary and secondary schools of Japan. In their drive to educate all citizens to the level of high school completion, the Japanese have virtually eradicated illiteracy, producing a population of school students whose average level of achievement exceeds the highest levels achieved by schoolchildren in most other developed nations in the world (Husen, 1967). Cummings (1979), who has studied the Japanese school system extensively, believes that the success of these lower schools can be attributed to their freedom from corporate and governmental intrusion. Commenting on Cummings's work, Walzer (1983) concludes, "It is often said that the decision to educate everyone necessarily leads to a lowering of standards. But this is true only if the schools are weak, incapable of resisting the pressures of a hierarchical society" (p. 205). In the same vein, Willie (1982) observes, "In the world of education, the illusion often is that quality is the opposite of quantity and that a society with an excellent system of higher education cannot have both quality and quantity. The Japanese experience contradicts this illusion" (p. 20). Willie also points out that, in a democratic society, the quality of collective decision making is likely to increase as the educational level of the entire population rises.

Underlying all these statements is the fundamental notion that the purpose of educational institutions is to *educate* their students and that the quality of a society improves as the population becomes more educated. This is obviously a talent development conception, in that the excellence of the system is defined by its ability to develop the talents of all its citizens. According to this conception, the education of those students who perform best on admission tests is not necessarily more important than the education of students at other levels of performance. Indeed, certain social policies might dictate that even greater attention be given to the education of underprepared students.

Perhaps the biggest obstacle to the joint pursuit of excellence and equity is the resources view of excellence. According to this view, the underprepared student (and, in certain institutions, the average student as well) is a liability. Admitting such a student leads to a lowering of the average test score of entering students (selectivity) and, therefore, diminishes the "excellence" of the institution. At the same time, teaching the poorly prepared student is considered a low-level enterprise, often left to part-time faculty members hired specifically for this purpose. The talent development view, on the other hand, would regard as excellent any teacher who is capable of producing significant improvements in the performance of students, whatever their performance level at college entry.

To summarize: The fundamental conflict between excellence and equity seems to stem from our acceptance of the reputational and the resources views of excellence. The talent development conception not only represents an alternative view that promises a good deal more equity in the system but also offers the significant possibility of upgrading the overall excellence of the system. At this point, it seems appropriate to recall the words of a Carnegie Commission on Higher Education report (1968) published more than fifteen years ago: "What the American nation now needs from higher education can be summed up in two words: quality and equality. Our colleges and universities must preserve academic quality if our intellectual resources are to prove equal to the challenges of contemporary life. And the campuses must act boldly to open new channels to equality of opportunity" (pp. 53–54).

The Underprepared Student

In fulfilling its talent development mission, American higher education faces some formidable challenges. Perhaps the most immediate challenge is that of dealing effectively with the underprepared student. *Underprepared* is, of course, a relative term, since there is no precise dividing line between well-prepared and underprepared students. Most academics seem to use the term for students who are not presently able to do "college-level" work (another relative term) or who function at a level below that of most other students at the institution.

That American higher education has been confronted with increasingly larger numbers of underprepared students is clear (Cross, 1971). As everyone knows, scores on nationally administered college entrance examinations have declined precipitously in recent years. And declining test scores are not the only evidence of underpreparation. In 1983, more than two out of every five freshmen said that a desire to "improve my reading and study skills" constituted a very important factor in their decision to go to college (Astin and others, 1983). This figure is nearly double what it was twelve years ago. Similarly, over the past dozen years, the proportion of freshmen saying they will need tutoring help in specific courses has almost doubled.

The largest test score declines have occurred on measures of verbal ability. This fact may explain why today's college students are reluctant to undertake courses of study that challenge their verbal skills. Thus, the proportions of freshmen planning to major in English, foreign languages, literature, history, and philosophy have dropped sharply since the 1960s (Astin, 1983c; see also Chapter Eight). All these fields demand reading and writing skills, as well as critical and analytical ability.

I have already pointed out that the underprepared student is regarded as a liability by those who embrace the reputational, resources, and outcomes views of excellence. Faculty members, in particular, are reluctant to deal with underprepared students for several reasons. As undergraduates, most faculty members were outstanding students themselves; as graduate students they associated almost exclusively with other outstanding students. By the time they receive their doctorates, few new college faculty members are interested in teaching—much less well-prepared to teach—underprepared students, many of whom function below the secondary-school level in their verbal skills.

But even if faculty members are willing to teach underprepared students, the task is not easy. Among other things, most underprepared students do not have the basic academic skills (reading, writing, analytic thinking) necessary to deal with college-level material. And since they have not yet developed their learning skills to the point where academic work is intrinsically rewarding, their motivation is often marginal. Under these conditions, learning is a difficult chore for the students, and teaching such students is an even more difficult chore for professors.

How widespread is the problem of underpreparedness? Consider the following statement from a professor and former dean:

> Some [students], whether because their previous education has been scanted in deference to no doubt well-meant social experimentation or for other reasons unknown to me, arrive seriously underprepared in English, foreign languages, history or mathematics, and not infrequently in all those subjects. The Committee on Admissions and Financial Aids, rightly impressed by these individuals' motivation and promise, simply has to gamble on their ability, once in college, to make up for lost time; and the gamble pays off in a gratifyingly large percentage of cases. Nevertheless, the diversion of effort into essentially remedial learning and the resultant foreclosing or at least postponement of other curricular possibilities imposes a tax one can't help feeling sorry to see levied against the progress of undergraduates. Its cost is further compounded by the fact that it can easily extend beyond the baccalaureate, continuing to be a burden to students pursuing professional studies at the graduate level [Ford, 1984, p. 32].

The author of this statement, Franklin L. Ford, is McClean Professor of Ancient and Modern History at Harvard. From 1962 to 1970 he served as dean of the Faculty of Arts and Sciences. He is, of course, talking about Harvard undergraduates.

The University of California at Los Angeles, where I teach, is presumably a selective public research university; it accepts only those applicants who graduate in the top one-eighth of their high school senior class. Yet more than half of all UCLA freshmen are required to take Subject A, a noncredit remedial course in English composition unflatteringly referred to as bonehead English. Clearly, the problem of underpreparedness is not unique to community colleges or to other relatively nonselective institutions.

Some college faculty members respond to this problem in unrealistic and unproductive ways. A common approach is just to try to avoid the problem altogether by raising admissions standards. This "solution" was the one advocated by the National Commission on Excellence in *A Nation At Risk*; the major recommendation aimed at higher education was to raise admissions standards. My intuition tells me that this approach simply will not work. For one thing, ethnic minorities and low-income students will resist any attempts to reverse the hard-won gains made during the 1960s and 1970s. Just as important, higher education cannot afford to lose the bodies. The size of the college-age population will continue to decline into the mid 1990s, and since most institutions are dependent on enrollment-driven funding formulas, they really have no alternative but to continue admitting underprepared students. The real issue, then, is what they *do* with such students.

Traditionally, efforts to educate underprepared students have been guided by two radically different philosophies. The elitist philosophy is to let them sink or swim, with the expectation that most of them will sink. This philosophy was at one time common in some of the large midwestern state universities that practiced open admissions. In effect, a high dropout rate was considered a mark of excellence in these institutions.

The second philosophy holds that by admitting under-prepared students the institution has implicitly agreed to provide whatever educational programs and services are necessary to help them reach their degree objectives. This philosophy, in essence, expresses a talent development view. It regards the underprepared student as an educational challenge rather than as a liability. It is, I might add, an active philosophy, as opposed to the basically passive sink-or-swim approach. Under the sink-

or-swim philosophy, the educational institution presents itself as a kind of academic obstacle course, and students are expected to negotiate the course without any particular assistance or special treatment.

A more subtle problem is the belief, widespread among college faculty members, that underprepared students are simply not capable of profiting from higher education. This belief may represent the most serious obstacle of all to the education of underprepared students, since it can lead the faculty member to assume that all underprepared students are going to fail. The self-confirming nature of such a negative attitude is obvious. The educability of underprepared students ought to be viewed as an empirical question: Are students who, at college entry, lack the academic skills necessary for college-level work to be regarded as beyond all hope? Considering the importance of this question, it is remarkable that so little research has been done on it. What evidence does exist, however, suggests that the noneducability of underprepared students is a myth. Saint Edward's University, in Austin, Texas, has for several years operated a unique undergraduate program for children of migratory farm workers (Dennar, 1982). Even though the students entering this program perform very poorly on traditional measures of academic competence, nearly half have been able to complete their bachelor's degrees and many of these have subsequently entered and completed graduate and professional degree programs.

Still other evidence on the educability issue comes from a large-scale study of the City University of New York (CUNY), which in 1970–71 initiated an open admissions policy whereby any graduate of a city high school was eligible to attend one of the CUNY campuses. In this study (Rossmann and others, 1975), open admissions students (those admitted under the new policy) were compared with regularly admitted students (those qualified for attendance under CUNY's previous admissions policies). As expected, at the time of entry to college, the verbal and mathematical skills of the open admissions students were substantially less developed than those of the regular students. By the end of the first academic year, however, the skills of the open admissions students had improved substantially. While they had not necessarily caught up with regular students, they were performing at the level that the regularly admitted students had reached at the time they entered college. In short, this study suggests that underprepared students are educable, that higher education institutions are capable of delivering an effective education to these students, and that—given adequate time and resources—such students can develop their skills to the point of performing college-level work. In Chapter Seven, I will propose certain approaches to providing effective educational programs for underprepared students.

The educability question is not new to American higher education. Robert Maynard Hutchins, regarded by some as a true elitist in his controversial views about higher education, was nevertheless one of the first educators to argue that everyone is capable of learning the material of higher education: "I insist, however, that the education I shall outline is the kind that everybody should have, that the answer to it is not that some people should not have it, but that we should find out how to give it to those whom we do not know how to teach at present" (Hutchins, 1936, p. 61).

Summary

Educational equity is by no means a new idea. In the United States, it became a major issue when American higher education embarked on its major expansion during the 1950s and 1960s and, in particular, when many institutions responded to the civil rights movement by attempting to recruit larger numbers of ethnic minority students.

In this chapter, I have argued that equity cannot be equated simplistically with access: that is, with the availability of *some* kind of higher education opportunity. The quality of the opportunity must also be taken into account. Basically, I have proposed that "equality of opportunity" should be viewed in terms of educational benefits: Two opportunities are not equal if they would lead to different outcomes for a given individual. When individuals are denied access to the best opportunities by selective admissions practices or other means, they are being denied an equal opportunity.

I have also pointed out that the practices of testing and selective admissions derive from our hierarchical conception of American higher education and our acceptance of the traditional views of excellence. The major problem with hierarchical systems and with selective admissions practices is that they operate differentially to deny equal opportunities to minority and low-income students.

I have also pointed out that the talent development view of excellence represents one way out of this dilemma, in that it values the education of all students equally and does not favor the well-prepared student over the underprepared student. Underpreparation is, of course, a disadvantage that plagues many minority and low-income students. It must be dealt with effectively if the talent potential of our population is to be developed to the full.

In short, the conflict between excellence and equity would seem to derive primarily from our traditional conceptions of excellence. By embracing a talent development view of excellence, I believe that we can make great strides toward the simultaneous achievement of educational equity and excellence.

Chapter Five

Rewarding Good Teaching and Improving Teacher Quality

In this chapter I shall examine the teacher-training function and the role of education schools and departments in American higher education. Given the broad scope of the issues covered in the preceding chapters, the reader may reasonably ask why the focus of this chapter is so specialized. Why not a chapter on departments of arts and humanities, schools of engineering, medical schools, and the like? My answer is that the teacher-training function is the principal means through which higher education influences elementary and secondary education. Higher education bears exclusive responsibility for selecting and training teachers and administrators for the lower schools. Moreover, since higher education's very existence depends on the quality and quantity of students produced by the secondary schools, its stake in this enterprise is immense.

But the topic of teacher training and education departments bears even more directly on the issues covered in this book: the hierarchical nature of American higher education, the continuing dominance of the resources and reputational views of excellence, the need to pay greater attention to higher education's talent development function, and the need to promote greater educational equity. Specifically, I shall point out how the problems currently besetting teacher training and schools of education result in part from continued reliance on the reputational and resources views of excellence and how greater fidelity to a talent development view will not only strengthen teacher training but also ensure greater educational equity in this country.

The teacher-training function of American higher education is in serious trouble, as is evidenced by several phenomena: the low status of education schools and departments within academia, the sharply declining interest in teaching at all levels, and the poor preparation of students who aspire to careers in teaching. Let us consider each of these problems in turn.

Status of Education as a Field

"Educators . . . are in charge of the transmission of the culture, especially of what might be called the 'extra-familial culture.' If this function is badly performed, society could easily deteriorate with alarming rapidity. From the point of view of social priorities, one would think, therefore, that schools of education should have the highest status on the campus rather than the lowest" (Boulding, 1975, p. 300). Here we have one of the most bewildering paradoxes in American higher education: *Educational* institutions have relegated their departments of education to a position of very low esteem. Why should this be so? There are, I think, several explanations that merit some discussion.

First, many American academics are unwilling to grant that education is a legitimate discipline. The question of how a discipline differs from a nondiscipline is somewhat arcane, and I will not debate it here. To my mind, education fits nicely within the social sciences and may be regarded as a kind of hybrid social science drawing from psychology, sociology, history, anthropology, and the like. Be that as it may, the fact remains that education is considered a professional field rather than an academic discipline, and most academic departments tend to regard so-called professional fields with some disdain. This attitude probably derives from the high prestige accorded "pure" or "basic," as opposed to "applied," fields.

But the lowly status of education departments is not attributable solely to their "applied" nature. After all, schools of medicine, law, and engineering are accorded relatively high status within academia. Thus, a second explanation lies in the comparative status of the practicing professionals in the various fields. Doctors, lawyers, and engineers enjoy much higher prestige and earn much higher salaries than schoolteachers. Moreover, like schools of education, the professional schools of social work, library science, and nursing—which also train professionals for relatively low-status occupations—are assigned low status.

What accounts for the relatively low status of these professionals? In the United States, schoolteaching, nursing, social work, and other low-status, low-paying fields have traditionally been populated by women and, to a lesser extent, by minority-group members. And until very recently, American society tacitly and willingly accepted the idea that women and minorities "deserve" lower status and less pay than white males. That idea has, of course, been seriously challenged by the women's movement and the civil rights movement. Nonetheless, as Judith Lanier, dean of the College of Education at Michigan State University, observes, "Affirmative action efforts focus initial attention on helping women and minorities gain access to what has been traditionally men's work, rather than on upgrading the quality of what has been traditionally women's work. This is the agenda we must still address, and the teaching profession is among the most obvious to be addressed" (Lanier, 1983, p. 4).

A third explanation for the low prestige of education schools lies in the quality of the students they enroll. Education schools tend to attract students who are poorly prepared, compared with students majoring in other fields (see Table 10). Given the high value attached to high-performing students, it follows that the status of education departments suffers. Similarly, the fact that law students and medical students are generally better prepared academically than are education students helps to explain the wide status differences between these professional schools.

Here we have a clear example of how the resources conception of excellence contributes to, and influences, the hierarchical thinking of academics: Not only institutions but also disciplines within institutions are assigned status in accordance with their ability to attract well-prepared, high-performing students. It might be added that, even within traditional academic disciplines, subspecialties connected with education have low status. Within the field of psychology, for example, school psychology and educational psychology have much less prestige than experimental, physiological, social, or clinical psychology.

Another reason for the low position of education schools and departments is their mixed mission. Originally established to provide training for elementary and secondary schoolteachers, many such schools and departments have recently instituted major programs of research and hired faculty members who are trained in other disciplines. This development—which was probably prompted by a desire to achieve greater prestige and respectability within the larger academic community—has inevitably led to conflicts within education schools and departments. Most of the older faculty members were trained in education, are committed to teacher training, and have only a modest commitment, if any, to scholarship and research. The newer faculty members identify primarily with the scholarly discipline in which they took their doctorates (psychology, economics, sociology, and so on), have little or no interest in teacher training, are committed to research and scholarship, and may even tend to denigrate the field of education. Some of the major research universities have created graduate schools of education where research receives the highest priority and where teacher training, if given any priority at all, is confined largely to postgraduate education. Again, the impetus for these trends seems to be the desire to gain greater respectability within the institution.

In a penetrating essay on what he calls "the schools of the minor professions," Nathan Glazer (1974) notes that the professional degree in education (the Ed.D.), unlike the medical and law degrees, has less status in its own field than does the Ph.D. He also points out that education schools usually pay more attention to those planning to become administrators or scholars than to would-be teachers: "The problem . . . of getting enough attention and resources devoted to teacher training in the school of education—an activity which should, by definition, be one of its major roles—is one that is never quite solved" (p. 357).

Perhaps the most impressive evidence of the low status of the field of education is the demise of the teachers college. In the 1950s there were more than 200 teachers colleges in the United States. Today there are virtually none. Almost all of the teachers colleges or normal schools in the public sector were converted into so-called state colleges and state universities during the period when most of the states began to develop hierarchical systems of public higher education. The process was as follows: Because the teachers colleges were considerably inferior in status, relative to the flagship universities, they received relatively meager funding. The most obvious way to improve their status was to emulate the institutions at the top of the hierarchy. Among other things, this meant minimizing the teacher-training function (a symbol of low status), developing a general-purpose liberal arts curriculum, and expanding their graduate programs and research capabilities. Hence, as Dunham (1969) observes, many first-rate teachers colleges became third-rate universities.

Underlying the status problems afflicting schools and departments of education is the simple, though paradoxical, fact that the art and profession of teaching is seriously undervalued in academia, especially in the more research-oriented institutions at the top of the hierarchy. Such institutions may pay lip service to the importance of effective teaching, but invariably the emphasis is on "publish or perish." A faculty member's performance is evaluated primarily in terms of scholarly accomplishments and professional activities and only secondarily in terms of teaching skill. Any reader who doubts this should sit in as a silent observer on any meeting of a recruitment or promotion committee in a major university. Such committees often give very little, if any, attention to assessing the candidate's performance as a teacher or a mentor.

These attitudes are reflected in the way future college professors are trained. Thus, most doctoral programs emphasize the development of research and scholarly skills but virtually ignore the development of pedagogical skills. Hutchins (1936) commented that "the students who are going to be teachers are put through a procedure which was designed to produce investigators" (p. 3), and the situation has not changed since his day. Academicians apparently believe that no particular training or preparation is required to produce a good teacher; anyone who mastered the subject matter can teach well. Similarly, newly hired faculty members are given very little formal training or supervision in teaching and advising students. Their research and scholarly work is closely scrutinized, however, particularly as the time for a tenure decision approaches.

The low status of pedagogy in the academy is summarized by Boulding (1975): "One of the major problems of the university is the weakness of its ostensibly primary function—teaching. It is universally admitted that university teaching is pedestrian and ill-rewarded. While there may be exceptionally good teachers here and there, on the whole, the level of teaching is mediocre to poor, and there seem to be no institutional mechanisms for improving it" (p. 301). Boulding goes on to argue that teaching might be more highly valued and rewarded if it were as open to public scrutiny as the fruits of the professor's research and scholarly work: "The faculty member whose main concern is good teaching has his product invisibly distributed over silent students and alumni. . . . A reputation for good teaching is made only by gossip in an essentially collegial situation, and under these circumstances it is not surprising that it is poorly rewarded" (p. 301).

I believe that our traditional conceptions of excellence must also be blamed for the low value assigned to teaching. Given Boulding's point that the products of good research and scholarship are more visible and quantifiable than those of good teaching, it follows that an institution's prestige can be enhanced much more easily by recruiting outstanding scholars than by recruiting outstanding teachers. Nationally visible scholars are also more useful than outstanding teachers in attracting more money, more bright students, and other resources. In contrast, under a talent development view, outstanding teachers would probably be the most valued members of the academic community, since they would be making the greatest contributions to the institution's excellence.

Declining Interest in Teaching

Since the early 1970s, students' interest in teaching careers at all levels—elementary, secondary, and postsecondary—has declined precipitously (Figure 2). The magnitude of this drop is remarkable. In the late 1960s, nearly one freshman in four aspired to a career in elementary or secondary school teaching. By the early 1980s, the figure had dropped to only one freshman in twenty. Since women have traditionally accounted for 75 percent of the freshmen planning to become teachers, part of the decline is attributable to women's increasing interest in what were formerly male occupations: business, law, medicine, and engineering (Astin, 1983c). Proportionately, however, the decrease of interest in teaching is just as great among men as among women. Indeed, the decline has been greatest at the postsecondary level, where men have traditionally outnumbered women by about two to one.

These changes in freshman aspirations are reflected in declines in the actual number of teachers coming out of the higher education system. Thus, the estimated number of teacher-education graduates dropped from 289,000 in 1973 to 135,000 in 1983 (" 'Up to half . . . ,'" 1984). A recent article in *Newsweek* entitled "Why Teachers Fail" (1984) reports substantial shortages of teachers in many states and projects that, over the next several years, the demand for new teachers will substantially outstrip the supply.

Several factors account for this alarming trend. During

Figure 2. Trends in the Interest of College Freshmen in Teaching Careers,
1966-1983.

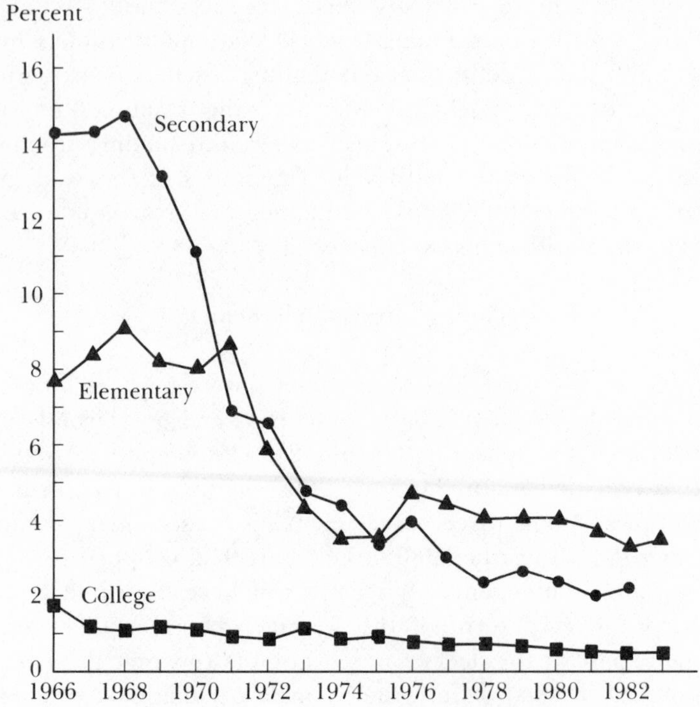

Percent

Source: Higher Education Research Institute, 1984.

the late 1960s and early 1970s, there was an oversupply of
teachers that received widespread attention from the media.
Changes in freshman career aspirations no doubt represent a response to that situation, an interpretation confirmed by the fact
that the sharpest decline in student interest in teaching as a career occurred during the early 1970s (see Figure 2). The decline
has continued, however, even though labor market conditions
have changed dramatically, suggesting that other forces are at
work. I believe that two seemingly unrelated phenomena have
combined to prolong the decline. One is pay and working conditions; the other is the changing American value system.

As far as pay is concerned, the *Newsweek* article also reports that new college graduates who take teaching jobs earn

substantially less than graduates in almost any other field. Thus, the 1984 starting salary for new schoolteachers averaged $14,500, compared with $19,300 for liberal arts graduates, $20,500 for graduates in economics or finance, $24,200 for chemistry graduates, and $26,800 for engineering graduates. Moreover, between 1970 and 1980, the proportion of employed teachers who say that if they could start over again, they would certainly not become teachers increased sharply (from 3.7 percent to 12 percent); the proportion saying they would probably not become teachers rose from 8.9 percent to 24 percent ("Why Teachers Fail," 1984). This increased rate of dissatisfaction is probably attributable to poor salaries, poor working conditions, or both.

Longitudinal data from a 1980 follow-up of respondents who were originally surveyed as entering freshmen in 1971 confirms the impression that the poor remuneration for schoolteachers may help to explain why interest in teaching as a career has declined. On the follow-up, respondents were asked to indicate their current job and their degree of satisfaction with various aspects of the job. Looking only at those respondents who had full-time jobs at the time of the follow-up, we find that elementary and secondary teachers expressed about the same level of overall satisfaction with their jobs as those in other occupations and that they tended to be much more satisfied with working conditions, job challenge, and their opportunities to be creative, to use their college training, and to contribute to society. At the same time, however, they tended to be much less satisfied than respondents in other occupations with their salaries, fringe benefits, and opportunities for promotion.

Such practical and economic considerations may also account for students' declining interest in college teaching. During the early 1970s, new doctorate-recipients found it increasingly hard to get jobs in academia. Tales of unemployment and underemployment—of Ph.D.s driving taxicabs—became increasingly common. Moreover, during the past decade, college faculty members have lost 20 percent of their purchasing power because their salaries have simply not kept pace with inflation (National Center for Education Statistics, 1983, Table 2.11, p. 100).

The second major factor in the decline of interest in

teaching as a career is the radical change in students' values and attitudes, revealed by data from the Cooperative Institutional Research Program (CIRP), which for the past nineteen years has conducted national surveys of first-time, full-time freshmen. For the purposes of this discussion, the most relevant changes are a sharp increase in materialism and in the desire to be very well off financially and a concomitant decrease in altruism and in concern for the good of society (see Chapter Eight). Those careers that have increased most in popularity among entering freshmen also tend to pay well: law, business, engineering, and computer science. Conversely, those career fields suffering the greatest drops in popularity tend to be relatively low-paying: teaching, social work, nursing, allied health, and the clergy—generally known as the human service occupations.

In short, it would appear that many students have lost interest in teaching not only because it pays rather badly but also because making money is more important to students than it used to be, while the goals of serving others and contributing to society have become less important (see Chapter Eight for more discussion of these changes). What we are witnessing here, I think, is a profound change in the dominant values of American society. If this shift continues in the same direction, and if teachers' salaries are not increased substantially, then we can probably expect even further declines in the number of students aspiring to careers as teachers.

Talent Supply for Teaching

The preceding discussion underscores a serious quantitative problem. Schoolteachers are already in short supply, and the shortage will probably become more severe. But what about the qualitative issue? What kinds of students now aspire to teaching as a career? We know that the pool of candidates is much smaller. Has it also become more select? One important clue to the quality of people entering different fields is their performance on standardized tests of academic ability. Table 10 shows the 1974–75 test scores of high school seniors, classified by race and by intended major field of study in college. To

Table 10. Scholastic Aptitude and American College Test Scores
of Entering Freshmen by Race and Intended Major Field of Study.
(High School Seniors of 1974-75)

| | Mean Composite SAT Score | | | | |
Intended Major Field	Blacks	Chi-canos	Puerto Ricans	Ameri-can Indians	Whites
Physical sciences and mathematics	845	1,016	915	979	1,142
Engineering	848	1,018	918	969	1,109
Biological sciences	807	921	897	855	1,066
Social sciences	735	866	796	839	1,029
Allied health	710	846	800	868	958
Business	695	807	814	798	950
Arts and humanities	732	845	831	808	930
Education	632	751	738	755	884
Rank of education among eight fields	8	8	8	8	8

Note: ACT scores have been converted to SAT equivalent (verbal
plus mathematical) scores, following Astin, Christian, and Henson (1978).

Source: Astin, 1977, p. 70.

give the broadest possible picture of the national talent supply,
we combined data from the two major college admission testing programs—the Scholastic Aptitude Test (SAT) and the
American College Test (ACT)—by converting ACT scores into
SAT equivalents (see Astin, Christian, and Henson, 1978). Note
that students planning to major in education rank last in all five
ethnic groups. And the differences are not trivial. For example,
the difference between the scores of education students and
those of students in the next-lowest groups (arts and humanities, business, and allied health) averages around 75 points. The
difference in scores between education students and the top-
ranked students (those planning to major in physical science
and mathematics and in engineering) averages more than 200
points! Clearly, at the high school level, students who aspire to
careers in teaching are among the least well prepared of all as-
pirant groups.

The relatively poor preparation of students planning on
teaching careers is not a recent development. Indeed, more than

forty years ago, Learned and Wood (1938) observed the same phenomenon. But the situation seems to be going from bad to worse. According to the recent *Newsweek* article ("Why Teachers Fail," 1984), the average test scores of prospective education majors have declined even more sharply than the national average, so that the gap between potential education majors and other students actually widened between 1973 and 1983. These trends are confirmed by an independent analysis of high school seniors who participated in the National Longitudinal Studies of 1972 and 1980 (Peng, 1982). Although the scores of high school seniors in general on vocabulary and reading tests dropped significantly, the decrease was greater for prospective education majors than for noneducation majors. It might also be pointed out that these declines were limited to women, who account for about three-fourths of all prospective education majors. The scores of men planning to major in education changed very little.

To analyze the quality question in terms of high school grade average, another important indicator of talent, I used data from the Cooperative Institutional Research Program to compute the proportions of 1966 and 1982 freshman aspirants to teaching careers who made A or A- averages in high school and examined their rank among forty-two career groups. The results showed that in the fall of 1982, the pattern—with respect to talent as measured by high school grades—formed a perfect hierarchy. Those freshmen planning to become college teachers were the best prepared: Close to half (48.5 percent) earned A or A- averages in high school; only two other career choices—foreign service and medicine—included a higher proportion of A students. Next came those who planned to become secondary teachers: 30.9 percent (close to the median of 30.6 percent) had earned A or A- averages in high school, and this group ranked twenty-first among the forty-two career groups, almost exactly the midpoint. Only 21.1 percent of the freshmen planning to become elementary schoolteachers had A or A- averages. Those planning to become school principals had the poorest high school records of all, with only 14.7 percent earning A or A- averages. Indeed, this career group had lower grades than all other career groups except freshmen planning to become

housewives, skilled tradesmen, law enforcement officers, sales-
men, and business owners.

This comparison also indicated that, between 1966 and
1982, the relative ranking, among forty-two career groups, of
freshmen aspiring to teaching careers declined. Although the
percentages with A averages increased over the sixteen-year interval for three of the four groups pursuing teaching careers,
this increase is attributable to the widely publicized grade inflation that occurred over the same period. Also during this interval the data show a drop in rank for all four career groups: from
first to third place for college teaching; from fifteenth to twenty-first for secondary teaching; from twenty-eighth to thirty-
first for elementary teaching; from twenty-second to thirty-
seventh for school principals. In terms of high school grades as
well as standardized test scores, then, the talent level of prospective teachers has dropped. These data provide convincing
evidence that the pool of prospective schoolteachers has declined not only in quantity but also in quality.

The quality of the teachers and administrators who staff
our public schools has important implications for educational
equity. If a student is not progressing well because of poor
teaching, highly educated parents may be able to compensate
by providing extra help and support at home. And affluent parents can hire tutors or elect to send their child to a private
school, but poor and less-well-educated parents do not have
such resources to compensate for ineffective teaching or badly
run schools. In short, when higher education sends out ill-prepared teachers and administrators to staff our public schools, it
is the disadvantaged student who pays the biggest price.

The current shortage of teachers could have been antici-
pated as early as the mid 1970s, when many school districts
around the country began reporting shortages of teachers in science and mathematics. The failure to anticipate such shortages
is in part attributable to the fact that very little attention has
been given to the distribution of prospective teachers among
major fields. Table 11—which shows the intended college majors
of those 1966 and 1982 entering freshmen (from the Cooperative Institutional Research Program) who aspired to careers in

Table 11. Intended Major Fields of Study of Freshmen Planning
on Teaching Careers, 1966 and 1982.

	Intended Major					
Career Choice	Arts and Humanities (%)	Biological Sciences (%)	Education (%)	Physical Sciences[a] (%)	Social Sciences (%)	Other (%)
College Teaching						
1966	45.2	3.8	10.2	20.9	11.5	8.4
1982	44.6	3.2	13.6	16.5	11.0	11.1
Secondary Teaching						
1966	34.6	4.9	21.0	13.2	3.8	22.5
1982	18.3	4.8	63.0	5.7	2.6	5.6
Elementary Teaching						
1966	13.8	0.4	75.4	3.0	2.0	5.4
1982	1.5	0.6	94.4	0.4	1.0	2.1
All Careers						
1966	17.5	3.7	10.6	17.6	15.0	35.6
1982	7.7	3.7	6.0	15.1	6.4	61.1

[a]Includes engineering and mathematics.

Source: Unpublished data, Cooperative Institutional Research Program.

elementary, secondary, or college teaching—throws some light on this question. Among prospective college teachers, by far the most popular majors in 1982 were the arts and humanities, whereas prospective secondary teachers overwhelmingly preferred education (63 percent), as did an even larger percentage of prospective elementary school teachers (94.4 percent). Even more interesting are the trends revealed. During the sixteen-year period, students planning to become elementary or secondary schoolteachers became much more likely to major in education than to take up one of the academic disciplines. This trend was particularly evident among prospective secondary schoolteachers, who were three times more likely to major in education in 1982 than in 1966. Conversely, the percentage of prospective schoolteachers planning to major in the physical sciences or in the arts and humanities declined radically. When this decline is viewed in light of the parallel reduction in the size of the total pool of prospective teachers that occurred during the same period (see Figure 2), it is easy to understand why science and mathematics teachers are in such short supply in the lower schools. Moreover, given the equally dramatic decline in the proportions of prospective elementary and secondary teachers planning to major in the arts and humanities, we can anticipate similar shortages in such fields as English, history, and the fine arts.

No such decline has occurred among prospective college teachers, however; the proportion planning to major in the arts and humanities fell only slightly between 1966 and 1982. These findings suggest that while student demand for course work in the arts and humanities has dropped sharply (see Chapter Eight), there has been no corresponding decrease in the proportion of prospective college teachers who anticipate teaching in these fields. Thus, the current oversupply of arts and humanities doctorates in American higher education threatens to get worse.

Although many critics of teacher education programs have argued that students should major in the discipline they intend to teach rather than in education, these findings show the reverse trend: Prospective teachers are increasingly likely to major in education. While this argument about which major is most appropriate has not, to my knowledge, ever been tested empirically, the fact that most prospective schoolteachers now choose to major in education further discourages students in the most selective institutions (which do not permit such a major) from pursuing teaching careers.

Certain other attributes distinguish potential teachers from other students. Table 12 compares teaching aspirants with aspirants to other careers, using three measures of socioeconomic status: parental income, father's educational level, and mother's educational level. To simplify the comparisons, the table shows the proportions of prospective teachers who come from high-income ($50,000 or more a year) families and whose parents have college degrees. Clearly, freshmen aspiring to become elementary and secondary teachers come from relatively low socioeconomic backgrounds, falling well below the norm for the forty-two career groups on all three measures. This is particularly true of those planning to go into secondary school

Table 12. Socioeconomic Status of Freshmen Planning on
Teaching Careers.

Career Choice	Parental Income[a]		Father's Education[a]		Mother's Education[a]	
	Percent-age Earning $50,000 or More	Rank of Percent-age Among 42 Careers	Percent-age with College Degree	Rank of Percent-age Among 42 Careers	Percent-age with College Degree	Rank of Percent-age Among 42 Careers
College teaching	19.0	21	55.7	5	42.6	3
Secondary teaching	11.8	38	37.7	34	28.5	32
Elementary teaching	15.5	31	43.2	32	26.5	34
Median[b] career group	18.9	—	48.5	—	33.9	—

[a]The percentages on each socioeconomic status item were calculated for each of 42 career groups and then ranked (1–42).

[b]The mean of the 21st and 22d ranked careers.

Source: Unpublished data, Cooperative Institutional Research Program, Fall 1982 survey of entering freshmen.

teaching, who rank thirty-eighth in terms of parental income. Only students aspiring to careers in law enforcement, pharmacy, medical technology, and clerical work come from families with lower incomes. Prospective secondary teachers rank slightly lower than prospective elementary teachers in terms of father's education but slightly higher in terms of mother's education.

Prospective college teachers come from considerably higher socioeconomic backgrounds. They rank right at the median for all forty-two career groups in terms of parental income, and they rank close to the top in terms of parents' education. Indeed, if we considered the proportion whose parents have graduate degrees (data not presented in the table), we would find that they rank first in terms of mother's education and second in terms of father's education. Thus, while the income level of their parents is no more than average, students aspiring to careers in college teaching come from the best-educated families.

Table 13 shows the racial composition of the various teacher-aspirant groups in 1982 and ten years earlier. The most

Table 13. Racial Distribution of Freshmen Planning on Teaching Careers, 1972 and 1982.

Career Choice	Black (%)	Chicano (%)	Puerto Rican (%)	American Indian (%)	Asian (%)	White (%)
College teaching						
1972	14.8	0.8	0.6	0.5	2.2	81.2
1982	6.2	0.9	1.5	0.6	5.1	85.8
Secondary teaching						
1972	7.9	2.1	2.1	0.4	1.7	89.7
1982	3.6	1.9	1.0	1.2	1.0	93.3
Elementary teaching						
1972	9.3	1.0	0.6	0.8	0.2	88.3
1982	3.8	1.2	0.6	0.4	0.4	94.3
All 42 careers combined						
1972	8.7	1.5	0.6	1.1	1.1	87.3
1982	8.5	0.9	0.9	1.0	1.4	88.2

Note: The percentages do not add up to 100 across the rows because the category "Other" has been omitted.

Source: Unpublished data, Cooperative Institutional Research Program.

dramatic shifts in minority representation have occurred among blacks. At all three levels of teaching, the proportion of blacks declined by more than half between 1972 and 1982. These trends are all the more remarkable when one realizes that the proportion of blacks among all career groups has remained virtually unchanged over the same period. Thus, in 1982, the percentage of blacks among freshmen aspiring to teaching careers at any level fell well below the percentage of blacks in all career groups. It would seem, then, that the well-known overrepresentation of blacks in the field of teaching (Astin, 1982) will soon be a thing of the past. At the same time, the proportion of whites among teachers at all levels will probably increase.

The data for the four other minority groups (Chicanos, Puerto Ricans, American Indians, and Asians) should be interpreted with caution, given the very small percentages involved. This is particularly true for American Indians, since students' self-reports for this category are highly unreliable (see Astin, 1982). Perhaps the most noteworthy trend among these smaller minority groups was the increase in the percentage of Asians among freshmen aspiring to become college teachers. By 1982, Asians were overrepresented among prospective college teachers (relative to their representation in all career groups) by a factor of three to one.

I have frequently talked with representatives of teachers' unions and with deans of education schools about the relatively poor academic preparation of teaching aspirants. Typically, they tell me that the data cannot be trusted because students frequently change their plans after entering college. Thus, they claim, the people who end up working as schoolteachers are probably very different from what one would suppose from the data on high school seniors or on entering college freshmen. The implication is that schoolteachers are a much more competent and talented group than those students who, early in their college careers, say they plan to become teachers.

An opportunity to test this argument was afforded by the previously mentioned 1980 follow-up study of entering freshmen. Since the typical undergraduate completes the baccalaureate within four or five years after entering college, this nine-year interval presumably constitutes sufficient time to determine which students actually end up being employed as teachers. This analysis involved only those respondents who, at the time of the 1980 follow-up, had attained at least a baccalaureate. The idea was to see whether the academic credentials of 1971 teaching aspirants were any different from the academic credentials of those employed as schoolteachers nine years later. Table 14 compares the three groups of 1971 teaching aspirants with the three counterpart groups of 1980 teachers on four measures: high school grade average, high school class rank, election to a high school honor society, and recognition in the National Merit Scholarship Program. This last measure is of particular interest, since recognition in the National Merit Program is based strictly on the student's scores on either the Preliminary Scholastic Aptitude Test or the Scholastic Aptitude Test; only

Table 14. Teaching Aspirants in 1971 Versus Employed Teachers in 1980: A Comparison of Academic Credentials. (Baccalaureate Recipients Only)

| | Percentage Among Persons in | | | | | |
| | Elementary Teaching | | Secondary Teaching | | College Teaching | |
Academic Credentials	1971 Freshman Aspirants (N = 647)	1980 Employed Graduates (N = 622)	1971 Freshman Aspirants (N = 689)	1980 Employed Graduates (N = 455)	1971 Freshman Aspirants (N = 105)	1980 Employed Graduates (N = 59)
High school grade average:						
A- or better	24.6	23.7	29.5	25.5	48.6	40.6
B+ or better	45.8	42.3	55.6	49.2	61.0	64.3
Graduated in top quarter of high school class	55.8	54.5	63.7	61.1	81.0	79.7
Elected to high school honor society	38.6	38.7	45.0	44.0	54.3	52.5
Received recognition in National Merit Program[a]	8.0	6.3	13.6	11.9	21.9	28.8

[a]Certificate of Merit or Letter of Commendation.

Source: Unpublished data, Cooperative Institutional Research Program.

those who make very high scores are awarded a Certificate of Merit or a Letter of Commendation.

As Table 14 shows, those respondents who ended up being employed as elementary or secondary schoolteachers earned lower grades in high school than did those who, as entering freshmen, aspired to these careers. The results for the college teaching groups were less clear-cut: Aspirants were more likely than employed teachers to have high school grades of A– or better, whereas employed teachers were more likely than aspirants to have high school grade averages of B+ or better. Apparently, people who made B+ averages in high school are especially likely to end up being employed as college teachers.

When it comes to graduation in the top quarter of their high school class, all three groups of employed teachers come out worse than their counterparts among entering freshmen. It should be emphasized, however, that the differences on this variable are very small, as are differences with respect to membership in a high school honor society. The proportions were about the same at the elementary level, while at the secondary and college levels, slightly larger proportions of aspirants than of employed teachers had been elected to such societies.

With respect to recognition in the National Merit Program, aspirants again come out ahead of employed teachers at the elementary and secondary levels. At the college level, however, those respondents who ended up being employed as teachers in 1980 were substantially more likely (28.8 percent) than those who had, as freshmen, aspired to college teaching (21.9 percent) to have received a Certificate of Merit or a Letter of Commendation in the National Merit Program.

In short, the data in this table would seem to refute the contention that the pool of potential teachers improves significantly during the college years and that those who end up as teachers are of much higher quality than those who aspire to teaching careers as high school seniors or college freshmen.

Summary

As this chapter has no doubt made clear, it is my impression that most academicians—especially those in the major research universities—tend to regard schools or departments of education as something of an embarrassment. Indeed, several leading universities have recently attempted to get rid of their education schools altogether. For example, in 1982 the faculty at the University of California at Berkeley recommended that the Graduate School of Education be eliminated, but this recommendation was overruled by the chancellor.

Why do schools of education have such low status in the eyes of academicians?

At the root of the problem, I think, is the value system of college professors and administrators. Most of the faculty members I know embrace the resources approach to excellence and therefore place a very high value on the intellect and on scholarship. They themselves tended to be outstanding students, both in high school and in college, and were heavily rewarded for their academic achievements. They are usually very deferent to their most brilliant peers, and they favor their most "brilliant" students (meaning the most verbally fluent as well as the most outstanding in research and scholarship). In other words, academicians value the *demonstration* of intellect over the *development* of intellect (talent development). At the same time, they value pure (often called theoretical or basic) knowledge over practical (often called applied or technical) knowledge. This latter bias suggests that academics place greater emphasis on having knowledge ("academic" departments) than on applying knowledge ("professional" schools).

As it happens, education schools fail to pass muster on all counts: They train practitioners who are supposed to apply knowledge rather than generate it; and, when they do conduct research, it tends to be applied rather than theoretical. But most important, the students attracted to programs in education tend to be among the least well-prepared (least "brilliant") of all college students. Students aspiring to become schoolteachers are thus regarded as a liability because their relatively poor academic preparation dilutes the "selectivity" (resources and reputation) of the institution.

The data presented in this chapter give a rather bleak picture of both the quantity and the quality of prospective teachers. The pool of students interested in teaching at any level has

declined sharply over the past fifteen years to the point where
most states are now experiencing severe shortages of teachers.
Although college teachers come from the ranks of the best-
prepared students, those who plan to enter elementary and secondary teaching are among the most ill-prepared of all career
groups. Moreover, the academic disadvantagement of prospective schoolteachers seems to have increased in recent years, so
that the gap between students pursuing teaching careers and students pursuing other careers has widened. These findings suggest
that the current teacher shortage will get worse before it gets
better and that the problem of recruiting academically talented
people into teaching will become increasingly severe.

These difficulties are compounded by the negative attitudes of academics, referred to earlier. This negativity is especially acute in the prestigious institutions, most of which do not
even permit their undergraduates to major in education. Since
these institutions enroll a disproportionate share of the best-
prepared students, their disdainful attitudes have exacerbated
the problems of finding and training highly able people to teach
in our public schools.

These negative views of the field of education and the
profession of teaching are reinforced in many of our universities, where teaching and pedagogical ability are not highly valued and where research and scholarship are the top priorities.
It seems likely that the millions of students who have passed
through our colleges and universities during the past several decades have picked up their professors' attitudes. Such attitudes
are exemplified by the recent cover story in *Newsweek* entitled
"Why Teachers Fail" (1984). The cover picture showed a crude
chalkboard drawing of a teacher wearing a dunce cap.

If institutions were to embrace a talent development view
of excellence, at least some of the problems confronting education and teacher training would be mitigated. Outstanding teachers would receive the same rewards as outstanding scholars, and
pedagogy would be elevated to a much higher status within the
academy. In all likelihood, such a change in institutional values
would also serve to attract better-prepared students to careers as
schoolteachers.

Chapter Six

Student Involvement:
The Key to Effective Education

How do we go about facilitating talent development in higher education? What are the most effective methods? What theories of student learning seem to be most valid? Even a casual reading of the extensive literature on student development in higher education can be a confusing and perplexing experience. One finds not only that the problems being studied are highly diverse but also that investigators who claim to be studying the same problem frequently do not look at the same variables or employ the same methods. And even when they are looking at the same variables, different investigators may use very different terms in describing and discussing them.

The theory of student involvement presented in this chapter has direct implications for the talent development view of excellence. It has several other virtues as well. First, it can be stated simply: *Students learn by becoming involved.* I have not found it necessary to draw a maze consisting of dozens of boxes interconnected by two-headed arrows in order to explain the basic elements of the theory to others. Second, the theory provides a context for understanding the diverse literature in this field because it seems to explain most of the empirical knowledge gained over the years about environmental influences on student development. Third, the theory embraces principles from such widely divergent sources as psychoanalysis and classical learning theory. Fourth, the involvement concept applies equally to students and to faculty. And finally, the theory of involvement is a useful tool that can be used both by researchers, to guide their investigation of student and faculty development, and by college administrators and faculty, as they attempt to design more effective learning environments.

What I mean by involvement is neither mysterious nor esoteric. Quite simply, student involvement refers to the amount of physical and psychological energy that the student devotes to the academic experience. A highly involved student is one who, for example, devotes considerable energy to studying, spends a lot of time on campus, participates actively in student organizations, and interacts frequently with faculty members and other students. Conversely, an uninvolved student may neglect studies, spend little time on campus, abstain from extracurricular activities, and have little contact with faculty members or other students. Let me emphasize that these hypothetical examples are intended to be illustrative only. There are many other possible forms of involvement, which I will discuss in more detail later on.

Although we shall focus our attention here on the student, faculty members too can be characterized in terms of their relative degrees of involvement. A highly involved faculty member would put a lot of time and energy into teaching activities, regularly seek out student advisees to monitor their progress, actively participate in departmental and institutional functions, and make a conscious effort to integrate research and teaching activities.

In some respects the concept of involvement resembles the Freudian concept of cathexis. Freud believed that people invest psychological energy in objects outside themselves. In other words, people can cathect on their friends, families, school-work, jobs, and so on. The involvement concept is also very similar to what learning theorists call "vigilance" or "time-on-task." The concept of "effort," though much narrower than that of involvement, is also relevant here.

To give a better sense of what I have in mind, I want to share with you the results of several hours spent looking into dictionaries and a thesaurus for words or phrases that captured some of the intended meaning. Because involvement is, to me, an active term, the following list uses verb forms:

attach oneself to	plunge into
commit oneself to	show enthusiasm for
devote oneself to	tackle
engage in	take a fancy to
go in for	take an interest in
immerse oneself in	take on
incline toward	take part in
join in	take to
partake of	take up
participate in	undertake

Most of these terms have a behavioral meaning. I could have included words and phrases more interior in nature (value, care for, stress, accentuate, emphasize). But in the sense in which I am using the term, involvement implies a behavioral component. This is not to deny that motivation is an important aspect of involvement but rather to emphasize that the behavioral aspects, in my judgment, are critical. It is not so much what the individual thinks or feels but what he or she does that defines and identifies involvement.

At this stage in its development, the involvement theory comprises five basic postulates:

1. Involvement refers to the investment of physical and psychological energy in various "objects." The objects may be highly generalized (the student experience) or highly specific (preparing for a chemistry examination).

2. Regardless of its object, involvement occurs along a continuum. Different students manifest different degrees of involvement in a given object, and the same student manifests different degrees of involvement in different objects at different times.

3. Involvement has both quantitative and qualitative features. The extent of a student's involvement in, say, academic work can be measured quantitatively (how many hours the student spends studying) and qualitatively (does the student review and comprehend reading assignments, or does the student simply stare at the textbook and daydream?).

4. The amount of student learning and personal development associated with any educational program is directly proportional to the quality and quantity of student involvement in that program.

5. The effectiveness of any educational policy or practice is directly related to the capacity of that policy or practice to increase student involvement.

These last two propositions are, of course, the key educational postulates, since they offer clues about how to design more effective educational programs for students. Strictly speaking, however, they do not qualify as postulates, since they are subject to proof by empirical test. As a a matter of fact, much of the recommended research on involvement (discussed later in this chapter) is intended to test these two propositions.

Implicit Pedagogical Theories

The theory of student involvement has important implications for classroom teaching. Whether they admit it or not, all faculty members rely on some sort of pedagogical theory in carrying out their teaching activities (Hunt, 1980). Though these theories are sometimes not clearly stated, they nevertheless govern much of the typical teacher's effort. What is particularly interesting about some of these theories is that they appear to have their roots in traditional conceptions of excellence—in particular, the resources and content views.

In developing the theory of student involvement, I was

prompted in part by a dissatisfaction with these implicit ideas about teaching because of their tendency to treat the student as a kind of black box. On the input end of this black box are the various policies and programs of a college or university, and on the output end are various types of achievement measures such as gradepoint average or scores on standardized tests. What seems to be missing is some mediating mechanism that explains how these educational programs and policies are translated into student achievement and development. The inadequacies of these theories are compounded by their implicit, unexamined nature. Even when faculty members and administrators are aware of the theories that guide their actions, they seem to accept them as gospel rather than as testable propositions.

So far I have identified three such implicit pedagogical models: the content, the resources, and the individualized (or eclectic) theories. As I examine them, I shall show how the theory of student involvement can help tie them more directly to talent development.

The Content Theory. This first concept of pedagogy, which might also be called the subject-matter theory, is very popular with college faculties. According to this theory, student learning and development depend primarily on exposure to the right subject matter. Thus, a liberal education consists of an assortment of "worthwhile" courses. Individual courses, in turn, are evaluated in terms of their content, as reflected, for example, in course syllabi. In fact, it is a common practice for most academics to evaluate their colleagues' teaching performance by inspecting course syllabi. Given this strong emphasis on course content, it is not surprising that the practitioners of this theory tend to believe that students learn by attending lectures, doing the reading assignments, and working in the library. Rarely do they use oral presentations by the student as learning tools, and then they generally require that the presentations focus on the content of the reading or the lecture.

Under the content approach to learning, those professors with the greatest specialized knowledge of a particular subject matter have the highest prestige. Thus this approach appears to encourage the fragmentation and specialization of faculty interests and to equate scholarly expertise with pedagogical ability. But perhaps the most serious limitation of the content theory is that it assigns students a passive role in learning. The "knowledgeable" professor lectures to the "ignorant" student so that the student can acquire the same knowledge. Such an approach clearly favors highly motivated students and those who tend to be avid readers and good listeners. Students who read slowly or who have no intrinsic interest in the subject matter of a particular course are not well served by this approach. In fact, recent attempts to expand educational opportunities for underprepared students have probably been hindered by the continued adherence of most faculty members to the content theory of learning (Astin, 1982).

The Resources Theory. This theory derives directly from the resources conception of institutional excellence. While most faculty members would support this theory in principle, it is a particular favorite among administrators and policy makers. The term *resources,* as used here, includes a wide range of things that are thought to enhance students' learning: physical facilities (laboratories, classrooms, libraries, audiovisual aids), human resources (well-trained faculty members, teaching assistants, counselors, and support personnel), and monetary resources (financial aid, endowments, extramural research funds). In effect, proponents say, if adequate resources are brought together in one place, student learning and development will occur. And the more resources there are, the better the learning is. Many college administrators, it should be noted, view the acquisition of resources as their most important function.

One resource measure that is particularly popular with administrators is the student-faculty ratio. It is generally believed that the lower the ratio, the greater the student's learning and personal development. But the resources theory has qualitative as well as quantitative aspects. Thus, the data reported in Chapter Two on undergraduate quality ratings suggest that many faculty members subscribe to the belief that increasing the proportion of high-quality professors on the faculty (quality in this instance being defined primarily in terms of scholarly productivity and national visibility) strengthens the educational environment. As a matter of fact, many research-oriented institutions could probably afford to hire more faculty members if they were less committed to recruiting and retaining faculty members who are highly visible within their disciplines. In short, such policies involve a trade-off between quantity and quality.

Subscribers to the resources theory of pedagogy also tend to regard high-achieving students as a resource. Thus, many faculty members and administrators believe that having substantial numbers of high-achieving students on the campus enhances the quality of the learning environment for all students. Acting on this belief, some institutions invest a lot of money in recruiting high-achievers.

The resources theory of pedagogy has some of the same limitations as the resources conception of excellence. First, certain resources, such as bright students and prestigious faculty, are finite. As a result, the institutional energies that might otherwise be invested in the teaching-learning process are instead expended in recruiting high-achieving students and prestigious faculty. From a systems perspective, these recruitment activities merely redistribute these finite resources from one institution to another rather than add to the total pool of such resources. In other words, while a successful faculty or student recruitment program may seem, from a resources standpoint, to benefit a particular institution, such benefit comes at the expense of other institutions. As a consequence, widespread acceptance of the resource theory of pedagogy tends, paradoxically, to reduce the total amount of resources available to the higher education community at large.

The second problem with this pedagogical approach is that it focuses institutional attention on the mere accumulation of resources and shifts attention away from the utilization or deployment of such resources. For instance, having established a multimillion-volume library, the administration may ignore the question of whether students are using it effectively. Similarly, having successfully recruited a faculty "star," the college may pay little attention to whether or not the new faculty member works effectively with students. In fact, when institutions are trying to recruit stars, one of the perks commonly offered is a low (or no) teaching load.

The Individualized (Eclectic) Theory. Since this theory is not derived directly from any of the traditional views of excellence, it is not widely practiced by college faculty members. This theory—a favorite with many developmental and learning psychologists (Chickering and Associates, 1981)—assumes that no single approach to subject matter, teaching techniques, or resource allocation is adequate for all students. Rather, supporters of this approach attempt to identify the curricular content and instructional methods that best meet the needs of the individual student. Given its emphasis on borrowing what is most useful from other pedagogical approaches, this flexible approach might also be termed eclectic.

In contrast to the content approach, which generally results in a fixed set of curricular requirements (courses that all students must take, or "distributional requirements"), the individualized approach emphasizes electives. As a matter of fact, most college curricula represent a mixture of the content and individualized theories, in that students must take certain required courses or satisfy certain distributional requirements but also have the option of taking a certain number of free elective courses.

But the individualized theory goes far beyond the issue of curriculum. Among other things, it emphasizes the importance of advising and counseling and of independent study on the part of the student. It should be noted here that the philosophy underlying most student personnel work (guidance, counseling, selective placement, and student support services) implicitly incorporates the individualized or eclectic theory of student development. It is perhaps no accident that those few institutions that openly advocate an individualized approach to instruction (Empire State College, the Evergreen State College, and Hampshire College, for example) tend to be relatively new (founded since 1960) and therefore are not bound by traditional views of excellence.

The individualized approach is also associated with particular instructional techniques: for instance, self-paced instruction, contract learning, and independent study. In addition, this theory has led some educators to espouse the "competency-based" learning model (Grant and others, 1979; Mentkowski and Doherty, 1984), whereby common learning objectives ("competencies") are formulated for all students, but the time allowed to reach these objectives is highly variable, and the instructional techniques used are highly individualized.

Although the individualized theory has certain obvious advantages over the content and resources theories, it can be extremely expensive to implement, since each student normally requires a great deal of individualized attention. In addition, because there are virtually no limitations to the possible variations in subject matter and in pedagogical approach, the individualized theory is difficult to define with much precision. Further, given the current state of research on learning, it is impossible at this point to specify which types of educational programs or teaching techniques are most effective with which types of learners. Beyond an "individualization of approach," it is difficult to know just *what* approaches are likely to work best with *what* type of student. In other words, while the theory is appealing in the abstract, it is extremely difficult to put into practice.

The Place of the Theory of Student Involvement

How does the theory of student involvement relate to these traditional pedagogical theories? In my judgment, it can provide a link between the central variables in these theories (subject matter, resources, and individualization of approach) and the learning outcomes of concern to the student and the professor. According to the theory of student involvement, if a particular curriculum or a particular array of resources is to have its intended effects, it must elicit enough student effort and investment of energy to bring about the desired learning and development. Simply exposing the student to a particular set of courses may or may not work. The theory of involvement, in other words, provides a conceptual substitute for the black box that is implicit in the three traditional pedagogical theories.

The content theory, in particular, tends to assign students

a passive role—as recipients of information. In contrast, the theory of involvement emphasizes the active participation of the student in the learning process. Recent research at the precollegiate level (Rosenshine, 1982) suggests that learning will be greatest when the learning environment is structured to encourage active participation by the student.

On a more subtle level, the theory of student involvement encourages educators to focus less on what they do and more on what the student does: how motivated the student is, how much time and energy the student devotes to the learning process. It holds that student learning and development will not be very great if educators focus most of their attention on course content, teaching techniques, laboratories, books, and other resources. Under this approach, student involvement—rather than the resources or techniques typically utilized by educators—becomes the focus of concern.

As this discussion suggests, the construct of student involvement in certain respects resembles a much more common construct in psychology, that of motivation. I personally prefer the term *involvement,* however, because it connotes something more than just a psychological state; it connotes the behavioral manifestation of that state. Involvement is more susceptible to direct observation and measurement than is the more abstract psychological construct of motivation. Moreover, involvement seems to be a more useful construct for educational practitioners: "How do you motivate students?" is probably a more difficult question to deal with than "How do you get students involved?"

During the past few years, developmental theories have been receiving a good deal of attention in the higher education literature. These theories are of at least two types: those that postulate a series of hierarchically arranged developmental stages (see, for example, Heath, 1968; Kohlberg, 1971; Loevinger, 1966; Perry, 1970), and those that view student development in multidmensional terms (such as Brown and DeCoster, 1982; Chickering, 1969). (For recent comprehensive summaries of these theories, see Chickering and Associates, 1981, and Hanson, 1982.) The theory of student involvement, however, differs qualitatively from these developmental theories. Whereas they focus primarily on developmental outcomes (the "what" of student development), the theory of student involvement is concerned more with the behavioral mechanisms or processes that facilitate student development (the "how" of student development). Later in this chapter, I discuss how the two types of theories might be studied simultaneously.

Student Time as a Resource

Although higher education administrators are constantly preoccupied with accumulating and allocating fiscal resources, the theory of student involvement suggests that the most precious institutional resource may be student time. According to the theory, the extent to which students are able to develop their talents in college is a direct function of the amount of time and effort they devote to activities designed to produce these gains. To take a specific example: If a greater understanding of history is regarded as an important talent development goal for history majors, the extent to which students reach this goal is a direct function of the time they spend listening to professors talk about history, reading books about history, discussing history with other students, and so forth. Within certain broad limits, the more time students spend in such activities, the more history they learn.

The theory of student involvement explicitly acknowledges that the psychic and physical time and energy of students are finite. Educators are in reality competing with other forces in the student's life for a share of that finite time and energy. The student's investment in matters relating to family, friends, job, and other outside activities represents a reduction in the time and energy the student has to devote to his or her educational development.

In applying the theory of student involvement, administrators and faculty members must recognize that virtually every institutional policy and practice (class schedules; regulations on class attendance, academic probation, and participation in honors courses; policies on office hours for faculty, student orientation, and advising) can affect how students spend their time and how much effort they devote to academic pursuits. Moreover, administrative decisions on many nonacademic issues (the location of new buildings such as dormitories and student unions; rules governing residency; the design of recreational and living facilities; on-campus employment opportunities; the number and type of extracurricular activities and regulations regarding participation; the frequency, type, and cost of cultural events; roommate assignments; financial aid policies; the relative attractiveness of eating facilities on and off campus; parking regulations) also can significantly affect how students spend their time and energy. Ultimately, these allocations of time and effort should have important effects on how well students actually develop their talents.

While this discussion has focused primarily on student involvement, the involvement of faculty and staff members in institutional activities also has potentially important implications for the effectiveness of the institution's educational program. At least two forms of faculty "noninvolvement," for example, would appear to detract from program effectiveness: part-time status and excessive engagement in outside consulting and other professional activities. In both instances the faculty member's time on campus is significantly reduced, and a good deal of professional time and energy is invested in activity unrelated to the institution's educational activities. Clearly, if institutions were to embrace involvement as a critical factor in assessing faculty performance, outside professional and consulting activities would come under much closer scrutiny.

Relevant Research and Its Findings

The theory of student involvement has its roots in a longitudinal study of college dropouts (Astin, 1975) aimed at identifying factors in the college environment that significantly affect the student's persistence in college. As it turned out, virtually every significant effect could be explained in terms of the involvement concept. Every positive factor was one that would be likely to increase student involvement in the undergraduate experience, while every negative factor was one that would be likely to reduce involvement. What were these significant environmental factors? Probably the most important and pervasive was the student's residence. Living in a campus residence was positively related to retention, and this positive effect occurred in all types of institutions and among all types of students regardless of sex, race, ability, or family background. Similar results had been obtained in earlier studies (Astin, 1973a; Chickering, 1974) and have subsequently been replicated on several occasions (Astin, 1977, 1982). It is obvious that students who live in residence halls have more time and more opportunity to get involved in all aspects of campus life. Indeed, simply by virtue of eating, sleeping, and spending their waking hours on the college campus, residential students stand a better chance than do commuter students of developing a strong identification with and attachment to undergraduate life.

These longitudinal studies also showed that students who join social fraternities or sororities or participate in extracurricular activities of almost any type are less likely to drop out. Participation in sports—particularly intercollegiate sports—has an especially pronounced effect on persistence, despite the many stories about college athletes who are exploited and never finish college. Other activities that enhance retention include enrollment in honors programs, involvement in ROTC, and participation in professors' undergraduate research projects.

One of the most interesting environmental factors in retention was holding a part-time job on the campus. Though it might seem that having to work while attending college takes time and energy away from academic pursuits, part-time employment in an on-campus job actually facilitates persistence. It would appear that such work (which also includes the federal College Work-Study program) operates in much the same way as residential living: Because the student spends time on campus, he or she is more likely to come into contact with other students, professors, and college staff. On a more subtle psychological level, reliance on the college as a source of income may serve to develop a greater sense of attachment to it.

Retention suffers, however, if the student works off campus at a full-time job. Clearly in this case the student is spending a lot of time and energy on nonacademic activities that are usually unrelated to student life. Full-time off-campus work thus reduces the investment the student can make in studies and other campus activities.

Findings concerning the effects of different types of colleges are also relevant to the theory of involvement. Thus, the most consistent finding—reported in virtually every longitudinal study of student development—is that the student's chances of dropping out are substantially greater at a two-year college than at a four-year college. The negative effects of attending a community college are observed even after the effects of the students' entering characteristics and the lack of residence and work are taken into account (Astin, 1975, 1977). Community colleges are places where the involvement of both faculty members and students appears to be minimal: All students are commuters, and most are part-timers. Thus they presumably manifest less involvement simply because of their part-time status. Similarly, a large proportion of faculty members are employed part-time.

The 1975 study of dropouts also produced some interesting findings regarding the fit between student and college: Students are more likely to persist at religious colleges if their own religious background is similar; blacks are more likely to persist at black colleges than at white colleges (now that white colleges are more fully integrated, however, this finding may no longer hold; see Astin, 1982); and students from small towns are more likely to persist in small colleges. It seems reasonable to suppose that the mechanism for such effects is the student's ability to identify with the institution. One has an easier time becoming involved when the college environment seems comfortable and familiar.

Further support for the involvement theory can be found by examining the reasons that students give for dropping out of college. In the case of men, the most common reason is "boredom with courses." Boredom clearly implies a lack of involvement. In the case of women, the most common reason for dropping out is "marriage, pregnancy, or other family responsibilities." Here we have a set of competing objectives that drain away the time and energy that women might otherwise devote to being students. The persister-dropout phenomenon provides an ideal paradigm for studying student involvement. If we conceive of involvement as occurring along a continuum, the act of dropping out can be viewed as the ultimate form of noninvolvement; it anchors the involvement continuum at the low end.

In view of the apparent usefulness of the involvement theory as it applied to this research on dropping out, I decided to investigate the involvement phenomenon much more intensively in a subsequent study of college impact on a wide range of other outcomes (Astin, 1977). This study, which used longitudinal data on more than 200,000 students and examined more than eighty different student outcomes, focused on the effects of several different types of involvement: place of residence, honors programs, undergraduate research participation, social fraternities and sororities, academic involvement, student-faculty interaction, athletic involvement, and involvement in student government. To understand the effects of these various forms of involvement, one should keep in mind the overall results of this study: College attendance in general serves to strengthen students' competence, self-esteem, artistic interests, liberalism, hedonism, and religious apostasy, and to weaken their business interests.

Perhaps the most important general conclusion to emerge from this elaborate analysis was that *nearly all forms of student involvement are associated with greater-than-average changes in the characteristics of entering freshmen.* And for certain student outcomes, *involvement is more strongly associated with change than either entering freshmen's characteristics or institutional characteristics.*

The following is a summary of the results related to specific forms of involvement.

Effect of Place of Residence. Leaving home to attend college makes a substantial impact on most college outcomes. Students who live on campus show greater gains than do commuters in artistic interests, liberalism, and interpersonal self-esteem.

And living in a dormitory is positively associated with several other forms of involvement: interaction with faculty members, involvement in student government, and participation in social fraternities or sororities.

Further, living on campus substantially increases the student's chances of persisting and of aspiring to a graduate or professional degree. Residents are more likely than commuters to achieve in such extracurricular areas as leadership and athletics and to express satisfaction with their undergraduate experience, particularly in the areas of student friendships, faculty-student relations, institutional reputation, and social life. Residents are also much more likely to become less religious and more hedonistic (*hedonism* here refers to drinking, smoking, sexual activity, and the like).

Effect of Honors Program Involvement. Students who participate in honors programs gain substantially in interpersonal self-esteem, intellectual self-esteem, and artistic interests. They are more likely than are those who do not take part to persist in college and to aspire to graduate and professional degrees. Honors participation is also positively related to student satisfaction in three areas—quality of the science program, closeness to faculty, and quality of instruction—and negatively related to satisfaction with friendships and with the institution's academic reputation. These findings suggest that honors participation enhances faculty-student relationships but may isolate students from their peers.

Effect of Academic Involvement. Defined as a complex of self-reported traits and behaviors (such as the extent to which students work hard at their studies, the number of hours they spend studying, their degree of interest in their courses, good study habits), academic involvement produced an unusual pattern of effects. Heavy academic involvement tends to retard those changes in personality and behavior that normally result from college attendance. Thus, students who are heavily involved academically are less likely than are average students to show an increase in liberalism, hedonism, artistic interests, and religious apostasy or a decrease in business interests. The only personality change accentuated by academic involvement is the need for status, which is strengthened. Being academically involved is strongly related to satisfaction with all aspects of college life except friendships with other students.

This pattern reinforces the hypothesis that students who get heavily involved in their college studies tend to become isolated from their peers and consequently to be less susceptible to the peer group influences that seem critical to the development of political liberalism, hedonism, and religious apostasy. On the other hand, they experience considerable satisfaction, perhaps because of the many institutional rewards for good academic performance. Although most research on classroom learning has been carried out at the precollegiate level, the bulk of the evidence from this research provides strong support for the concept of involvement as a critical element in the learning process. "Time-on-task" and "effort," for example, appear frequently in the literature as key determinants of a wide range of cognitive learning outcomes (Bloom, 1974; Fisher and others, 1980).

Effect of Student-Faculty Interaction. Frequent interaction with faculty members is more strongly related to satisfaction with college than any other type of involvement or, indeed, any other student or institutional characteristic. Students who have many contacts with the faculty are more likely than those who do not to express satisfaction with all aspects of their institutional experience, including student friendships, the variety of courses, the intellectual environment, and even the administration of the institution. It would seem that finding ways to encourage greater student involvement with faculty members (and vice versa) might be a highly productive activity on most college campuses.

Effect of Athletic Involvement. Interestingly enough, the pattern of results associated with involvement in athletic activities closely parallels the pattern associated with academic involvement. Students who become heavily involved in athletic activities show smaller-than-average increases in political liberalism, religious apostasy, and artistic interests and a smaller-than-average decrease in business interests. Athletic involvement is also associated with satisfaction in four areas: the institution's academic reputation, the intellectual environment, student friendships, and institutional administration. These results suggest that athletic involvement, like academic involvement, tends to isolate students from the peer group effects that normally accompany college attendance. For the studious person, this isolation results from the time and effort devoted to studying. For the athlete, the isolation may result from long practice hours, travel to athletic competitions, and special living quarters.

Effect of Involvement in Student Government. Participating in student government is associated with greater-than-average increases in political liberalism, hedonism, artistic interests, and status needs, as well as with greater-than-average satisfaction with student friendships. This pattern of relationships supports the hypothesis that the changes in attitudes and behavior that usually accompany college attendance are attributable to peer-group effects. That is, students who become heavily involved in student government interact frequently with their peers, and this interaction appears to accentuate the changes normally resulting from the college experience.

Applications of the Theory by Campus Staff Members

The theory of involvement has a number of interesting implications for practitioners in higher education. Let us briefly consider some of the possible uses that faculty members, administrators, and student personnel workers might make of it.

Faculty Members and Administrators. As already suggested, the content and resources theories of pedagogy tend to favor the well-prepared, assertive student. In contrast, the student involvement theory suggests the need to give greater attention to the passive, reticent, or underprepared student. Of course, not all passive students are uninvolved in their academic work, nor are they necessarily experiencing academic difficulties. But passivity is a warning sign that may denote a lack of involvement. Moreover, devoting more attention to passive students may well serve the interests of greater educational equity, since passivity often characterizes minority and disadvantaged students (H. S. Astin and others, 1971; Astin, 1982).

Perhaps the most important application of the student involvement theory to teaching is that, as I mentioned earlier, the instructor focuses less on content and on teaching techniques and more on what students are actually doing: how motivated they are and how much time and energy they devote to the learning process. Teaching is a complex art. And, like other art forms, it may suffer if the artist focuses too exclusively on technique. Instructors can be more effective if they focus on the intended outcomes of their pedagogical efforts: maximizing student involvement and learning. (Final examinations monitor learning, but they come too late in the learning process to be of much value to the individual student.)

The same point can perhaps be better illustrated with an example from sports. Any professional baseball player will tell you that the best way to develop skill in pitching is to focus not on the mechanics but on the intended result: getting the ball over the plate. If the player overemphasizes such technical matters as the grip, the stance, the windup, and the kick without attending to where the ball goes, he will probably never learn how to pitch well. As a matter of fact, the technique involved in pitching a baseball, shooting a basketball, or hitting a golfball is really unimportant as long as the ball goes where the player wants it to. If the ball fails to behave as intended, *then* the player begins to worry about adjusting his or her technique.

Counselors and Student Personnel Workers. If an institution commits itself to maximizing student involvement, counselors and other student personnel workers will probably occupy a central role in institutional operations. Since student personnel workers usually operate on a one-to-one basis with students, they are uniquely positioned to monitor the involvement of their clients in the academic process and to work with individuals to maximize that involvement. One of the challenges confronting such workers these days is to find a hook that will get students more involved in the college experience: by taking a different array of courses, by changing residential situations, by joining student organizations or participating in various kinds of extracurricular activities, or by associating with new peer groups.

The theory of involvement also provides a potentially useful frame of reference for working with students who experience academic difficulties. Perhaps the first task in working with such students is to understand the principal objects on which the student's energy is focused. It might be helpful, for example, to ask students to keep a detailed time diary, showing when and for how long they study, sleep, socialize, daydream, work at a job, commute to and from college, and so on. From such a diary the counselor can identify the principal activities in which the student is currently involved and the objects on which he or she cathects, and can thereby determine whether the academic difficulties stem from competing involvements, poor study habits, lack of motivation, or some combination of these factors.

In short, the theory of student involvement provides a unifying construct that can help to focus the energies of all institutional personnel on a common objective.

Need for Feedback

A critical consideration in implementing the student involvement theory is to make sure that students, faculty members, and administrators have adequate feedback. In the preceding section I used such phrases as "focus more on what students are actually doing," "monitor the involvement of their students," and "understand the principal objects on which the student's energy is focused." The importance of feedback may be best illustrated by returning to the art form analogy for a moment.

An essential ingredient in performing artists' development of techniques and skills is the opportunity to view the results of their work. Neophyte painters see what comes out on the canvas, aspiring musicians hear what they play and sing and adjust their behavior accordingly. And artists very often rely on technology to enhance the feedback process: dancers use mirrors, musicians use recording and amplification, and so on. If you have any doubts about the importance of feedback in learning a performing art, consider how it would be to try to learn to paint blindfolded or to play the violin with your ears plugged.

Now if teaching and administration are more like art

forms than like mechanistic activities that can be learned by following a how-to manual, then having adequate feedback is essential to learning how to be a good teacher or administrator. And if student involvement is a key ingredient in effective learning, then having regular access to certain information about student involvement would seem to be an essential part of learning and maintaining effective teaching and administration in our colleges.

Feedback on student involvement can be particularly valuable in helping administrators make better use of resources. Ideally, administrators should have regular feedback on the quantity and quality of students' involvement in a wide range of areas: studying, extracurricular activities, faculty members, other students, the library, laboratories, and so on. By monitoring such feedback on a department-by-department basis, administrators should be able to identify potential problem areas and to target resources accordingly (see Chapter Seven for further discussion of these matters).

For the student's part, the importance of feedback in learning is obvious. In the previous chapter I noted that a large body of research (Gagne, 1977) suggests that students learn better when they have a "knowledge of results" (feedback on how well their talent is developing). This sort of feedback occurs, for example, when students have a chance to go over any test they have taken and analyze their errors. And if student involvement is an important ingredient in the learning process, then students would also stand to profit from a better understanding of how they are spending their time and energies and whether they might be able to modify their way of allocating these resources to facilitate their academic progress.

Subjects for Further Research

Applying the theory of student involvement to my research work over the past several years has generated a great many ideas for further study. This research is concerned not only with testing the theory itself but also with exploring educational ideas that grow out of the theory. The following are just a few examples of how institutions might explore the implications of the involvement theory for their own programs and policies.

Different Forms of Involvement. Clearly, one of the most important next steps in developing and testing the involvement theory is to examine ways to evaluate different forms of involvement. As already suggested, a time diary might have considerable value in determining what priority the student gives to various objects and activities. From my experience with such time diaries (Astin, 1968a), I know that students spend very different amounts of time on studying, socializing, sleeping, daydreaming, and traveling. How frequently students interact with each other, with faculty members and other institutional personnel, and with people outside the institution is another matter that should be investigated. Finally, the extracurricular activities in which the student participates should be identified, and the time and energy devoted to each activity should be assessed.

Quality Versus Quantity of Involvement. C. Robert Pace, my colleague at UCLA, has developed an extensive battery of devices to assess the quality of effort that students devote to various activities (Pace, 1982). Pace has assembled an impressive body of evidence showing that talent development may be heavily dependent on both the quality and the quantity of students' involvement. A number of research questions arise in connection with the quality-versus-quantity issue: To what extent can high-quality involvement compensate for lack of quantity? Can students be encouraged to use time more wisely? To what extent does low-quality involvement reflect a lack of motivation, personal problems, and so on?

Involvement and Developmental Outcomes. The research reviewed earlier (Astin, 1977) suggests that different forms of involvement lead to different developmental outcomes. The connection between particular types of involvement and particular outcomes is a problem of obvious significance that should be addressed in future research. For example, do certain kinds of involvement facilitate student development along the various dimensions postulated by theorists such as Chickering (1969),

Loevinger (1966), Heath (1968), Perry (1970), and Kohlberg (1971)? It would also be useful to know whether particular student characteristics (such as socioeconomic status, academic preparation, gender) are significantly related to different forms of involvement and whether a given form of involvement produces different outcomes for different types of students.

Role of Peer Groups. A considerable body of research on precollegiate education suggests that the student's commitment of time and energy to academic work is strongly influenced by his or her peers (Coleman, 1961; McDill and Rigsby, 1973). It would be useful to determine whether similar relationships exist at the postsecondary level and, in particular, whether different peer groups can be used consciously to enhance students' involvement in learning.

Locus of Control and Attribution. Learning and developmental theorists in recent years have shown an increasing interest in the concepts of locus of control (Rotter, 1966) and attribution (Weiner, 1979). A considerable body of research, for example, suggests that students' degree of involvement in learning tasks is influenced by whether they see their behavior as controlled by internal or external factors. Weiner argues that even if students view the locus of control as internal, their involvement may be contingent on whether they see these internal factors as controllable (effort, for instance) or as uncontrollable (such as ability). Clearly, the effectiveness of any attempt to increase student involvement may depend heavily on the student's perceived locus of control and attributional inclinations.

Other Topics. Among the other questions that might be explored in future research on the involvement theory are the following: What are the characteristics of the exceptions to the rule—the highly involved students who drop out and the uninvolved students who nonetheless manage to persist in college? Are there particular developmental outcomes for which a high degree of involvement is contraindicated?

Two students may devote the same total amount of time and energy to a task but may distribute their time very differently. For example, in preparing a term paper, one student may work for one hour each night over a period of two weeks, while another may stay up all night to do the paper. What are the developmental consequences of these different patterns?

How do different kinds of involvement interact? Does one form of involvement (in extracurricular activities, for example) enhance or diminish the effects of another form (such as academic work)? What are the ideal combinations for facilitating the maximum learning and personal development?

Although the theory of involvement generally holds that more is better, there are probably limits beyond which increasing involvement ceases to produce desirable results and even becomes counterproductive. Examples of excessive involvement are the "workaholic," the academic "nerd" or "grind," and other personality types who manifest withdrawal and obsessive-compulsive behavior. What are the ideal upper limits for various forms of involvement? Are problems more likely to develop when the student is excessively involved in a single object (academic work, for instance) than they are when he or she focuses on a variety of objects (such as academic work, a part-time job, and extracurricular, social, and political activities)?

And what about the participation of campus educators? Can student involvement be increased if professors interact more with students? Can administrators bring about greater faculty-student interaction by setting an example themselves? Does focusing on student involvement as a common institutional goal tend to break down traditional status barriers between faculty members and student personnel workers?

Summary

In this chapter, I have presented a theory of student development—the student involvement theory—which, in my view, is at once simple and comprehensive, a theory that not only elucidates the mass of findings that have emerged from decades of research on student development but also offers higher education practitioners a tool for designing more effective learning environments.

Student involvement refers to the quantity and quality of

the physical and psychological energy the student invests in the college experience. Such involvement takes many forms: absorption in academic work, participation in extracurricular activities, interaction with faculty members and other institutional personnel, and so forth. According to the theory, the greater the student's involvement in college, the greater the learning and personal development. From the standpoint of the educator, the theory's most important point is that the effectiveness of any educational policy or practice is directly related to its capacity for increasing student involvement.

The principal advantage of the student involvement theory over traditional pedagogical approaches (including the content, the resources, and the individualized or eclectic theories) is that it directs attention away from subject matter and technique and toward the motivation and behavior of the student. It views student time and energy as institutional resources, albeit finite ones. Given this view, all institutional policies and practices—those relating to nonacademic as well as to academic matters—can be evaluated in terms of the degree to which they increase or reduce student involvement. Similarly, all higher education practitioners—counselors and student personnel workers as well as faculty members and administrators—can assess their own activities in terms of their success in encouraging students to become more involved in the college experience.

Chapter Seven

Practical Steps
for Involving Students
and Developing Their Talents

In this chapter, I will take up the very practical question of how American higher education can go about implementing some of the concepts presented in the preceding chapters, in order to upgrade the overall excellence of the system and to make it more equitable for poor and minority students. In their catalogs and other official publications, most colleges and universities in the United States espouse a talent development philosophy. But merely paying lip service to this philosophy is no longer enough. The time has come for all of our institutions to rededicate themselves to this fundamental educational task.

This chapter first suggests some practical strategies for increasing students' involvement in college. Next, I look at public policy, outlining some of the actions that external agencies can take to assure that academic institutions will give higher priority to their talent development mission. The chapter then considers two types of institutions—the research university and the commuter college—that pose special problems when it comes to implementing the talent development conception. In the following section I will point out some of the sources of inertia and conservatism within the higher education system that make it highly resistant to change. Finally, I will argue the need for strong and creative leadership on the part of administrators and discuss ways in which we might be able to improve our selection of administrators.

In the preceding chapter we saw that one of the best ways to develop talent to the maximum is to get students actively involved in their own learning. Involvement has both quantitative and qualitative aspects: the amount of time the student devotes to learning and the effectiveness of any given investment of time and energy as far as learning outcomes are concerned. Any institution wishing to stimulate participation has available to it three major vehicles: instruction, student life, and assessment and feedback.

Using Instruction to Increase Involvement

Perhaps the most direct and potent way to get students to take an active part is through instruction, seen very broadly. I will discuss here several types of teaching and related practices that offer promise for heightening students' involvement: better use of resources, active modes of teaching, learning communities, individualized instruction, curricular innovation, increased student-faculty contact, and faculty development. Finally, I will reexamine the special problem of the underprepared student.

Better Use of Resources. In allocating instructional resources, colleges and universities traditionally invest the greatest amount in educating graduate and professional students; the next largest share goes to upper-division undergraduates; and lower-division undergraduates rate the smallest investment. Most states employ formulas that allocate resources to public institutions in this manner. The problem with this pattern is that the investment is smallest at the level where involvement problems appear to be greatest. Most students who fail to complete the baccalaureate drop out of college during their freshman or sophomore years. Thus, it would seem appropriate to devote the most money and effort to educating freshmen and sophomores. In its final report, the Study Group on the Conditions of Excellence in Higher Education (1984) recommended just that: a major reallocation of resources so that lower-division students—in particular, new freshmen—receive a much more substantial portion of instructional resources than they currently do in most institutions. (This process was labeled front loading.) The Study Group also recommended that institutions revise their current practice of hiring part-time instructors for economic reasons (because part-time instructors, who usually do not receive fringe benefits, cost the institution less than full-time instructors). It argued that because part-time instructors tend to be less involved in their work at the institution, three or four part-time faculty members are simply not equivalent to one full-time faculty member in terms of commitment to and involvement with students. Finally, the Study Group recommended that, in the faculty recruitment and review process, considerably more weight be given to teaching.

Another issue relating to resource use is the academic calendar. While the relative merits of a quarter, semester, trimester and other plans are not clear, there are certain approaches that offer some promise of increasing student involvement. For example, in the so-called four-one-four plan, students can use the intervening one month as a time to concentrate their energies on a single subject or project, without the sense of discontinuity and fragmentation that frequently occurs when students study four or five different subjects simultaneously. The point here is that academic administrators and planners should begin to view the academic calendar as a tool for enhancing involvement and learning.

Active Modes of Teaching. In Chapter Six, I described the content view of excellence and noted that it tends to result in passive learning: The "knowledgeable" faculty member lectures to the "ignorant" student. Student involvement under these conditions is likely to be minimal. The Study Group made a number of recommendations concerning greater use of active teaching modes, whereby students take much more responsibility for their own learning. Among the many techniques available for encouraging greater student responsibility are supervised independent study, internships, taking part in faculty research activities, and participation in small discussion groups.

Learning Communities. Students attending the larger colleges and universities often have difficulty becoming full participants in college life because they have only limited opportunities to identify with other students. Therefore, the Study Group recommended that institutions make special efforts to create small subgroupings of students called learning communities and characterized by a common sense of purpose. Such communities can be organized along curricular lines, common career interests, avocational interests, residential living areas, and so on. These can be used to build a sense of group identity, cohesiveness, and uniqueness; to encourage continuity and the integration of diverse curricular and co-curricular experiences; and to counteract the isolation that many students feel.

Individualization. As noted in Chapter Six, the individualized approach to instruction offers yet another means of promoting student involvement. Although such an approach may be difficult to implement, most institutions, even large ones, should make a concerted attempt to experiment with different forms of individualization. Among the most articulate and comprehensive treatises on the subject are "Individualized Education" (Clark, 1981) and *The Personalized System of Instruction* (PSI) (Keller and Koen, 1976). The PSI has been subjected to extensive research and found generally superior to traditional lecture methods. Briefly, PSI involves organizing the material of a course in several dozen units, each with its own study guide telling students what to read and what they must know in order to master the unit. Each unit requires an average of two hours to master. A key element in PSI is the use of student proctors who have already mastered the material and who administer examinations to current learners. If the learner scores below 90 percent, the proctor provides appropriate feedback and suggests how the learner might go about mastering the material. Clearly, under the PSI approach—and indeed, most other forms of individualized instruction—students proceed at their own pace. Thus, the lockstep approach to undergraduate learning, whereby each student is expected to complete the bachelor's degree within four years, does not accommodate well to individualized instruction.

Another promising form of individualization is contract learning. Here the student negotiates with the professor, sometimes called a mentor, agreeing to perform a certain amount of work for which a certain amount of credit will be granted. A substantial amount of evidence suggests that contract learning elicits considerable student involvement. Once again, the time required to complete a given contract varies from student to student (Chickering, 1974; Cross, 1976).

Curricular Innovation. The traditional liberal arts curriculum tends to reflect the interests of individual professors; it is not organized or presented in such a way as to appeal to students. These days, a number of institutions are experimenting with curricular innovation designed to increase students' involvement: colloquies, integrated seminars, and similar devices of an interdisciplinary nature that attempt to integrate subject matter from different disciplines by focusing on contemporary issues and problems. Modern society offers a wide range of subjects that lend themselves well to such seminars: the environment, energy, the impact of technology, terrorism and disregard for international law, nuclear weapons, war and peace, and consumerism, to name but a few. It seems likely that students will devote more time and effort to academic work if at least some of that work focuses on issues they find interesting and meaningful.

Student-Faculty Contact. A large body of research (see Chapter Six) suggests that the best way to involve students in learning and in college life is to maximize the amount of personal contact between faculty members and students. Unfortunately, the policies of many institutions militate against such contact. Classes are held in large lecture sections, faculty office hours are limited, and advising is performed by nonfaculty personnel. I have already mentioned several methods for increasing student-faculty interaction (learning communities, student participation in faculty research projects); many other means are available. The important point is that direct contact between students and faculty members is a simple and effective way to interest students in learning. Thus, institutional planners and administrators would do well to ask how much contact their students currently have with professors and whether there are means available to increase this contact.

Faculty Development. Another aspect of faculty members' lives that bears directly on the involvement goal is faculty development. In most American colleges and universities faculty members are expected to perform at least two basic functions: teaching and research. Yet both graduate training and appointment procedures emphasize scholarly and research skills, and faculty members are hired and promoted primarily on the basis of their scholarly performance. Their pedagogical and mentoring skills, on the other hand, are given relatively little attention. Most graduate programs offer virtually no training in these abilities, and new instructors are usually given little or no direct supervision. It is simply assumed that they can teach and advise students effectively and confidently. All too frequently, this assumption is unfounded, as generations of undergraduates can attest.

The Study Group on the Conditions of Excellence in Higher Education (1984) recommended several changes in the graduate education and in-service training of faculty members that bear serious consideration. Specifically, it recommended that prospective and newly hired instructors receive much more extensive training in assessment procedures (designing, administering, and interpreting tests of various types) as well as in the basic teaching crafts of syllabus writing, lecturing, leading discussions, and designing individualized learning experiences. If faculty members become better teachers and mentors, students are likely to get more involved in their courses.

Underprepared Students. As I mentioned in Chapter Six, underprepared students have special problems with involvement. Because their learning skills are not well developed, they have difficulty comprehending traditional academic material.

Consequently, they become bored, discouraged, and alienated. Little wonder that so many of them drop out of college.

The gravity of this problem cannot be overestimated. Since faculty members cannot easily identify with such students, they are often reluctant to invest significant energy in teaching them. Perhaps more important, the presence of such students in the classroom creates problems for the professor in presenting the subject matter. If he or she pitches the material to the level of the underprepared students, the more advanced students feel cheated or bored. On the other hand, if the professor directs the material to the more advanced students, the underprepared student finds it almost impossible to survive. Some educators (Bowen, 1981b; Coleman, 1982) have argued that this problem calls for much more individualized instruction. It should be recognized, however, that individualization requires a considerable investment of the professor's time and that any given professor's time is limited.

The most realistic solution to this problem is to use student peers. Considerable research evidence suggests that peer tutoring is a highly effective means for dealing with a diversity of competence in the classroom (P. A. Astin, 1982). I have already mentioned that the Personalized System of Instruction (Keller and Koen, 1976), which uses student proctors, seems to produce better results than traditional methods. In Japan, where peer tutoring is widely practiced in the elementary schools, students seem to perform as well as or better than students in almost any other nation (Cummings, 1979).

Even more persuasive is the evidence from a recent survey of the literature by Levin, Glass, and Meister (1984), who compared the cost-effectiveness of four interventions—peer tutoring, computer-assisted instruction, lengthened instructional time, and class size—in developing basic skills in mathematics and reading. Computer-assisted instruction tended to be more cost-effective than increased instructional time and reduced class size, and peer tutoring was more than twice as cost-effective as computer-assisted instruction.

The only objection to peer tutoring comes from those who claim that the more advanced students are being exploited.

One possible response to this objection is to pay the more advanced students for their tutoring help. But such a step may not be necessary. The Japanese experience suggests that tutoring slower students does not inhibit the achievement of the more advanced students. Indeed, one of the best ways to master a subject is to teach it. Moreover, the involvement of *both* the slower and the more advanced students is enhanced through peer tutoring.

Using Student Life Activities to Increase Involvement

Student life outside the classroom offers a number of levers for promoting greater involvement: academic advising, residential facilities, orientation, financial aid, counseling, and campus life in general.

Academic Advising. Academic advising seems to be one of the weakest areas in the entire range of student services. As a matter of fact, undergraduates are more likely to express dissatisfaction with one-on-one services (advisement, career counseling, job placement, and so on) than with other aspects of their college exposure (Green and others, 1983). In many large universities, faculty members have been relieved of virtually all academic advising responsibilities and replaced by a professional staff. While this practice may give faculty members more time for other endeavors, it also distances them from student life and makes it harder for them to identify with the typical student's problems in deciding on a major and on specific courses to take. In its recent report on undergraduate education, the Study Group on the Conditions of Excellence in Higher Education (1984) strongly recommended that all members of the academic community, including faculty members and administrators, participate in academic advisement as a means of familiarizing themselves with the curriculum of the total institution and of maintaining personal contact with at least some undergraduates.

Residential Life. Given the large body of research demonstrating the efficacy of the residential experience for increasing student involvement (Astin, 1975, 1977, 1982; Chickering,

1974), it is unfortunate that many institutions with residential facilities have never utilized the full potential of this experience. Since students spend so much of their time in residence halls, there is no reason why these facilities cannot be used to increase their academic involvement. For instance, faculty members might be encouraged to spend more time in the institution's residence halls, perhaps even to teach classes and hold office hours there. The possibilities are numerous and should be explored more fully. As a first step, administrators might perform time studies of students' behavior in residence halls; such studies would provide clues to how these facilities might be better utilized to support the institution's talent development mission.

Orientation. Many institutions view orientation not as a part of the academic program but as an introduction to college life. As such, orientation sessions might be more effectively used; for instance, to inform students about the importance of involvement and to alert them to early signs of low involvement, such as boredom with courses, academic difficulties, minimal contact with other students, and so forth. The orientation session could also be used to collect baseline data for assessing talent development. Finally, institutions should consider offering a first-term orientation course, which would give students an in-depth picture of the facilities and curricular opportunities on the campus and would also allow them to explore, under controlled conditions, the possible connections between their college experiences and their long-term life plans. Such an exploration would serve not only to increase involvement in college life by demonstrating its relevance to their later lives but also to open up new career possibilities and other life options.

Financial Aid. Studies of the impact of financial aid programs (Astin, 1977) suggest that part-time on-campus employment is an effective tool for enhancing student involvement. As long as such work does not require more than twenty hours a week, it apparently does not interfere significantly with the student's academic work. Thus, institutions should explore ways of making more part-time job opportunities on campus available to students.

Counseling. Like academic advising, counseling is one of the face-to-face services that tend to get low ratings from undergraduates (Green and others, 1983). Existing campus resources for this kind of direct contact tend to be passive and therefore underutilized. Counselors simply sit around waiting for students to come in for help. Because the clients for such services are self-selected, the students most in need of help—particularly those bored with the college experience and on the point of dropping out—often do not get it. If counseling is to be effective in promoting student involvement, it must take a more aggressive stance, seeking out those students who could benefit most.

Campus Life in General. Perhaps the best way to assess the adequacy of campus life in general, insofar as stimulating student involvement is concerned, is to pose a series of questions. To what extent does campus life provide opportunities for students to take part? What changes in the physical plant and surroundings might make the campus a more exciting place? What special provisions are made for commuter students? Are social and cultural events scheduled so as to encourage students' participation? Are enough extracurricular activities offered to permit most students to get involved in at least one?

Using Assessment and Feedback to Increase Involvement

As someone with nearly twenty-five years' experience with various types of student assessments, I have concluded that information gathering is one of the weakest parts of the institutional process. I believe that any good college or university assessment program must satisfy two fundamental criteria: It should be consistent with a clearly articulated philosophy of institutional mission, and it should be consistent with *some* theory of pedagogy or learning. Given the philosophical and theoretical position of this book, then, I believe that such an assessment program should be consistent with the institution's talent development goals and with the theory of involvement.

A related philosophical question has to do with the implicit purposes of any information-gathering activity. Unfortunately, most institutional assessment is done for evaluation purposes; that is, the performance of students and faculty members is judged on the basis of the information gathered. I see two problems with this approach. First, it is essentially adversarial: Students are tested and graded to determine whether they should be admitted, awarded credit, or permitted to graduate; and faculty members are assessed to decide whether they should be hired, promoted, or given tenure. Under such conditions, assessment is bound to be perceived as a threat. The second problem is that this approach is basically passive: Students and professors submit to the assessment process and try to show themselves in the most favorable light possible.

The talent development and involvement concepts demand a very different purpose for assessment. In this case, assessment would be used primarily for feedback to increase the involvement of students and faculty members and to develop their talents as completely as possible. Such assessment is active rather than passive, since it is designed to facilitate and improve performance. Furthermore, the information gathered is used to benefit the parties involved rather than to pass judgment on them. In examining various issues related to assessment and feedback, I shall focus on three topics: implementing appropriate procedures, assessing students' cognitive performance, and assessing faculty performance.

Implementing Appropriate Procedures. The ultimate responsibility for implementing appropriate procedures rests with the top administrators of any college or university. Although most college catalogs claim that talent development is a fundamental institutional purpose, the planning and decision-making process in higher education typically ignores the student development implications of various courses of action. This tendency is exemplified by the computer-based management information systems now used by many colleges and universities (Baldridge and Tierney, 1979). Except for simplistic data on enrollments and fields of study, these systems provide virtually no information on what is happening to students at the institution. The same goes for the information typically gathered by administrators for periodic meetings of the board of trustees; except for enrollment figures, the data provided to trustees usually concern fiscal matters. (Indeed, even enrollment data are of interest primarily because of their fiscal implications.) Administrators who rely exclusively on this type of information implicitly see resource acquisition as their primary function. The benefit side of any decision equation, as it reflects the probable consequences for talent development, receives scant attention at best and in most cases is ignored altogether in making decisions.

The best starting point for academic leaders who want to improve the institution's assessment procedures, then, is a thorough examination of the current information system. How much is known about how involved or uninvolved students are? Is information concerning student involvement (or lack of it) available to key personnel? Do classroom instructors and faculty advisors regularly have access to data on students' academic involvement? Do student personnel administrators periodically receive information on students' extracurricular participation? Do appropriate data get disseminated in a comprehensible form and in time to take any necessary remedial action?

Institutional leaders should also consider their own needs for information. Traditionally, academic administrators have been more means-oriented than ends-oriented. The. reward structure in higher education clearly reinforces this tendency, since administrators are rewarded not for maximizing the talent development of their students but rather for acquiring money, bright students, and highly trained and prestigious faculty members. Under a talent development and involvement approach, on the other hand, administrators will seek a very different kind of information. The information should include the following core elements:

1. *Successful completion of a program of study.* In its simplest form, this measure would involve a dichotomy: the student either completes a degree or drops out. More sophisticated approaches to such a measure would involve determining whether a student's undergraduate achievements are consistent with his or her degree plans at college entry.

2. *Cognitive development.* The basic purpose here is to

determine whether the institution is achieving its basic instructional purpose: to develop the cognitive abilities of its students. (Special problems connected with assessing cognitive development are discussed below.)

3. *Student involvement and satisfaction.* Students' satisfaction with the institution's program is one of the most important indications of an institution's effectiveness. Students should be asked not only about their overall satisfaction but also about their satisfaction with more specific matters: the quality of teaching, advising, curriculum, facilities, extracurricular activities, and various student services. Perhaps the best way to assess involvement, as I suggested earlier, is to ask students to keep time diaries indicating how much time (per week, for example) they spend in various activities (studying, interacting with each other and with professors, working at an outside job, engaging in athletics and other activities, and so forth).

The sad fact is that academic administrators seldom receive regular feedback on student development and involvement, even though such outcomes are the heart of the institution's educational purposes. Perhaps the best way to communicate the seriousness of this situation is to consider what would happen if corporate business managers concentrated solely on resource allocation without regard to whether or not the organization was making a profit (the business analog of learning and student development). Without feedback, academic administrators cannot hope to plan and to make decisions that will enhance the student's learning and involvement.

Assessing Cognitive Performance. Since the talents most institutions attempt to develop inevitably include various cognitive skills, being able to measure improvements in those abilities is essential to any assessment program carried out as part of a talent development approach. The Study Group on the Conditions of Excellence in Higher Education (1984) identifies six cognitive skills that are basic to a liberal education: verbal ability, quantitative ability, analytical reasoning ability, the ability to synthesize, organizational and human relations skills, and an understanding of cultural diversity. (For additional suggestions concerning cognitive skills, see Chapter Three.)

Despite (or perhaps because of) the fundamental importance of cognitive development, attempts to assess changes in cognitive skills can be extremely threatening to both faculty members and students. Professors, in particular, seem to prefer traditional course grades and tend to resist the use of nationally standardized tests for examining cognitive performance. The fundamental problem with traditional course grades is that they do not necessarily assess change or improvement in the student's cognitive skills. Rather, they measure the performance of students relative to one another at the end of the course. As noted in Chapter Four, students who end up with mediocre grades may have developed their talents just as fully as students who end up with high grades. It all depends on a given student's level of cognitive development at the beginning of the course. Bright or well-prepared students may coast along without improving their skills significantly and still earn an A or B; dull or underprepared students may work hard, learn a great deal, and make significant gains in cognitive ability but still earn no more than a C.

That faculty resistance to longitudinal assessment of students' cognitive development can be overcome is evidenced by the findings of a study of Alverno College conducted by Mentkowski and Doherty (1984). These investigators found that the data produced by the repeated testing of undergraduates generated considerable analysis and discussion on the part of faculty members, who ultimately became enthusiastic supporters of the assessment program. Involving faculty in either the development or the selection of the measures to be used seems to be one effective way of enlisting their support. Mentkowski and Doherty also found that the student's high school grade average does *not* predict the growth of cognitive skills during the undergraduate years.

Most colleges and universties have long required that students take nationally standardized tests for admission both to college and to graduate school, and an increasing number of in-

stitutions now administer various competence tests during the
junior and senior years. Since these tests are, in essence, measures of cognitive performance, it is unfortunate that the most
prominent testing organizations are reluctant to provide feedback on the results for individual test questions. The reason
usually given for this reluctance is the need to protect test security. This argument has always puzzled me, given the theory
underlying the construction of most achievement tests. Briefly,
the items for such tests are selected from a hypothetical domain
of all possible test questions that could be asked about the particular subject in question. If providing individual-item feedback
to institutions violates the security of a particular set of items,
then the test company can simply write new items each year.
(This would, of course, entail additional expense, but the extra
costs would represent only a tiny fraction of the total revenues
generated by these tests every year.) If the domain is finite,
then once all possible test items have been written and made
public, the test-makers can simply sample randomly from this
domain in constructing a new test each year. It might be argued
that under these conditions professors will simply encourage
their students to study for the test by learning the answers to
all the items. But what is wrong with this? If the student knows
the answers to all possible questions that could be asked about a
particular body of knowledge, then that student knows, by definition, that body of knowledge.

If the institution had access to the results for individual
test questions on, say, the aptitude and achievement tests of the
College Entrance Examination Board, it could repeat some of
these tests after one, two, or four years to measure improvements in students' performance on specific items. Moreover, if
testing organizations could be persuaded to perform studies
equating the major college admission tests (SAT and ACT) with
the Graduate Record Examination (GRE), the results of these
tests could be used to measure improvements in cognitive performance during the undergraduate years. Some faculty members may feel that the capacities measured by these tests are
not relevant to the goals of the academic program. But this objection seems frivolous, since the same faculty members are will-

ing to use these tests as a basis for admission to undergraduate, graduate, and professional schools. My main point here is that if faculty members and testing organizations changed their attitudes, institutions would be able to take advantage of the fact that students are already taking these tests, and they could score students' test performance in such a way as to measure improvements.

While academic departments probably have no great difficulty devising local instruments to measure improvements in specific fields of study, the problem of measuring the impact of a liberal or general education is not so easily resolved (Pace, 1979). As was mentioned in Chapter Three, however, efforts are currently under way to develop instruments that will handle this problem. One promising device is the American College Testing Program's College Outcomes Measurement Project (COMP) Battery, which uses a novel set of test stimuli (audio recordings, filmstrips, and so on) and requires students to respond in several modes: multiple choice, essay, and oral (Forrest and Steele, 1982). Another promising device is the McBer Company's Behavioral Event Interview (Klemp and McClelland, 1984), in which the student is interviewed in depth about several real events in his or her recent past; the student's responses are then subjected to a detailed analysis for what they reveal about the student's skills. Both of these instruments produce scores on such capacities as communication skills and critical thinking ability.

Assessing Faculty Performance. So far in this section I have been concerned only with students, but I believe faculty members are also learners who need feedback just as much as students do, especially in developing their pedagogical skills. Like institutions, professors can pursue their talent development mission more effectively if they make better use of existing knowledge about human learning. Perhaps the two most important principles of learning are "knowledge of results" (feedback) and "time-on-task" (involvement).

Three steps can be taken to improve the quality of feedback for faculty members. First, institution-wide evaluations of classroom instruction by students should be mandated, with the proviso that the results be for the instructor's eyes only. Under these conditions, it would be important to design the ratings to provide feedback about specific changes that would improve the course. Student ratings of instruction are fairly common, but in most cases these ratings are used in ways which run contrary to the principles of good feedback for learners. When ratings are made public (for instance, in student-published guides) or are made a basis for personnel decisions, the instructor is motivated to manipulate the ratings rather than to use them as suggestions to improve his or her own teaching. In such circumstances, the potential learning value of the feedback is compromised. Moreover, when low ratings are made public, the professor is tempted to rationalize the results away rather than to learn from them. If institutions feel that students' evaluations must be made public or used in personnel actions, then it is probably best to employ two sets of ratings, one for the record and one for the private edification of the professor.

Since student ratings of classroom instruction are so common, institutions might usefully invest in evaluating and improving the procedures used. Evidence suggests, for example, that student ratings are subject to biases that have little if anything to do with the quality of instruction. Courses having a quantitative content, for instance, tend to get lower ratings than qualitative courses (Bassin, 1974). If the academic community were made aware of these biases, the results of student ratings could be interpreted more accurately and used more effectively.

Second, teaching consultants should make periodic visits to the classrooms of all instructors. The purpose of these visits would be to provide feedback in the form of consultation and constructive criticism from a trusted colleague or an outside teaching consultant. Such consultation would help faculty members "examine and enrich their current assumptions and skills in a supportive but challenging climate" (Carrier, Dalgaard, and Simpson, 1983, p. 196). Few faculty members can view their own classroom performance objectively. Thus, a consultant who observes the class directly can help the faculty member see the implicit theories on which he or she is operating (Argyris and Schön, 1974; Hunt, 1976). If a faculty colleague rather than an outside teaching consultant serves in this capacity, that colleague should be exempted from participating in any personnel decisions involving the instructor in question.

Third, nonclassroom contacts between faculty members and students (advising, mentoring, informal interactions) should be used as a source and a subject of feedback to the faculty. Since faculty-student contact plays such an important role in increasing students' involvement (Astin, 1977), faculty members need information not only on their classroom performance but also on their behavior with students outside the classroom. Such feedback could be obtained through simple surveys of students. The results of these surveys could be aggregated by major field and disseminated to each department, together with institution-wide norms. Depending on the size of the department, it might also be useful to aggregate the results separately by class (for freshmen, sophomores, and so on). Faculty members would then be asked to discuss the results at departmental meetings. If such ratings were made a regular (at least annual) part of the informational feedback to departments, professors would know whether the advisory process and other direct faculty-student contacts needed strengthening and whether their attempts to improve such contacts were actually working.

Public Policy

So far this discussion of reform has been limited to actions that institutions can take to promote the talent development view of excellence and to increase students' involvement. In this section, I shall discuss the implications of the talent development view for public policy. More specifically, I will suggest what policy makers might do in four areas—student involvement, teacher training, admissions, and research—to promote the talent development mission of higher education.

Policy Changes to Support Student Involvement. One obvious mechanism that can be used to enhance student involvement is the front loading of resources mentioned earlier in the chapter. If policy makers would increase substantially the funding formulas for lower-division students, institutions could de-

vote more of their resources to those learners, especially freshmen. If such revisions are made, however, states should hold
institutions accountable for substantial changes in the quality
and quantity of student-faculty contact, counseling, and other
direct services to students.

A similar reexamination of funding priorities should be
undertaken in the case of community colleges, which are generally funded on a lower formula basis than four-year institutions and which face more severe problems with student involvement. In view of the relatively poor academic preparation of
most community college entrants, policy makers should consider allocating resources to help community colleges develop
programs that will strengthen students' participation.

Similarly, part-time and commuter students tend to be
only weakly involved in the learning process and to suffer high
dropout rates. Thus, for community colleges and other commuter institutions, policy makers might want to consider funding policies that encourage full-time attendance and support
special programs (such as weekend "residencies") designed to
compensate for the relative lack of involvement that typically
results from the student's not living on campus.

A final suggestion relates to the movement to hold institutions accountable for their expenditures of public funds.
Rather than harrass institutions to produce detailed records on
how funds are spent, funding agencies might more productively
use this concern for accountability to increase students' involvement and learning. In particular, they might encourage
institutions to implement assessment and feedback procedures
that will yield better information on the effectiveness of their
talent development programs. Tennessee has already launched a
program to provide institutions with more money if they implement longitudinal assessments that demonstrate significant
cognitive growth among their undergraduates (Bogue and
Brown, 1982). Although the long-range effectiveness of the
Tennessee program has not yet been adequately evaluated, there
is good reason to believe that it has significantly improved the
information-gathering and dissemination procedures at almost
all of the public institutions in the state.

Policy for Improved Teacher Training. As was pointed out in Chapter Five, this nation faces serious problems with respect to the quantity and quality of elementary and secondary schoolteachers; and the states must assume the major responsibility for solving these problems. The most obvious solution is to recruit more students—and especially more of the better-prepared students—for careers as schoolteachers and school administrators. Among the many incentives available to states and the federal government for this purpose are scholarships and "forgivable" loans. Another possibility is to include schoolteaching among the options available for many of the programs of public service currently being considered at the national level.

The relationships that currently exist between state agencies and public institutions might also be used to ameliorate the problem. In particular, state funding agencies should consider offering incentives that will encourage the state universities to strengthen their education departments and their teacher-training programs. Considering the poor academic preparation of most of the undergraduates who pursue careers in teaching and considering that the major public research universities enroll disproportionate shares of the best-prepared students, state planners should find ways to encourage these institutions to expand and strengthen their involvement in teacher training. Ideally each of the major state universities should develop highly visible programs for preparing teachers and should try to attract their brightest undergraduates to these programs. If such programs include practice teaching as well as additional courses in a major, they would probably require five years for the student to complete.

Public Policy on Admissions. Of all the areas in which public policy can make a difference for higher education, admissions is perhaps the most critical (Green, 1981). As I have pointed out repeatedly, the talent development conception entails an approach to admissions that differs markedly from the approaches taken in support of traditional conceptions of excellence. Under the reputational and resources models, priority is given to high-performance students, whereas students who perform poorly are regarded as a liability. Under the talent development model, the state has a stake in educating people at all levels of competence and preparation.

The talent development model provides an interesting framework within which to examine some of our admissions policies and other basic public policies related to access and to the funding of higher education. As is well known, education confers certain benefits on society as well as on the individual (Bowen, 1977). Better-educated citizens are likely to contribute substantially to society in the form of tax payments. In contrast, people with little education are more likely to cost the society money, in the form of unemployment benefits, welfare payments, and the costs exacted by crime and by institutionalization.

Figure 3 illustrates these relationships in the form of two hypothetical functions. The descending curve shows simply that

Figure 3. Hypothetical Relationship Among Three Variables.

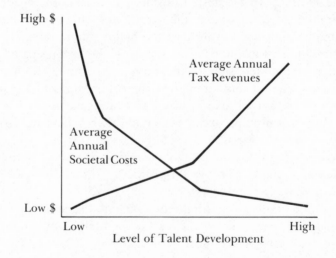

the lower the individual's level of developed talent, the more the individual will cost society in terms of welfare payments, institutionalization, and the like. The ascending curve shows that the higher the individual's level of developed talent, the greater the average tax revenues. The point where the curves cross is the societal break-even point, at which the average societal costs are balanced by the average tax revenues.

Note that because the cost curve descends very rapidly at the very low end of the developed talent range, a given increment at the low end of the talent continuum yields a much larger reduction in societal costs than an equal increment of talent higher up on the continuum. The reverse is true for tax revenues. A given increment of talent at the high end of the continuum produces a greater increase in tax revenues than an equal increment at the low end. I should emphasize that these curves are hypothetical and that the real curves might have somewhat different shapes. As the curves are drawn now, the sum total of the benefits (welfare savings plus additional tax revenues) deriving from a given increment of talent is roughly equivalent all along the talent continuum. If this were the real state of affairs in our society, it would presumably justify equal educational investments at all levels of developed talent.

But how much does it really cost to develop talent at different levels? Although there is distressingly little empirical evidence bearing on this critical question, let us consider another hypothetical case: Figure 4 shows the hypothetical costs

Figure 4. Hypothetical Costs of a Given Increment of Talent at Different Levels of Developed Talent.

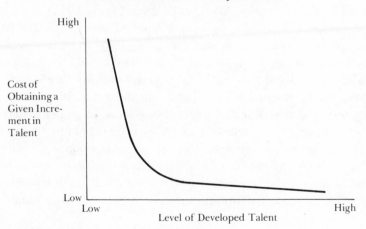

of obtaining a given increment of talent at different levels of developed talent. The curve indicates that developing the talent of people at the low end of the continuum is much more costly than developing the talent of people at the high end. (Such a result would be consistent with the widespread belief that remedial education tends to be costly.) Note, however, that the real curve might be much flatter, indicating that a given investment of educational resources produces roughly equal increments of talent at all levels of developed talent. If empirically based functions like the ones shown in Figures 3 and 4 could be constructed, it would then be possible to formulate an educational policy that would maximize the overall economic benefits to society.

Another important policy issue for state planners and policy makers is the poor representation of minority and low-income students in the more selective public institutions. Obviously, if the talents of these underrepresented individuals are to be developed, they must first be admitted to the institutions. Even though the *Bakke* decision prohibits the use of numerical quotas in admissions, it provides that some weight can be given to race. Nevertheless, many institutions are reluctant to use such criteria on the grounds that to do so constitutes reverse discrimination. But there are choices that avoid this problem. One such possibility is to give students "credit" for being disadvantaged. How such a system might work was demonstrated in a simulation study (Astin, Fuller, and Green, 1978) involving the applications of a national sample of more than 100,000 prospective college students. The purpose of the study was to determine what proportions of different racial/ethnic groups would be selected for admission under various conditions. A "disadvantagement index" based on three variables—parental income, father's education, mother's education—was calculated for each applicant, with the most disadvantaged applicants receiving the highest scores. The use of such an index assumes that affluent parents are in a better position to provide their children with the resources needed for intellectual development (space for studying, books, tutors and other special remedial assistance, and so forth) and that they are likely to live in communities where the local high schools are relatively rigorous.

Eight different admissions models—each based on a different combination of test scores, grades, and disadvantagement—were used. Three major findings emerged. First, minorities benefit considerably from the use of a disadvantagement index, but such an index must be given substantial weight to compensate for the handicap imposed by their low test scores and grades. Second, tests represent a much more formidable admissions obstacle for minority students (blacks in particular) than grades do. Consequently, the use of a disadvantagement index benefits minority students more if it is combined with grades alone rather than with grades and test scores. Third, the handicap imposed by the use of test scores and grades becomes greater as the selection ratio increases. For example, a simple combination of test scores and grades produces an 80 percent underrepresentation of blacks when only one applicant in four can be accepted for admission but only a 65 percent underrepresentation when the selection ratio is one in two. The disadvantagement index is especially appealing because it is color-blind and gives explicit attention to educational and economic disadvantagement. Thus, minorities who come from educated and affluent families do not benefit unfairly, and nonminority students who come from disadvantaged families are equally compensated for the disadvantagement.

Research and Public Policy. Funding agencies can contribute to the talent development mission of institutions and to the expansion of opportunities by supporting additional research on three topics: educational costs and benefits, the instruction of underprepared students, and alternative admissions procedures.

As Figures 3 and 4 indicated, additional knowledge is needed about the relationship between educational investments and educational benefits (talent development). Among the many questions that merit further exploration are the following: Does a given educational investment produce equivalent payoffs in terms of talent development at different points on the ability spectrum? Is the relationship between the amount invested and the degree of payoff linear, or is there a point of diminishing returns at the high end of the investment continuum? Is there a point at the low end of the continuum where the payoff drops sharply?

It would also be useful to know whether the shape of the investment-payoff function is different for students at different levels of ability or achievement. Similarly, does the shape of the investment-payoff function differ depending on the type of payoff being investigated (communication skills, interpersonal skills, and so on)? Finally, the relationships among different types of payoffs should be investigated. Do equal increments in cognitive performance at different points on the ability continuum lead to equal increments of earnings?

Questions related to teaching underprepared students also need research. As graduate students, most college faculty members were trained in departments where they had little or no contact with underprepared students. Consequently, these same faculty members encounter serious pedagogical problems when they take positions in institutions enrolling large proportions of underprepared students. At the same time, incumbent faculties in the very selective or even moderately selective institutions strongly resist any attempt to expand educational opportunities that would bring in more underprepared students. Teaching such students carries little reward and is not a valued activity within most academic disciplines. To make matters worse, many underprepared students have only a marginal motivation for academic work.

Considering that the number of such students entering higher education institutions is rapidly expanding, a concerted research effort should be made to identify effective pedagogical techniques. In particular, high priority should be given to studying ways to identify and train faculty members who can work effectively with such students.

The third topic that particularly deserves research support from public agencies concerns admissions criteria. Even if all institutions were to embrace a talent development approach to excellence and to make their admissions policies as flexible as possible, the number of applicants would still far exceed the number of spaces at some institutions. The issue here is just what admissions criteria make the most sense for a talent development approach. As already noted, the traditional personnel selection model based on test scores and grades does not necessarily identify those students who are most capable of profiting from higher education. The ideal would be to identify those students most likely to develop their talents to the fullest, given the particular programs and resources of the institution in question. Such admissions criteria would probably take into account the student's motivation, capacity for involvement, and so on.

One obstacle to such research is the time-honored practice of validating any admissions instrument by determining how it correlates with college gradepoint average. In Chapter Four, I argued that the gradepoint average is a poor measure of how much students are actually learning. If testing agencies and institutions embark on research programs to identify those students whose talents are most likely to develop at particular institutions, then they must employ something other than gradepoint average as the dependent variable. The ideal would be to use longitudinal (pretest-posttest) assessments of cognitive performance. Such measures would provide much better criteria than the gradepoint average for assessing the validity of admissions instruments.

As suggested in earlier chapters, two types of institutions present special problems when it comes to implementing the talent development model: the research university and the commuter college. Let us consider just what these problems are and how they might be overcome.

Special Institutional Problems: The Research University

The sheer size and complexity of most research universities, particularly those in the public sector, make it difficult for them to give high priority to talent development and student involvement. But they have other more fundamental problems in this regard, the chief among them being intense internal pressure to enhance their position in the academic pecking order through the acquisition of faculty stars and research grants and contracts.

A Conflict of Values. As I will suggest in the later discussion of leadership, the administrators of most research universities send out mixed signals about institutional mission. In official documents and pronouncements, they claim to be strongly committed to undergraduate education and effective teaching, but their actual practices tend to belie this commitment. For example, in the recruitment, promotion, and tenuring of faculty members, most research universities give much greater weight to research and scholarly performance than to effectiveness in teaching and working with students. Despite much rhetoric to the contrary, then, the teaching-versus-research conflict has by no means been resolved in most of these institutions.

This problem is exacerbated by the intense competition within and between departments for scholarly recognition and by the increasing withdrawal of faculty members from meaningful interactions with undergraduates. At many research universities, as we have seen, nonteaching personnel assume the major responsibility for advising undergraduates. Moreover, the common practice of posting office hours—ostensibly so that undergraduates will have some opportunity to come in and talk personally with faculty members—is, in my opinion, a device for minimizing the amount of time that faculty members spend in direct student contact, by setting an upper limit (usually a modest one) on that time.

It is my impression that, implicitly, most research universities are oriented primarily toward self-aggrandizement. As an illustration of this value orientation, let me describe an event I recently attended honoring the head of one of our major research universities. Many prominent educators, politicians, and celebrities were present. Of the dozen or so speakers who recited the accomplishments of the president, not a single one said anything about the educational effectiveness or quality of the institution. All the comments were directed toward the institution's effectiveness in conducting research and its recent ascendancy in the National Academy of Science's ratings of graduate programs. A visiting Martian would have concluded that the university in question was a research institute rather than an educational institution.

The severe conflict between the values of research and of pedagogy was no doubt intensified by the ascendancy, during the 1950s and 1960s, of specialized research supported by federal funding agencies (Perkins, 1973). Such support has since decreased, but the frame of mind engendered by the dominance of research lingers on. Patullo has characterized the problem as follows: "Where the institution's basic raison d'être is the instruction and socialization of a cross section of the young, it is reasonable and appropriate to press responsible faculties by all available means to better performance of their first duty. At Harvard, I believe the reluctance of the faculty to embrace some of the reforms that seem so obviously needed from this perspective stems not from recalcitrance, blindness, or unconcern, but from a strong sense, hitherto unarticulated, that our most important responsibility lies elsewhere, and the changes which would be consistent with the one objective are quite inconsistent with our primary obligation to perpetuate a great scholarly community" (quoted in Rees, 1976, p. 84).

Despite these problems, some academic institutions have managed to blend research and teaching effectively. Notable among these are the University of Chicago, Harvey Mudd College in California, and a number of the more selective liberal arts colleges. I believe that these institutions have been able to achieve a rapprochement between the goals of teaching and those of research in two ways. First, they openly acknowledge that they accord research less time and emphasis than some of the more single-minded research universities. And second, they make a conscious effort to integrate their research and teaching. Edward H. Levi, former president of the University of Chicago, articulated this idea as follows: "[From] the very beginning . . . [the] University has attempted to make pervasive throughout the entire institution, and at all stages, its dual emphasis on the liberal arts and on investigation. . . . In short, it has never accepted the dichotomy which is supposed to separate teaching from research. It believes that discovery, itself, is the greatest form of teaching, and that mutual efforts to understand . . . not only give the institution its unity, but link scholars over time and across national boundaries and disciplines" (quoted in Rees, 1976, p. 85).

The "Jack Armstrong" Syndrome. The inability of many research universities to give more emphasis to undergraduate teaching and to integrate research and teaching can be attributed to what I call the Jack Armstrong Syndrome, which characterizes the faculty personnel policies of many research universities. As my middle-aged readers will recall, Jack Armstrong was a popular radio hero who could do everything well. He was handsome, intelligent, brave, strong, sincere, and moral. He was a great athlete and a great adventurer. He was, in short, the original all-American boy.

Anyone reading the typical job description of the faculty member in a major research university might be tempted to conclude that all faculty members are also supposed to be Jack Armstrongs. To merit promotion or tenure, the faculty member must do everything well: research and scholarship, teaching and mentoring, service to the university through committee membership and other activities, service to the community and general public, and outside professional activities. In theory, only those faculty members who excel at all of these functions are worthy of being hired and receiving tenure.

Anyone who has ever worked in a research university knows that Jack Armstrong is a myth. Very few faculty members excel at all these activities, and some excel at none. Furthermore, the information available to make judgments about the faculty member's performance in at least one of these areas —teaching and working with students—often leaves much to be desired. In these circumstances, it is not surprising that search committees and faculty review and promotion committees frequently use only a single yardstick: the candidate's scholarly record. Not only does this narrowing of focus simplify the decision process, it also focuses on the one aspect of the candidate's performance that is directly related to enhancing the institution's resources and reputation. In short, the typical faculty job description is a fantasy and a smoke screen. While officially rewarding a diverse set of faculty accomplishments, the institution is, in reality, rewarding only scholarly activity.

If an institution really wants to make the best use of its faculty resources for teaching and other purposes besides research, it should strongly consider diversifying faculty job descriptions. Some faculty members could be evaluated primarily or exclusively in terms of their research performance, some could be evaluated primarily in terms of their teaching or mentoring activities, some might be assessed primarily in terms of their contribution to the institution and their value as consultants to other faculty members, and still others might be evaluated on all these criteria. In this way, outstanding researchers who are incompetent teachers could be kept out of the classroom, and outstanding teachers and mentors who are not particularly adept at research could be relieved of the burden of grinding out meaningless potboilers in order to gain tenure or promotion. At the same time, the definition of research or scholarship might be broadened to include a range of scholarly activities far beyond the mere publication of articles in refereed journals. (For some more detailed suggestions concerning this broadened concept of scholarship, see the recent report of the Study Group on the Conditions of Excellence in Higher Education, 1984.) Most important, however, is that such diversification in job descriptions would allow institutions to reward at least some faculty members for their contribution to the talent development mission.

Collegiality and Community. Another problem that plagues many research universities is the absence of collegiality and of any real sense of community. Most faculty members identify primarily with their disciplines and their departments (and some, even with subspecialities within their departments), and departments tend to be highly competitive with each other. Under these conditions, few faculty members feel any identity with the institution as a whole or any motivation to cooperate with colleagues in other disciplines. The single-minded emphasis on research and scholarly performance exacerbates these problems by pitting individual faculty members and departments against each other in an environment where one person's success may come to symbolize failure for others. When some faculty members are outstandingly successful in their scholarly endeavors, the norms of performance are effectively raised for other faculty members. The social environment of many research universities is thus characterized by parochialism, jealousy, and denigration of the work of others.

While this environment may enhance scholarly involvement and thereby develop the research talents of some faculty members, it exacts a heavy price. Not only are faculty energies deflected from teaching and working with students, but many students—well aware of the faculty's pettiness, lack of community, and indifference to undergraduates—become cynical and alienated. Such an environment is certainly not conducive to increased student involvement and learning.

In my interviews with leading educators, I posed the following question: "How can the research university, with its strong emphasis on individual scholarly achievement and competition, hope to attain a greater sense of community and collegiality?" Their responses varied widely, as the following examples demonstrate:

> I think size has gotten a bit out of bounds at present. Perhaps institutions can take steps to break themselves up into colleges. The University of Toronto is a fine example of that. They've gone into the collegiate system. Oxford and Cambridge are obvious ones. Claremont is another one that seems to work well. . . . These institutions have the benefits of size and at the same time the benefits of smallness and personality. [Howard Bowen]
> The world would be a lot better off if universities could so construct themselves that they could get a team of people together to take on some real problem and solve it in an interdisciplinary fashion. [Russell Edgerton]
> I think you've got to get faculty members to engage in collective enterprises that cut across departmental lines. How you do that, however, is another thing. [Patricia Graham]
> It requires a very effective kind of leadership

by department chairs and a willingness to create
the kind of environment that gets folks to work in
a collaborative way. . . . But the size of departments is a big issue. It's one thing to do that in a
department of 10 or 12 or 20, where you can all sit
around and get to know each other well enough to
make the trade-offs that are necessary to recognize
and respect individual differences. In a department
of 80 or 100, it is another matter. [Arthur Chick-
ering]

What, then, can research universities do to ensure that
higher priority is given to undergraduate teaching and student
development? Clearly, strong and effective leadership is needed
to improve the situation. Among other things, this leadership
must articulate a less ambiguous and contradictory set of institutional values. Administrators not only must pay lip service to
these values but must also introduce concrete policies and practices that are consistent with the institution's professed commitment to developing the talents of its undergraduates.

Special Institutional Problems: The Commuter College

More than any other type of institution, the commuter
college experiences severe problems in getting students involved in the learning process. Many students are enrolled part
time and spend only a modest amount of time on campus.
Many (if not most) of the faculty members are also part-timers.
Moreover, since the enrollments in many commuter institutions
are highly unstable, administrators are frequently preoccupied
with maintaining or increasing enrollments and thus devote little time to improving the teaching-learning process. Finally,
commuter institutions tend to enroll large proportions of students with marginal academic skills who find it difficult to get
heavily involved in academic work. As a result, attrition rates
are very high.

Transfer students (those who aspire to a baccalaureate
and who plan to enroll in four-year institutions after completing
the associate degree) find themselves in an environment domi-

nated by vocational students and by students not interested in a
degree of any kind. Lacking contact with a community of peers
who share their goal, many of these potential transfer students
lower their aspirations and drop out. Even though some community college spokespersons are inclined to downplay the
transfer function these days, the community college's piece of
the action in educating aspirants to the bachelor's degree is just
as important as it has ever been (Astin, 1983b).

There are several approaches to remedying the problems
of involvement for transfer students (Chickering, 1974; Educational Facilities Laboratories, 1977), but so far they have been
tried only sparingly. According to Lindquist (in press), commuter institutions can take four steps to generate greater involvement among their students:

1. Engage in brainstorming sessions with administrators, stu-
    dent service personnel, library staff members, and their
    community counterparts to discuss ways to work together
    in creating a rich environment for higher learning where
    commuters live.
2. Make administrative schedules flexible so that morning,
    noon, and night are covered to accommodate the diverse
    schedules of commuters.
3. Seek community and commuter experience in the staff-
    ing of the institution to generate a stronger capacity to em-
    pathize with commuters; and be sure that staff members
    whose only experience has been in residential colleges are
    thoroughly acquainted with the specialized needs of com-
    muters.
4. Conduct faculty development activities focusing on the di-
    verse learning objectives, backgrounds, styles, and espe-
    cially the contexts of commuter students; then help teach-
    ers redesign their courses to fit commuter profiles.

There are, of course, a number of other specific things
that commuter colleges can do to stimulate greater student involvement: establish disciplinary or career-related clubs that
cater to the special needs and interests of commuters, hold in-

tensive residential workshops on weekends, overnight, or during vacation periods, and design learning experiences that require commuter students to use initiative and to take a good deal of responsibility for their own learning. One institution that seems to have had a good deal of success in involving commuter students heavily in their academic work is Empire State College of the State University of New York. Students and faculty members negotiate learning contracts that typically require the student to do much more than simply read or write papers. Frequently these contracts commit students to visiting galleries, museums, laboratories, public libraries, or businesses; to conducting interviews or other types of survey research; and even to taking a course at a nearby college or university. For more details about such specific strategies for enhancing involvement among commuter students, see Chickering (1974).

For commuter institutions that wish to be more successful in their transfer mission, perhaps the greatest hope lies in rejecting traditional conceptions of excellence in favor of the talent development view. Since they are not handicapped by the single-minded commitment to research that one finds in most universities, commuter colleges are, at least in theory, much freer to embrace a talent development approach in all of their activities. For example, if traditional testing and grading procedures are replaced by the pretesting-posttesting assessment model, commuter institutions may be able to create an environment in which all members of the academic community develop a commitment to student involvement and personal development. Indeed, it may well turn out that many commuter institutions will surpass universities in their ability to develop student talent. Commuter institutions have little to lose and much to gain by pioneering the adoption of a talent development approach in their teaching and assessment activities.

The Challenge of Change

The American higher education system is characterized by certain features that make it highly resistant to change and innovation. Three major sources of resistance can be identified:

the institutional hierarchy itself, the internal structure and operation of institutions, and the traditional roles of faculty members and administrators. Let us consider each of these in turn.

Resistance from the Institutional Hierarchy. The hierarchical organization of American higher education represents one of the most important—albeit least recognized or understood—sources of resistance to change. Chomsky (1968) has commented that intellectuals who have achieved power and influence in the larger society have a stake in accepting and perpetuating the status quo, no matter how much in need of reform or renewal it may be. The same would seem to apply to institutions that have achieved power and influence within the system. The institutions at the top of the hierarchy have very little incentive to change. Let us examine this proposition in more detail.

In Chapters One and Two, we observed that the most prestigious institutions in the country define the norm for excellence. They have outstanding reputations, exceptionally able student bodies, faculties composed of distinguished and highly visible scholars, and abundant financial resources. Given that they have already achieved excellence, according to the reputational and resources views, and given the competitive nature of the American higher education system, it is understandable that these institutions resist any changes that might threaten their high rank in the academic pecking order. After all, there is no guarantee that under a talent development view they would maintain their favored position. Thus, elite institutions are likely to feel that they have nothing to gain and everything to lose if excellence is defined in terms other than reputations and resources.

It is not surprising, then, that some of the most vociferous opposition to the talent development view of excellence has come from persons associated with the elite sector of higher education. For instance, when the Commission on the Higher Education of Minorities (1981) recommended that institutions revise their testing and grading practices to make them more consistent with the talent development mission, this proposal was sharply criticized by a former president of Stanford University (Lyman, 1982) and a vice-president of the Educational Testing Service (Manning, 1982).

American higher education is steeped in tradition, and this is especially true of the most elite private institutions, which were founded much earlier than the majority of less elite institutions and which enjoy the support of large numbers of wealthy and powerful alumni. Because these alumni tend to donate substantial amounts of money to the institution, and because they are frequently involved in institutional activities through boards of trustees, they exert a great deal of influence on high-level policy making. Indeed, in many prestigious public and private colleges and universities, the chief executive officer spends much of his time catering to such individuals, who are usually anxious to maintain the institution's current elite status and who thus resist any attempts to move it in new directions. Obviously, anyone concerned with introducing major changes into the institution must consider how these important people will respond. I should add here that even elite institutions *can* change, as is evidenced by the conversion of several Ivy League men's colleges into coeducational institutions during the 1970s. When this transformation was first proposed, many alumni protested against the violation of a tradition that, in some cases, went back several hundred years. Eventually, however, the majority of alumni came to accept and support coeducation. Nonetheless, any such major change requires careful planning and forceful persuasion.

Nor is it just those persons directly connected with the elite institutions—as faculty members, administrators, current students, or alumni—who have a vested interest in preserving their high status and in perpetuating the reputational and resources conception of excellence. The hierarchical folklore is deeply imbedded in our national psyche, and many disparate groups seem to derive satisfaction from associating themselves with the institutions at the top of the hierarchy. For instance, politicians, entertainers, and other people in public life enjoy being invited to lecture or perform at elite institutions. Similarly, powerful people from the corporate and banking world take advantage of the opportunity to associate themselves with such institutions through membership on boards of trustees and advisory councils. Moreover, high school teachers and counselors, as well as many students and their parents, regard highly selective institutions as a kind of exclusive club, which bestows a special grace and distinction on those accepted as members; the possibility of membership in the club often serves as an incentive to high school students, a goal toward which they strive. In short, the larger society supports the notion that the higher education system boasts only a limited number of centers of excellence and that association with these institutions is desirable and satisfying.

It is often said that hierarchical systems can change only from the top down, since those further down in the hierarchy depend on those at the top for leadership and are reluctant to undertake any change that has not first been approved at the top. And, as the foregoing discussion makes clear, institutions at the top have little incentive to change. Furthermore, rational arguments by themselves are insufficient to refute the folklore or to undermine the established pecking order of institutions.

But the situation is not as hopeless as it may seem. There is evidence that if institutions further down in the hierarchy embrace a talent development view, they can make a difference. For instance, Northeast Missouri State University began implementing the talent development concept (which it calls the value-added approach) more than ten years ago; this approach involves a wide-ranging program of assessment to measure the talent development of its students (McClain, 1984). The university regularly assesses its freshmen using a mix of national and locally devised instruments, and then retests some of the same students as sophomores. It also assesses its graduating seniors each year with a battery of instruments that includes standard examinations required for admission to graduate or professional schools. These assessments are used not to "evaluate" faculty and students but rather (a) to provide feedback to faculty members and departments that can be used to strengthen the academic program and (b) to monitor the impact of efforts to strengthen the academic program and to improve student performance. The university has produced impressive longitudinal evidence

(McClain, 1984) suggesting that this program has already had a positive impact on student learning. In addition, the program has stimulated a major reexamination and modification of the curriculum, revisions in admissions and grading procedures, improvements in academic advising, greater student involvement in academic and career planning, and greater student satisfaction with the academic program. The university has also established a comprehensive data base and communication system that facilitates the exchange of information among departments about strategies that turn out to be especially effective.

Alverno College in Wisconsin (Mentkowski and Doherty, 1984) has likewise launched a comprehensive program focused directly on the development of talents related to the student's chosen career. During the past decade the faculty at Alverno has engaged in a joint effort that has three major objectives: (a) to identify those student talents and capacities that relate both to the goals of a liberal education and to effective performance at work, and to devise ways of assessing these student outcomes; (b) to determine how effectively the curriculum and academic program contribute to the enhancement of these outcomes and to make appropriate revisions; and (c) to assess empirically how what is learned in college affects performance on the job. Among other things, the Alverno experience shows that faculty members can become active and even enthusiastic participants in an institutionwide effort to strengthen a college's talent development mission.

And even as I write this chapter, I have been informed that the Fund for the Improvement of Postsecondary Education has awarded a grant to the Higher Education Research Institute at UCLA to implement the talent development approach in seven diverse colleges and universities across the country. Each institution in the consortium will be testing its new students with a comprehensive battery of instruments designed to assess the cognitive and affective outcomes of a liberal education. The same students will be reassessed at the end of their second undergraduate year. Since the top academic administrators and key faculty members at each institution will be actively involved in disseminating and interpreting the results of these assessments, it is expected that the project will eventually lead to a wide-ranging examination of the curriculum, teaching practices, and advisory programs at each institution. The consortium members will be meeting regularly to exchange information and ideas about effective implementation and dissemination strategies. One long-range goal of the project is to develop at each institution a "student-based management information system" (Astin and Scherrei, 1980) to be used for institutional self-evaluation, resource allocation, and planning.

The talent development approach pays off. In 1984, Northeast Missouri State University received the Theodore G. Mitau Award for innovation and excellence from the American Association of State Colleges and Universities. This relatively unknown institution has become highly attractive to prospective students, including many of the state's ablest high school graduates. According to President Charles McClain, the word has gotten out that Northeast Missouri State is a good place for undergraduates, that it is determined to give them the best possible education. Thus, the efforts of one institution have been successful in challenging the conventional folklore, and Northeast Missouri State has acquired prestige by its adherence to the talent development view.

Institutional Structure and Operation as Resistance. People who work in colleges and universities often forget that the routine operations of these institutions have become highly ritualized. Much of this ritual is keyed to the calendar, so that fundamental functions are repeated on an annual or seasonal basis almost like clockwork: student recruitment activities, application deadlines, letters of acceptance, orientation, registration, class schedules, midterms, finals, vacations, commencement, and so forth. These regularly programmed activities create an annual operational cycle that is repetitive, predictable, and hence highly resistant to change.

The governance procedures of most institutions, particularly the larger universities, have also become highly bureaucratized. Not only is the formal administrative structure heavily laden with assistant and associate deans and vice-presidents, but also the faculty advisory and governance system has become a maze of councils, standing committees, ad-hoc committees, and task forces. Change under these circumstances is exceedingly difficult, since decision-making power is highly diffused and any proposal for change must run the gamut of review committees, departments, councils, administrators, and sometimes even trustees. Cohen and March (1974) have labeled this situation "organized anarchy." The only reasonable way to cope with this particular barrier to innovation and change is through creative leadership. I shall discuss this issue at greater length in the next section.

 Resistance from Faculty Members and Administrators. Faculty members probably have more personal and professional autonomy than any other group of professionals employed in structured organizations. They are usually free to decide what they will teach, how they will teach it, what they will study, how they will study it, and how they will spend their time. Indeed, beyond meeting classes, holding office hours, and attending departmental and committee meetings, faculty members have few set obligations as to where they will be at what time. This autonomy increases with seniority and tenure. Naturally, faculty members value their autonomy highly and guard vigilantly against attempts to limit it. Sometimes this attitude takes the form of blind resistance to almost any change.

 Faculty members are inclined to view administrators with a curious mixture of fear, suspicion, and contempt: fear because of the potential threat to their autonomy posed by the administrator's real or imagined power, suspicion because of a traditional dislike of authority, and contempt because of a belief that administrators are failed faculty members who do not have the talent to become competent teachers and scholars or who value power and authority more than teaching and scholarship. As a consequence of these attitudes, which have been reinforced by the recent emergence of collective bargaining and unionism, faculty members tend to reject out of hand any administrative proposal for change.

 For their part, academic administrators (most of whom were once faculty members) are inclined to accept the view that faculty autonomy must be protected at all costs and that authoritarian or otherwise nondemocratic practices must be avoided. Indeed, during my eight years at the American Council on Education, I got used to hearing college presidents say that they had "no real power," that they merely carried out the will of the faculty. Thus, they are usually unwilling to act on any proposal without first running it through the cumbersome faculty review and advisory mechanisms. More than anything else, these administrative attitudes are responsible for the organized anarchy identified by Cohen and March.

Even when a proposal for change originates within the faculty, the background and training of most academics militate against its being accepted. One major objective of graduate training in all disciplines is to develop the student's skill in critical thinking. Graduate students are constantly rewarded for demonstrating their critical abilities. All too often, however, critical thinking means detecting flaws in the views or the work of others and pointing out these flaws in public arenas, such as classroom seminars, departmental colloquia, and doctoral oral examinations. Little wonder, then, that the tendency to display one's superior critical ability by finding fault should carry over into faculty life or that the initial faculty reaction to any proposal for change is an analysis of its defects.

The inherent conservatism of faculties does not go unnoticed by faculty members themselves. Indeed, most professors will readily admit that "it's hard to get anything changed around here." Ironically, this partial recognition exacerbates the problem by creating an atmosphere of institutional pessimism, a belief that significant change is either impossible or, at best, very difficult to achieve. This pessimism, in turn, discourages many faculty members from actively supporting proposals they find attractive. Their efforts will be futile, they think, so why should they try?

When pushed to account for institutional inertia, faculty members often cite the cumbersome administrative structure or even the conservatism and obstreperousness of their own colleagues. They are unable or unwilling to face the fact that they personally contribute to the inertia: through their mistrust of and even contempt for administrators and outside agencies, their blind defense of faculty autonomy, their tendency to be critical of new ideas and to display their critical skills at every possible opportunity, their passivity in the face of obstructionist colleagues, their pessimism about the prospects of significant change, and their reluctance to devote time and effort to supporting those proposals they find promising.

On occasion, external agencies—including boards of trustees; alumni groups; and federal, state, and local governments—have provided the impetus for change (for example, in recruiting more minority-group members to join the faculty, staff, and student body). Unfortunately, they have more often served as a catalyst for considerable institutional resistance to change. As the trend toward more centralized planning and budgeting has gained momentum, and as outside agencies (legislatures, state budget offices, coordinating boards) have increasingly pressed for greater accountability, faculty and institutional conservatism has hardened. No matter how it is presented, such central coordination is interpreted as a potential threat to autonomy, and academics respond to such threats by rushing to the defense of the status quo. Because of their tendency to man the barricades when confronted with external demands, innovation is stifled. Traditional practices and policies, which might otherwise be subjected to regular and rigorous review, are accepted as gospel. In short, the influence of external agencies is more symbolic than real. Most colleges and universities still exert considerable control over their most vital functions: admissions, orientation, course placement, course content, teaching techniques, the awarding of credits and degrees, hiring policies, and promotion and tenure policies.

The interplay of all these elements—the faculty's zealous protection of its own autonomy, the administration's acquiescence in this attitude, the long-standing academic tradition of criticism, and the tendency of both faculty members and administrators to resist external pressures—means that any proposal for change has a dubious future in most institutions. Even if a new idea is attractive enough to appeal to a majority of faculty members, their support is generally so fragile that a sufficiently determined and articulate critic can usually scuttle the proposal. In this sense, individual faculty members can wield a great deal of negative power.

If this theory of academic conservatism (Astin, 1976) is valid, the possibility for significant change within the system may seem feeble indeed. One can only agree with Patullo (1972) when he says, "Those who understand and empathize with the needs of the majority of undergraduates can only feel enormous frustration at the glacial pace of change of most colleges and universities" (p. 26). Nonetheless, there are ways of dealing with faculty members' resistance to change and of overcoming or reducing the other obstacles identified in this section. A special kind of administrative leadership is required.

Leadership

If American higher education is ever going to revise its traditional conceptions of excellence in favor of the talent development view, the responsibility for initiating and guiding such a transformation rests with its leaders. By leaders I mean primarily the chief executive officers of our colleges and universities, but I would also include here the top academic officers of the institution, trustees, leading scholars of higher education, officials of state systems, and state and national policy makers. To simplify my discussion of leadership, I will concentrate on the chief executive officers.

Clear Statement of Values and Purpose. In their best-selling book on effective business organizations, Peters and Waterman (1982) conclude that a leader who articulates and promotes a clear view of the organization's mission is essential. But in many colleges and universities, particularly the larger and more complex ones, the institutional leader fails to state goals clearly and frequently gives mixed signals about what the institution's primary purpose really is. For example, the same president who tells visiting parents that the institution is committed to excellent teaching may also try to lure a faculty star with the promise of little or no teaching load. Similarly, a president who tells the faculty senate that "scholarship is the number-one priority in this university" may agree to pay a higher salary to a football coach than to the faculty's Nobel Prize winner.

One way to resolve this ambiguity in institutional values is to make explicit the values that are implicit in such mixed messages. Indeed, one reason why the resources and reputational conceptions of excellence go unchallenged is that they are implicit rather than explicit. It is one thing for an institutional leader to take pride in enhancing the institution's resources and reputation, but it is quite another to say, flat out, that the principal mission of the institution is to acquire resources or to promote its own reputation. Institutional leaders must be more willing to make explicit statements about the institution's mission and values and to underscore these statements with concrete actions.

As a first step in implementing the talent development approach, the chief executive officer should state, directly and forthrightly, that the institution's most important and fundamental aim is to develop the talents of its students and faculty members to their fullest. These values must be stated on every possible occasion. The long-term goal here is to develop a clear-cut concept of institutional purpose that is shared by all members of the academic community. Only to the extent that talent development becomes a collective enterprise will the institution succeed in that mission.

Under such an approach, what becomes of the resources and reputational views of excellence? Given the pervasiveness of these traditional views, they cannot be ignored by even the most reform-minded administrator. The real question is their relative importance vis-à-vis the talent development concept. Thus, the administration would continue its efforts to acquire resources, but *always* with an eye toward how these resources can be deployed to enhance the student's educational and personal development. In other words, in the talent development view, resources are never an end in themselves. Similarly, in the long run, the best way for an institution to acquire a reputation for excellence may be to produce graduates who are satisfied with their educational experience and who spread the word to other prospective students and their parents. Eventually, such

word-of-mouth advertising will work its way into the local folklore, thus enhancing the institution's reputation. The example
of Northeast Missouri State University cited earlier is a case in
point. Moreover, most of us are familiar with institutions that
are not well known nationally but that have excellent local reputations for their outstanding educational programs. In short, embracing a talent development view of institutional mission and
implementing that view with concrete actions may be one of
the best ways for institutional leaders to enhance the institution's reputation, acquire more resources, and thus assure the
long-term viability of their institutions.

    Communication. Chief executives who wish to promote
a talent development view of excellence face a real challenge in
getting their ideas across to the rest of the academic community. Whereas abstract ideas in the natural sciences can be
communicated reasonably well through the language of mathematics, concepts in education and the social sciences are not so
easily conveyed. One method is to repeat the idea in many different contexts (speeches, symposia, memoranda, articles, and
so on), using as rich an array of styles and rhetorical devices as
possible.

    But perhaps the most effective means of communicating
abstract ideas is through concrete demonstration. Many avenues
are available for demonstrating the concepts of talent development and student involvement: changing the criteria used for
hiring and promoting faculty members, collecting and disseminating data that reflect changes in students over time, sponsor-
ing conferences and symposia on college teaching, providing
in-service training programs for newly hired faculty members,
increasing support for teacher-training programs and for schools
and departments of education, and establishing centers for
teaching and learning. (Some of these techniques are discussed
in more detail later.)

    Working with the Faculty. A recent study of college
presidents in forty-seven institutions (Astin and Scherrei, 1980)
suggests that dealings with faculty members represent the most
frequent source of severe conflict and frustration. The attitudes
of college presidents toward their faculty can best be described

as ambivalent. On the one hand, they generally respect the faculty's teaching skills and ability to work with students; on the other hand, they view faculty participation in governance with some hostility, their most frequent complaint being that the faculty is highly resistant to new ideas and proposals for change. Since faculty members are heavily involved in the governance process at most institutions, through academic senates and institutional committees, the chief executive officer must find effective ways of minimizing their negative influence while at the same time capitalizing on their expertise to solve institutional problems.

While faculty conservatism is indeed a force that must be taken into account, administrators must also recognize that any proposal for change almost inevitably makes demands on the faculty member's time and energy. Most faculty members are already extremely busy carrying out their teaching and scholarly responsibilities; so they are likely to resent and oppose administrative proposals for change unless those proposals are accompanied by concrete suggestions for appropriate trade-offs in faculty time. The Astin-Scherrei study suggests that the faculty's administrative work comes at the expense of time devoted to teaching. Thus, administrative suggestions to give more effort to the talent development (learning) process should probably be accompanied by plans to reduce faculty involvement in administration.

How can the administrator minimize, or perhaps even use to advantage, the academician's penchant for criticizing new ideas? The first step is to recognize that faculty members like to have a forum—for instance, a departmental meeting or a meeting of the faculty senate—in which to display their critical skills. The canny administrator thus will avoid introducing new ideas or asking for decisions on new proposals in such a forum, which almost invites rejection. One alternative, though not widely used, is to distribute drafts of the proposal and then hold hearings where any interested faculty member can come to offer his or her reactions and criticism. No votes should be taken and no decisions made at such hearings. Instead, they should be used as a mechanism for refining and improving the proposal as well as for smoking out the opposition. Once all interested faculty members have had an adequate opportunity to comment on the draft, it is revised and then either resubmitted for further hearings or submitted to the faculty for a vote. If the latter, the vote should probably be taken by ballot. If the vote is called at an open meeting, some faculty member is likely to seize the chance to display his or her critical abilities. Voting by ballot minimizes the probability that individual faculty members will be temporarily swayed by a brilliant critique and increases the likelihood that they will take the trouble to read and analyze the proposal on their own. So long as each faculty member is given an opportunity to speak at the hearings and later to vote on the proposal, the democratic process is preserved.

One proposal that will surely be made if a talent development approach is followed—and just as surely be opposed—is to implement assessment procedures that show how students are actually changing and developing. Faculty members tend to see such a comprehensive evaluation program as at best a drain on their time and at worst an administrative strategem for monitoring their teaching performance and a basis for rewarding or punishing them. To minimize this resistance, the administrator must make clear from the outset just how this longitudinal information on students will be used. It should not be used as a basis for rewarding and punishing professors. A much more productive tack is to view the information as an integral part of an educational process. One goal of this process is to promote a sense of mission among all members of the academic community. Unless everyone shares the conviction that student development should have the highest priority, a comprehensive assessment program is difficult to justify. But when this aim has general agreement, it follows that faculty members will feel a need to know just how their students are doing in this respect.

My sense is that most faculty members and administrators in higher education have at least some commitment to student development, as well as a desire to know how their students are faring. All too frequently, however, these concerns are subverted by more immediate priorities: professional advancement, institutional survival, fund raising, and so forth. Col-

lege presidents must therefore set an example by putting their
money where their mouth is, so to speak. They must make it
clear, by their concrete actions, that their primary goal is to
improve the quality of the undergraduate experience and that
all their other activities—fund-raising, public relations, and so
on—are merely means to this end.

*Reducing Resistance by Offering Alternatives to Talent
Development.* Having been personally involved over the years in
several attempts to implement a talent development concept, I
must admit that some faculty members are simply not psycho-
logically ready to accept such an approach in theory. In those
cases where strong faculty resistance seems a certainty, the chief
executive officer might consider instead introducing one of
three other choices. These options—labeled the quality-of-life,
degree-of-fit, and resource use approaches—are consistent with
the spirit of talent development but, because they do not require such extensive pretesting and posttesting of students, are
less likely to generate strong faculty opposition.

The quality-of-life approach relies primarily on the subjective reports of students about their educational experiences.
Samples of students are asked, by means of questionnaires or
interviews, to assess the quality of such aspects of college life as
classroom instruction, academic and career advising, relations
with faculty members, administrative procedures, student support services, and the general social and intellectual atmosphere.
The results of such judgments can be reported separately by
school, department, class, or student type. Not only can professors and administrators make practical use of such information,
but the very fact that the chief executive regularly seeks such
information as a basis for action sends an important message to
the rest of the academic community. In effect, it says that the
college president gives high priority to the talent development
and involvement notions. I might add here that the same quality-
of-life approach can be used to identify faculty problems that
need attention.

The degree-of-fit approach attempts to determine the extent to which the institution's course offerings and other activities are congruent with the student's needs and goals. The im-

plementation of this concept requires comprehensive information on the intellectual performance and aspirations of entering students. Such data can be used to place students in appropriate courses and to evaluate the curriculum and other aspects of the academic program, with an eye to possible modification or revision. Assessing the degree of fit is especially important in view of the changes in students' interests, the rapidly expanding knowledge base, and the emerging technologies. Like the quality-of-life approach, the degree-of-fit approach can also be applied to the faculty.

The resource use approach can take a variety of forms. Many institutions already survey faculty members to determine how they spend their time. But, as was noted in Chapter Six, one of the most important resources is student time. Any institution seriously concerned about maximizing students' involvement should also be concerned about how students are spending their time and whether they are devoting sufficient time to learning. This approach can also focus on the use of various physical resources such as laboratories, libraries, media centers, computers, and so forth. Periodic evaluations of how much and how well students are using such resources provide important clues to the extent of students' involvement in the learning process.

Selecting Leaders. According to some organization theories, the best way to change an organization is to change the people who run it. Having worked for eight years at the American Council on Education, which some observers jokingly call the college presidents' club, I am convinced that our traditional methods of selecting college presidents need a major overhaul. Let me first share my view of how the process actually works and then suggest some revisions that might produce substantially better results.

The selection process has three major phases: the preliminary screening of a large number of individuals, the development of a short list of candidates who are then scrutinized more carefully and often invited to the campus for a visit, and the final selection decision (which is often highly politicized). What kinds of people survive this process and are offered the job? My impression is that only three types of people stand a reasonable chance of being offered a college presidency: insiders (those already employed at the institution) who are well regarded either by the academic community in general or by particular persons associated with the search process; highly visible or famous people; and persons who hold, or have held, high-level administrative positions in other academic institutions.

Well-regarded insiders are usually, but not always, high-ranking administrators, most often provosts, vice-presidents, or deans. The second category includes politicians, high-ranking military officers, Nobel Prize winners, and the like. The third category includes administrators at other institutions who wish to improve their status either by moving to a higher-level position (from vice-president to president, for example) or by moving from one presidency to another at an institution higher up in the academic hierarchy. With respect to this last category, the relative status of the two institutions is important. For example, the search committee at an institution of only moderate prestige may be willing to offer the presidency to a relatively low-level administrator (a dean, for example) from an institution substantially higher up in the hierarchy. But when the two institutions are relatively close on the ladder, the search committee generally considers only top administrators (provosts or vice-presidents). Search committees at the prestigious research universities are inclined to reject applicants from the smaller colleges unless they happen to be presidents of one of the few elite (highly selective) small colleges. In fact, movement from the presidency of an elite small college to the presidency of a major university is a common career path. All this convinces me that the entire search process is heavily influenced by the institutional hierarchy and by concern about the institution's reputation. This latter concern explains why nationally visible figures (the second category) with no knowledge of academia and no background in education are sometimes chosen as college presidents.

It seems to me that different motives inform the choice of one particular type of candidate over another. In selecting the insider, the search committee is often motivated by a desire to avoid controversy; an insider is a safe appointment. In choosing a nationally famous person, the committee is trying to attract attention to the institution. In selecting an administrator from another institution, the search committee is trying to make the appointment seem as plausible as possible. While each of these motives is understandable, satisfying such motives is not necessarily in the best interests of the institution. What do I mean by best interests? Perhaps the gravest defect of the current search process is the failure to develop an appropriate job description. Reading through the employment section of the *Chronicle of Higher Education,* one finds that the advertisements for presidential vacancies are remarkably simplistic and homogeneous. Usually, prior high-level administrative experience is a prerequisite, as is the Ph.D. At most institutions where research is important, the candidate is required to be a scholar as well. At most community colleges, the candidate is required to have had experience working in a community college.

Such job descriptions are at once too inclusive and too exclusive: too inclusive because too large and too diverse a group of people qualify, and too exclusive because too many people who may have exactly the right qualities fail to qualify. I am thinking here of outstanding faculty members who understand academia but who do not wish to go through the usual progression (from department chair to dean to vice-president) that would put them in a position to qualify for a presidency. Such job descriptions also exclude people from government and private industry who might make excellent presidents but who do not have the required degrees or the necessary experience in academic administration.

Most practicing administrators, of course, will object strongly to the suggestion that previous administrative experience may not be that important in identifying the best prospects for top administrative posts. Like any other practicing professionals, college administrators are likely to feel that their prior experience in the field has been extremely valuable in sharpening their administrative skills and talents. But is it not also the case that candidates from administrative posts outside academe have had "prior experience" which may also facilitate their performance as academic administrators? So far as I know, there is no empirical evidence suggesting that top administrators who have come up through the ranks perform any more effectively than those who have not.

But perhaps the major difficulty with traditional search procedures is that they tend to favor the most ambitious candidates. It was my impression while working at the American Council on Education that many of the people who participated in Council affairs were administrators on the make. They saw their career development in hierarchical terms: each new job was no more than a stepping stone to a higher position. Thus, they would never consider making a lateral movement (say, from vice-president to vice-president or from president to president) unless it entailed progression up the ladder to an institution with substantially higher prestige. At the same time, they were willing to leave their current institution to join one of comparable, or sometimes even lower, prestige if the move represented increased responsibility (say, from vice-president to president).

What was even more troubling, the most active candidates were often those people who seemed to be doing the poorest job. Search committees apparently make little effort to determine how well an administrator is performing at his current institution. The assumption is "If the person has the job, the person must be performing the job satisfactorily." Search committees seem to make themselves highly vulnerable to incompetent candidates.

Because search committees generally do not write meaningful job descriptions and because they tend to prefer national celebrities or high-level academic administrators, many begin their activities by generating a list of names. If they find they need more names, they call the American Council on Education or presidents of neighboring institutions to solicit suggestions. It was my impression that the most ambitious (and sometimes the most incompetent) administrators went to enormous lengths to make their availability known to other college administrators and to staff members of the American Council on Education. Again, search committees seem to be open themselves up to some of the worst candidates.

It is my belief that search committees should begin their

deliberations not by developing a list of names but by delving deeply into the institution's problems and needs with the ultimate aim of creating a comprehensive job description. First and foremost, the description should focus on some shared conception of the institution's purpose. If talent development is a core part of the institution's mission, then consideration should be given only to those candidates who share this view and who have the ability to articulate and promote it within the institution. Each institution, of course, will have its own unique problems and goals. The point is simply that until the search committee has a clear understanding of what course the institution should pursue, any attempt to screen possible candidates for the presidency is futile. Once a comprehensive analysis of the institution's mission and needs is completed, and its future course charted, the search committee will have some basis for deciding what to look for in a candidate. Such personal qualities as intelligence, persuasiveness, and knowledge of academia should probably be given more weight than academic degrees or prior administrative experience.

Some search committees do develop fairly detailed job descriptions. But all too often these descriptions embody the resources and reputational views. Thus, the music behind the words in some advertisements for presidential vacancies is that the person ought to be good at fund raising. These days, search committees seem to favor candidates with good connections. My main point here is that if an institution wants to pay more than lip service to its talent development mission, it ought to attach great importance to the candidate's ability to further that goal.

Chapter Eight

The Changing College Student: Challenges Facing American Higher Education

A chapter focusing on the student seems an appropriate conclusion to a book on excellence in higher education. My view of American college students is heavily influenced by almost two decades of experience as director of the Cooperative Institutional Research Program (CIRP), which annually surveys the entering freshman classes of a large-scale national sample of colleges and universities. Originally intended to provide baseline information for the longitudinal follow-ups that constitute the empirical research whose findings are cited throughout this book (Astin, 1975, 1977, 1982), the freshman survey has in recent years become a subject of interest in and of itself for the insight it gives into the changing character of first-time, full-time college freshmen. By comparing the results of the eighteen consecutive freshman surveys (1966–1983), one can get a clear picture of trends in the characteristics of the nation's college-going young people. These trends are both fascinating and disturbing. As a scholar, I am fascinated by the complexity of the changes and by what they reveal about changes in the larger society. But as an educator, I am disturbed by the nature of these changes and by their potential effects on the higher education system. In this chapter, I will first review some of these trends, then discuss their significance in terms of the larger society and their implications for the excellence of the American higher education system.

Trends in Student Characteristics

Students' characteristics can be examined under three broad headings: academic skills and preparation, educational and career aspirations, and personal values.

Academic Skills and Preparation. The decline in college admission test scores has been widely publicized. For instance, it provides much of the empirical base for *A Nation at Risk* (National Commission on Excellence in Education, 1983). That this decline is not an isolated phenomenon is suggested by a number of trends in the annual freshman surveys. Better than two out of every five of today's freshmen (42 percent) say that one "very important" factor in their decision to go to college was a desire "to improve my reading and study skills." This figure is nearly twice what it was ten years ago. Similarly, over the past ten years, the proportion of freshmen saying that they will need "tutoring help in specific courses" nearly doubled.

Considering this apparent decline in academic competence, it is perhaps surprising that students' high school grades have improved dramatically over the same period (see Figure 5). In the late 1960s, freshmen entering college with C averages outnumbered those with A averages by better than two to one; by 1978 the A students outnumbered the C students. This grade inflation trend peaked in 1978 and has actually regressed slightly since then. Interestingly enough, the trend in test scores has followed a reverse pattern, reaching a low in the late 1970s and stabilizing until the present day. Moreover, students themselves confirm this grade inflation. A solid majority of the 1983–84 freshmen (58 percent) agreed that "grading in the high schools has become too easy" (Figure 5).

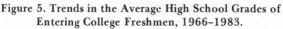

Figure 5. Trends in the Average High School Grades of
Entering College Freshmen, 1966–1983.

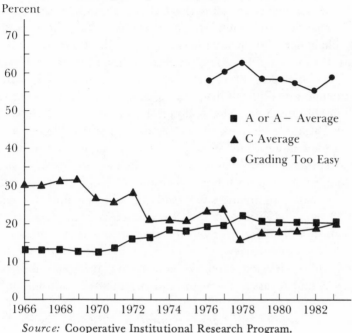

Source: Cooperative Institutional Research Program.

Even though many freshmen realize that grading standards in the secondary schools have declined, grade inflation may have prompted them to become unduly optimistic about their probable academic success in college. Thus, since 1967 the proportions of freshmen who expect to earn at least a B average in college, to be elected to an academic honor society, and to graduate with honors have increased, while the proportion expecting to fail a college course has declined.

Unpublished data from the National Commission on Excellence (Adelman, 1983) suggest that changes in the high school curriculum may be partly responsible for the decline in test scores and the rise in grades. Today's high school students are taking fewer solid academic courses (particularly English) and more "soft" courses such as marching band and driver training. Because grading standards tend to be less stringent in elective courses than in basic academic courses, this curricular shift has the effect of inflating students' grade averages but simultaneously leaving their basic academic skills undeveloped.

Other evidence from the CIRP surveys suggests that today's entering freshmen are reluctant to take college courses that challenge their academic skills, especially their verbal skills. Thus, the proportions of freshmen intending to major in English, foreign languages, literature, history, and philosophy—fields that demand reading ability, critical and analytical thinking, and skill in composition—have declined sharply since the 1960s.

These trends make it clear that American higher education today is enrolling an unprecedented number of underprepared students with serious deficiencies in basic learning skills. As long as the reputational and resources conceptions of excellence remain dominant, such students will continue to be regarded as a liability, and the "excellence" of American higher education will suffer. Conversely, institutions that embrace the talent development view of excellence will have a much stronger incentive to develop effective educational programs for these students and to assist them in realizing their educational objectives.

Educational and Career Aspirations. Despite the declines in academic skills over the past fifteen years, more freshmen than ever before aspire to advanced study, but only that leading to high-level professional degrees (in medicine, dentistry, law, and so on). The proportions of freshmen aspiring to higher academic degrees (the master's and the doctorate) have actually declined. This reduction, which closely parallels students' lessening interest in college teaching (Chapter Five), clearly spells trouble for our graduate programs in years to come.

Some of the most pronounced changes with respect to educational aspirations involve intended major fields of study. Since 1966, the fields of business, computer science, and engineering have become markedly more popular, while the market for the traditional liberal arts fields has become increasingly bearish. The fields experiencing the sharpest declines in popularity include the humanities (English, literature, foreign language, philosophy, theology), the fine and performing arts (art, music, speech, and theater), and the social sciences (anthropology, economics, geography, history, political science, psychology, social work, and sociology) (Figure 6). These three broad disciplinary

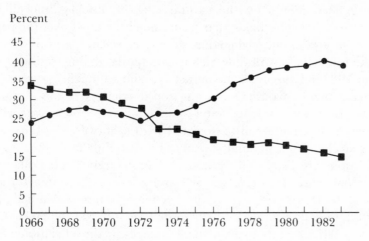

Figure 6. Trends in the Probable Major Fields of Entering College Freshmen, 1966–1983.

● Business, Engineering,
   and Computer Science

■ Humanities, Fine Arts,
   and Social Science

Source: Cooperative Institutional Research Program.

areas accounted for about one in three freshmen in 1966 but only about one in seven of today's freshmen. Some of these fields suffered more severe losses than others. For instance, between 1966 and 1983, the proportion of freshmen planning to major in English and literature dropped by more than 80 percent.

Student interest in the natural sciences also declined, though less precipitously, over the eighteen-year period. Thus, 2.6 percent of 1983 freshmen, compared with 3.3 percent of 1966 freshmen, intended to major in one of the physical sciences (astronomy, chemistry, earth science, and physics). The proportion planning to major in the biological sciences (biology, botany, and zoology) remained stable (3.7 percent in 1966, 3.8 percent in 1983).

Looking at more recent trends, we find that, since the mid 1970s, the humanities, the fine and performing arts, and the social sciences have continued to decline in popularity and have been joined by the natural sciences, nursing, and allied health fields. The fields that have gained the most over the past decade are, again, engineering, computer science, and business, which reached an all-time high in popularity among freshmen in the 1983–84 survey. Concomitantly, education, the natural sciences, the humanities, and the social sciences hit an all-time low. In short, students' interest in education and in virtually every field traditionally associated with a liberal arts education has declined sharply and steadily. These trends in freshmen aspirations are paralleled by almost identical trends in baccalaureates awarded. In 1971, the arts and sciences accounted for almost half (49 percent) of the bachelor's degrees awarded; in 1982, they accounted for little more than a third (36 percent).

What factors explain these changes in the educational aspirations of freshmen? The most obvious answer to this question lies in the declining academic skill levels discussed earlier. Students who enter college with underdeveloped skills are understandably reluctant to major in English, foreign languages, and other fields that demand linguistic proficiency. The decline in academic skills may also explain the decreasing popularity of the doctorate and the increasing popularity of business, a field that tends to attract students with relatively low academic skill levels (see Chapter Five). Education, which also attracts underprepared students (Chapter Five), has also declined in popularity, as I have mentioned. Thus, many of the students who in the past would have majored in education appear to have shifted to business. But perhaps the most important factor is students' increasing interest in making money. Engineering and computer science are fields that offer high-paying jobs to baccalaureate-recipients; business, of course, holds the promise of very lucrative positions. In contrast, the college graduate who has majored in education or the humanities can ordinarily expect to get a relatively low-paying job. (I will return to the money issue shortly.)

These trends have profound implications for the college curriculum and should arouse particular concern in those who support the content view of excellence, which holds that the liberal arts and sciences constitute the highest form of education. Clearly, the traditional liberal arts fields—especially the humanities—are in serious trouble. Because of declining student demand, many institutions have been forced to reduce the size of their faculties in these fields, and some smaller institutions may even have had to eliminate certain of these departments entirely. At the same time, schools and departments of business and computer science have expanded rapidly. These changes make it increasingly difficult for institutions to offer their undergraduates anything resembling a liberal arts education. If broad exposure to the liberal arts is regarded as a critical element in a high-quality undergraduate education, then the excellence of undergraduate education in America is seriously threatened by the trends described in this section.

Trends in students' long-range career plans closely parallel trends in their major field preferences. The career field gaining the most in popularity since 1966 is business, which includes such career choices as accountant, business executive, business owner, and salesman or buyer. The proportion of freshmen naming these career choices almost doubled over the eighteen-year period, from 11.6 percent in 1966 to 20.4 percent in 1983. The two other career choices showing substantial increases in popularity were engineer and computer programmer or analyst. Since 1966 these three careers have just about doubled in popularity among entering freshmen (Figure 7).

In Chapter Five, I noted that careers in school and college teaching have declined in popularity by some 75 percent since the 1960s. Three other career choices have shown greater than 50 percent declines over the same period: clergyman, research scientist, and law enforcement official. The first two of these usually require advanced training beyond the bachelor's degree, whereas none of the career choices that increased in popularity (business person, computer programmer, and engineer) requires such training. During the past six or seven years, the career choices of nursing and social work have also fallen sharply in popularity among entering freshmen. As a matter of fact, the

Figure 7. Trends in the Career Choices of Entering College Freshmen, 1966–1983.

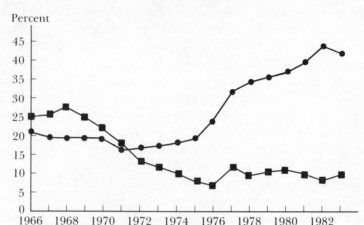

Percent

- ● Business, Engineering, and Computer Science

- ■ Clergy, Education, and Social Work

Source: Cooperative Institutional Research Program.

severest reductions have occurred among the human service occupations: teaching, nursing, social work, law enforcement, and the ministry. These careers also tend to be relatively low-paying and to require graduate training. In contrast, the careers increasing most in popularity do not require advanced training and tend to be relatively high-paying.

Personal Values. Since 1966, the freshman survey has included a list of fifteen to twenty "life goals" (statements reflecting personal values) and has asked students to indicate the relative priority they give to each. While the popularity of many of these life goals has fluctuated over the eighteen-year period, two of the statements show consistent—and contrasting—trends. The life goal of "being very well-off financially" has become steadily more popular. The proportion of freshmen regarding it as important has increased from 40 percent to nearly

70 percent over the past ten years (see Figure 8). The life goal of "developing a meaningful philosophy of life" has dropped

Figure 8. Trends in Two Student Life Goals Among
Entering College Freshmen, 1967–1983.

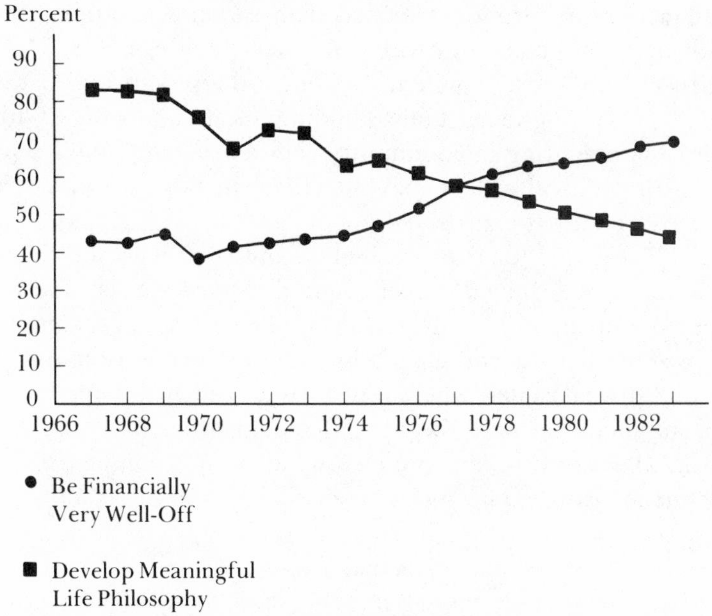

Percent

• Be Financially
  Very Well-Off

■ Develop Meaningful
  Life Philosophy

Source: Cooperative Institutional Research Program.

precipitously in popularity: Fifteen years ago, it was the most valued goal, being endorsed by 83 percent of entering freshmen, but by 1983-84 it had dropped to seventh on the list, being endorsed by only 45 percent.

One can speculate that the contrasting patterns for these two values are attributable to a common underlying shift in student values. More specifically, it could be argued that students who regard making a lot of money as an important life goal feel no need to develop a meaningful philosophy of life. Indeed, they may view the making of money as a kind of philosophy in itself. Most of the values given higher priority in recent years are concerned with money, power, and status: being very well off financially, being an authority, having administrative responsibility for others, and winning recognition. Moreover, two in three freshmen in 1983, compared with only half in the early 1970s, said that a major reason for their decision to attend college was to be able to make more money. Apparently, today's students are much more inclined than earlier generations to believe that learning is for earning. Conversely, life goals reflecting altruism and social concern—helping others who are in difficulty, promoting racial understanding, cleaning up the environment, participating in community action programs, and keeping up with political affairs—have declined in popularity, as have creative and artistic goals.

These value changes are highly consistent with the changes in student majors and career plans discussed earlier. Thus, increased student interest in business, engineering, and computer science has been accompanied by a strengthening of materialistic and power values, whereas decreased student interest in education, social science, the arts, the humanities, nursing, social work, allied health, and the clergy has been accompanied by a decline in altruism and social concern.

National Values

In attempting to understand what these student trends imply about the larger society, a historical perspective would be helpful. Has something unprecedented been happening in our society over the past two decades, or do these eighteen-year trends reflect cyclical phenomena, a repetition of the trends of earlier times? Is it possible, for example, that today's students are a throwback to the so-called Silent Generation of the 1950s? Unfortunately, national survey data on students' values were simply not collected before 1966. There are, however, earlier data on the fields of study in which students earned degrees (Adkins, 1975). For instance, between 1945 and 1975, the proportion of bachelor's degrees awarded in business fluctuated between 11 percent and 14 percent. Starting in 1975, this figure climbed steadily, reaching an all-time high of 18 percent in 1979. Trends in the major field aspirations of *freshmen* since the mid 1970s indicate that the percentages of business majors among baccalaureate-recipients will continue to climb at an even faster rate.

As for education, the trends are even more dramatic. Between 1945 and 1972, the proportions of education majors among baccalaureate-recipients showed modest increases and decreases from year to year. But after 1972, the proportion began to decline steadily, so that by 1980 the percentage of women earning bachelor's degrees in education had been cut in half, and the percentage of men had been reduced by one-third. Again, the freshmen surveys since the late 1970s suggest that these percentages will continue to decline.

In short, these analyses of degrees earned since the end of World War II suggest that the dramatic increase in the popularity of business and the concomitant decline in the popularity of education as a major are not merely a cyclical phenomenon making its periodic reappearance. Rather, it represents an unprecedented shift in American higher education.

To say that today's students are more materialistic and less altruistic is not intended as a criticism of the students themselves. On the contrary, to a large extent, the values of students are simply a reflection of the values of the larger society in which they grew up. As I write these words, Ronald Reagan has just been elected to a second term as president, and exit polls indicate that the pocketbook issues—taxes, inflation, and federal spending—were foremost in the voters' minds. Given that the losing Democratic challenger, Walter Mondale, campaigned on a platform which proposed raising taxes and increasing support for the disadvantaged, it is not surprising that the Republican incumbent won by such a large margin.

The current flurry of interest in the condition of education in the United States may be reassuring to some observers, but to me the concern seems to be extremely narrow. The much-heralded *A Nation at Risk* (National Commission on Excellence in Education, 1983), for example, argues that the United States must strengthen its educational system primarily for scientific and technological reasons (that is, to remain competitive in international trade and in the development of technology with possible military applications). Our ability to play an effective role in world affairs, however, does not depend solely on our scientific and technical skill. It also depends on our ability to understand and communicate effectively with other nations. Under these conditions, the precipitous decline in students' interest in the humanities, education, and the social sciences—together with the deemphasis on these fields that many institutions have felt constrained to implement—must be viewed with alarm. I might add here that the problems confronting education and the social sciences have been compounded by recent federal actions, including the attempt to phase out the social science and education programs of the National Science Foundation, the plan to eliminate the Department of Education, and the exclusion of social science research from the 1981 tax reform bill, which was intended to encourage private industry to invest more of its profits in research. To the extent that the federal government has shown any interest at all in supporting education, this interest has been confined to science and mathematics.

These trends are all the more chilling when one realizes that our nation has apparently chosen to regard the entire arms control and disarmament issue in terms of hard science and technology: Which side has the most weapons? How many and what type of weapons are necessary to launch a first strike? The prevailing belief seems to be that national security depends primarily on the development of more and better weapons. This kind of reasoning ignores the fact that a decision to engage in armed confrontation and a decision to employ nuclear weapons are *human* acts and that hard science and technology contribute very little to our understanding of how to anticipate or prevent such acts. For such understanding, we must turn to psychology, sociology, history, political science, anthropology, education, and related fields—the very fields that are on the decline at the institutional level and are being further crippled by the withdrawal of federal support.

Dealing effectively with any potential adversary requires first that we understand what makes the adversary tick: how he thinks, what his needs and basic interests are, how to educate him. And, I might add, it does not hurt to understand one's *own* motivation and national psyche as well. This kind of understanding of ourselves and our potential adversaries can never come from the hard sciences and technology alone.

The Values of Academia

The pattern of increasing student materialism and decreasing social concern is an interesting analogue to the various conceptions of excellence discussed throughout this book. The reputational and resources views, for example, parallel the increasing student interest in money, power, and status. In contrast, the talent development view parallels students' concern for others and for the society. Under the reputational and resources approaches, the institution devotes its energies to enhancing its power, prestige, and possessions. Under the talent development approach, the institution invests its energy and resources in helping students develop their talents and abilities to the fullest.

It is interesting to speculate on the extent to which the changing student values observed in the freshman surveys may be reinforced by the values to which students are exposed during the undergraduate years. What implicit values does higher education communicate to its students through its institutional policies and practices? Are our universities afflicted by the same materialism that seems to characterize college students and the larger society? Pick up any copy of the *Chronicle of Higher Education* and see how much space is devoted to matters relating to money, as opposed to matters relating, for example, to the improvement of undergraduate education. Or consider how our great universities get to be "great." Not necessarily by doing an outstanding job of educating their students, but by recruiting as many Guggenheim Fellows, National Academy of Science members, Nobel and Pulitzer Prize winners, and National Merit Scholars as possible; by garnering large research grants and contracts; and by amassing large endowments. *These* are the earmarks of excellence today, and they are clearly based on the resources and reputational views of excellence. Very few people stop to ask whether these resources are deployed effectively to enhance teaching and learning. In other words, many academics seem content to define educational excellence in terms of what we have, rather than what we do.

And to what extent do the internal operations of institutions reflect a common concern for the education of the student? To what extent do different operational units work cooperatively for common objectives, rather than competing with each other for greater institutional visibility and a larger share of the resources? There is no way to shield students from the value implications of how we deal with each other in our institutions.

That policy in American higher education is influenced more by economic than by educational considerations is apparent from a recent study of how college affects students' development (Astin, 1977). Even though the research evidence clearly indicates that student involvement and development are enhanced by living on campus, attending a four-year rather than a two-year institution, and attending a small rather than a large institution, the major trends in American higher education since World War II have all been in the opposite direction. That is, the proportion of commuter students has increased, two-year colleges have proliferated, and institutions have grown steadily larger. The impetus behind such trends is economic rather than educational. Commuter colleges obviate the need to construct expensive residential facilities, two-year colleges are cheaper to operate than four-year colleges, and large institutions presumably offer certain economies of scale.

It might be argued that academia, like its students, simply reflects the values of the larger society. But the real question, it seems to me, is whether higher education ought to be no more than a mirror. Perhaps we should introduce some alternative values to undergraduates. Instead of being merely materialistic, competitive, and acquisitive, and letting these values dominate our policies, perhaps we should start to think seriously about giving some other values—such as education, learning, talent development, the quest for truth, honesty, and concern for others—a higher priority.

Epilogue

In this book, I have attempted to articulate a view of excellence—the talent development view—that seems to offer significant advantages over the traditional views—the reputational and resources conceptions—that have come to dominate institutional policies and practices in American higher education. As long as our higher education institutions continue to give higher priority to resource acquisition and the enhancement of reputation than to anything else, they will simply reinforce the growing materialism and declining altruism that characterize the most recent generation of students. Do we want to see this happen? Is it appropriate that our institutions emphasize greed and self-aggrandizement above other motives and goals? Are these the values we want to encourage in our students?

Embracing a talent development view of excellence does not require that institutions abandon their research, certification, and public service missions. What is at issue here is the relative weight given to these various functions. In this connection, it is worth noting that research, certification, and public service are functions that can be carried out by research institutes, testing organizations, and other public and private agencies, whereas talent development is perhaps the only mission that our colleges and universities are uniquely qualified to perform.

Some readers may feel that my proposals are too utopian and that it is unrealistic to expect more of our colleges and universities to become truly dedicated to the talent development goal. But I am not so sure. First, it should be remembered that several institutions are already committed to talent development as a primary goal (see Chapter Seven). Indeed, most institutions espouse some sort of talent development view in their catalogues and other official publications. Moreover, students, their parents, and the public at large seem to support the idea that academic institutions should more fully commit themselves to maximizing student involvement and talent development. Finally, a recent survey of 194 members of the boards of re-

gional and national accrediting agencies suggests that support
for a talent development view of excellence may be just as
strong as support for the resource view (Kells, in press).

Imagine what it would be like to work in an institution
whose *only* mission was talent development, where the only activities encouraged or rewarded were those that facilitated the
student's personal and intellectual development, and where the
rewards were proportional to the institution's success in developing the talents of all its students. One could expect the following in such an institution:

- The entire academic community—faculty members, administrators, staff members, and students—would be united in
  working toward a common goal.
- Teaching and advising would be accorded much higher priority.
- The best students would be encouraged to help in teaching
  the slower students.
- More of the best students would be encouraged to take up
  teaching careers.
- No more faculty stars would be lured with the promise of
  low or no teaching loads.
- Administrators would be hired not so much to manage as to
  be educational leaders.
- Faculty members would use their research activities as a tool
  for enhancing the teaching-learning process.
- Assessment and evaluation would be used not so much for
  screening as for educational purposes (as a source of feedback to both professors and students).
- The admission and education of underprepared students
  would be given greater priority.
- Students would be exposed to an environment where the
  values of education and of serving others took precedence
  over the values of acquiring resources and improving status.

Those educators wishing to influence their institutions to
take a talent development approach may reasonably ask, at this
point: How do we start? Chapter Seven suggested a wide range

of specific actions to be taken in such areas as the selection of administrators, the reward system, the instructional process, the development of learning communities, student-faculty contact, student life, assessment and feedback, teacher training, and so forth. In addition, the recent report of the Study Group on the Conditions of Excellence in Higher Education (1984) provides guidelines for activities generally consistent with the talent development view of excellence. This report was the product of seven higher education scholars and administrators, working together under the sponsorship of the National Institute of Education and the U.S. Department of Education, and has already received a good deal of attention from the news media. It can usefully serve as a focal point for discussions—among faculty members, students, administrators, and other members of the academic community—on the quality of undergraduate education.

But perhaps the most important step that one can take is to initiate a campuswide discussion of institutional values. Such a discussion might center on the following questions: What are the implicit values underlying our current fund-raising activities, faculty hiring and promotion practices, methods of selecting trustees and administrators, student testing and assessment procedures, and student personnel practices? To what extent do our various activities reflect a commitment to promoting student involvement and developing talent? To what extent are they motivated by no more than a desire to acquire more resources and to enhance institutional reputation?

By becoming more conscious of the values underlying our current policies and practices, we can greatly increase the likelihood that, eventually, our academic institutions will indeed be able to realize their full educational potential.

References

Adelman, C. Personal communication, April 8, 1983.

Adkins, D. L. *The Great American Degree Machine.* Berkeley: Carnegie Foundation for the Advancement of Teaching, 1975.

American Association of State Colleges and Universities. *Quality and Effectiveness in Undergraduate Higher Education.* Washington, D.C.: American Association of State Colleges and Universities, 1971.

American Association of State Colleges and Universities. *Value-Centered Education and Moral Commitment.* Washington, D.C.: American Association of State Colleges and Universities, 1976.

Anrig, G. R. "Schools and Higher Education in a Period of Reform: Strengthening Standards and Performance." Paper presented at the annual meeting of the American Association for Higher Education, Chicago, March 15, 1984.

Argyris, C., and Schön, D. A. *Theory in Practice: Increasing Professional Effectiveness.* San Francisco: Jossey-Bass, 1974.

Ashby, E. *Any Person, Any Study.* New York: McGraw-Hill, 1971.

Astin, A. W. "A Reexamination of College Productivity." *Journal of Educational Psychology,* 1961, *52,* 173–178.

Astin, A. W. " 'Productivity' of Undergraduate Institutions." *Science,* 1962, *136,* 129–135.

Astin, A. W. "Differential College Effects on the Motivation of Talented Students to Obtain the Ph.D. Degree." *Journal of Educational Psychology,* 1963, *54,* 63–71.

Astin, A. W. "College Preferences of Very Able Students." *College and University,* 1965, *40,* 282–297.

Astin, A. W. *The College Environment.* Washington, D.C.: American Council on Education, 1968a.

Astin, A. W. "Undergraduate Achievement and Institutional Excellence." *Science,* 1968b, *161,* 661–668.

Astin, A. W. *Predicting Academic Performance in College.* New York: Macmillan, 1971.

Astin, A. W. "The Impact of Dormitory Living on Students." *Educational Record,* 1973a, *54* (3), 204–210.

Astin, A. W. "Measurement and Determinants of the Outcomes of Higher Education." In L. C. Solmon and P. J. Taubman (Eds.), *Does College Matter? Some Evidence of the Impacts of Higher Education.* New York: Academic Press, 1973b.

Astin, A. W. *Preventing Students from Dropping Out.* San Francisco: Jossey-Bass, 1975.

Astin, A. W. *Academic Gamesmanship: Student-Oriented Change in Higher Education.* New York: Praeger, 1976.

Astin, A. W. *Four Critical Years: Effects of College on Beliefs, Attitudes, and Knowledge.* San Francisco: Jossey-Bass, 1977.

Astin, A. W. *Minorities in American Higher Education: Recent Trends, Current Prospects, and Recommendations.* San Francisco: Jossey-Bass, 1982.

Astin, A. W. "Educational Excellence: Aspirations and Realities." In *Proceedings of the 97th Annual Convention, Middle States Association of Colleges.* Philadelphia: Middle States Association of Colleges, 1983a.

Astin, A. W. "Strengthening Transfer Programs." In G. B. Vaughan and Associates, *Issues for Community College Leaders in a New Era.* San Francisco: Jossey-Bass, 1983b.

Astin, A. W. "Today's College Student." Unpublished manuscript, Higher Education Research Institute, University of California, Los Angeles, 1983c.

Astin, A. W. "Student Involvement: A Developmental Theory for Higher Education." *Journal of College Student Personnel,* 1984, *25* (4), 297–308.

Astin, A. W. "Selectivity and Equity in the Public Research University." In L. Keopplin and D. Wilson (Eds.), *Project 2000: the NASULGC Project on the Future of the State University.* New Brunswick, N.J.: Rutgers University Press, forthcoming.

Astin, A. W., and Henson, J. W. "New Measures of College Selectivity." *Research in Higher Education,* September 7, 1977, pp. 1–9.

Astin, A. W., and Scherrei, R. A. *Maximizing Leadership Effectiveness: Impact of Administrative Style on Faculty and Students.* San Francisco: Jossey-Bass, 1980.

Astin, A. W., and Solmon, L. C. "Are Reputational Ratings Needed to Measure Quality?" *Change,* October 1981, pp. 14–19.

Astin, A. W., Christian, C. E., and Henson, J. W. *The Impact of Student Financial Aid Programs on Student Choice.* Final Report to the U.S. Office of Education, under Contract 300–75–0382. Los Angeles: Higher Education Research Institute, 1978.

Astin, A. W., Fuller, B., and Green, K. C. *New Directions for Higher Education: Admitting and Assisting Students After Bakke,* no. 23. San Francisco: Jossey-Bass, 1978.

Astin, A. W., Panos, R. J., and Creager, J. A. *National Norms for Entering Freshmen.* Washington, D.C.: American Council on Education, 1966.

Astin, A. W., and others. "Faculty Development in a Time of Retrenchment." *Change,* 1974.

Astin, A. W., and others. *The American Freshman: National Norms for Fall 1983.* Los Angeles: Higher Education Research Institute, Graduate School of Education, University of California, 1983.

Astin, H. S., and others. *Higher Education and the Disadvantaged Student.* Washington, D.C.: Human Services Press, 1971.

Astin, P. A. "Successful Intervention Is a Reachable Goal." Unpublished manuscript, Higher Education Research Institute, University of California, Los Angeles, 1982.

Baldridge, J. V., and Tierney, M. L. *New Approaches to Management: Creative Practical Systems of Management Information and Management by Objective.* San Francisco: Jossey-Bass, 1979.

Bassin, W. M. "A Note on the Biases in Students' Evaluations of Instructors." *Journal of Experimental Education,* 1974, *43,* 16-17.

Bloom, B. "Time and Learning." *American Psychologist,* 1974, pp. 683-688.

Bogue, E. G., and Brown, W. *Performance Incentives for State Colleges: How Tennessee Is Trying to Improve Its Return on Its Higher Education Investment.* Nashville: Higher Education Commission, 1982.

Boulding, K. E. "Quality Versus Equality: The Dilemma of the University." *Daedalus,* Winter 1975, *11,* 298-303.

Bowen, H. R. *Investment in Learning.* San Francisco: Jossey-Bass, 1977.

Bowen, H. R. *The Costs of Higher Education: How Much Do Colleges and Universities Spend Per Student and How Much Should They Spend?* San Francisco: Jossey-Bass, 1980.

Bowen, H. R. "Cost Differences: The Amazing Disparity Among Institutions of Higher Education in Educational Costs Per Student." *Change,* January/February 1981a, pp. 21-27.

Bowen, H. R. "The Baccalaureate Degree: What Does It Mean? What Should It Mean?" *AAHE Bulletin,* November 1981b, *34* (3), 11-15.

Breneman, D. W., and Nelson, S. C. *Financing Community Colleges: An Educational Perspective.* Washington, D.C., 1981.

Brown, R. D., and DeCoster, D. A. (Eds.) *New Directions for Student Services: Mentoring-Transcript Systems for Promoting Student Growth,* no. 19. San Francisco: Jossey-Bass, 1982.

California State Department of Education. *A Master Plan for Higher Education in California, 1960-1975.* Sacramento: California State Department of Education, 1960.

Carnegie Commission on Higher Education. *Quality and Equality: New Levels of Federal Responsibility for Higher Education.* New York: McGraw-Hill, 1968.

Carnegie Commission on Higher Education. *A Classification of Institutions of Higher Education.* Berkeley: Carnegie Commission on Higher Education, 1973.

Carrier, C. A., Dalgaard, K., and Simpson, D. "Theories of Teaching: Foci for Instructional Improvement Through Consultation." *The Review of Higher Education,* Spring 1983, 6, 195-206.

Cartter, A. M. *An Assessment of Quality in Graduate Education.* Washington, D.C.: American Council on Education, 1966.

Chickering, A. W. *Education and Identity.* San Francisco: Jossey-Bass, 1969.

Chickering, A. W. *Commuting Versus Resident Students: Overcoming Educational Inequities of Living Off Campus.* San Francisco: Jossey-Bass, 1974.

Chickering, A. W. *Quality from the Students' Point of View.* AASCU Studies 1983/1. Washington, D.C.: American Association of State Colleges and Universities, 1983.

Chickering, A. W., and Associates. *The Modern American College.* San Francisco: Jossey-Bass, 1981.

Chomsky, N. "The Responsibility of Intellectuals." In T. Roszak (Ed.), *The Dissenting Academy.* New York: Pantheon, 1968.

Clark, T. F. "Individualized Education." In A. W. Chickering and Associates, *The Modern American College.* San Francisco: Jossey-Bass, 1981.

Cohen, M. D., and March, J. G. *The American College President.* New York: McGraw-Hill, 1974.

Coleman, J. E. "Reconciling Access with Excellence: The Challenge of Educating Underprepared Students." In L. Wilson (Ed.), *New Directions for College Learning Assistance: Helping Special Student Groups,* no. 7. San Francisco: Jossey-Bass, 1982.

Coleman, J. S. *The Adolescent Society.* New York: Free Press, 1961.

Commission on the Higher Education of Minorities. *Final Report.* Los Angeles: Higher Education Research Institute, University of California, 1981.

Cross, K. P. *Beyond the Open Door: New Students to Higher Education.* San Francisco: Jossey-Bass, 1971.

Cross, K. P. *Accent on Learning: Improving Instruction and Reshaping the Curriculum.* San Francisco: Jossey-Bass, 1976.

Cummings, W. K. *Education and Equality in Japan.* Princeton: Princeton University Press, 1979.

Davis, D. E., and Astin, H. S. "Gender and Reputational Standing in Academe." Unpublished manuscript, Graduate School of Education, University of California, Los Angeles, 1984.

Dennar, B. "College Program Offers Chance to Break Migrant Cycle." *Dallas Morning News,* November 28, 1982, p. 1.

Dunham, A. *The Colleges of the Forgotten Americans: A Profile of State Colleges and Regional Universities.* New York: McGraw-Hill, 1969.

Educational Facilities Laboratory. *The Neglected Majority: Facilities for Commuting Students.* New York: Academy of Educational Development, 1977.

Ewell, P. T. "Dimensions of Excellence in Postsecondary Education." Unpublished paper prepared for the Study Group on the Conditions of Excellence in American Higher Education. Boulder: National Center for Higher Education Management Systems, 1984.

Feldman, K. A., and Newcomb, T. M. *The Impact of College on Students.* San Francisco: Jossey-Bass, 1969.

Fisher, C. W., and others. "Teaching Behaviors, Academic Learning Time and Student Achievement." In C. Denham and A. Lieberman (Eds.), *Time to Learn.* Washington, D.C.: National Institute of Education, 1980.

Ford, F. L. "Today's Undergraduates: Are They Human?" *Harvard Magazine,* March-April 1984, pp. 29–32.

Forrest, A., and Steele, J. M. *Defining and Measuring General Education, Knowledge and Skills. Technical Report, 1976-81.* Iowa City: American College Testing Program, 1982.

Friedenberg, E. Z. "Can Testing Contribute to the Quest for Community Among Students?" In Commission on Tests, *Report of the Commission on Tests: II, Briefs.* New York: College Entrance Examination Board, 1970.

Gagne, R. M. *The Conditions of Learning.* (3rd ed.) New York: Holt, Rinehart and Winston, 1977.

Gardner, J. *Excellence: Can We Be Equal and Excellent Too?* New York: Harper & Row, 1961.

Glazer, N. "The Schools of the Minor Professions." *Minerva,* 1974, *12* (3), 347–364.

Goodman, P. *The Community of Scholars.* New York: Random House, 1962.

Grant, G., and others. *On Competence: A Critical Analysis of Competence-Based Reforms in Higher Education.* San Francisco: Jossey-Bass, 1979.

Green, K. C. "Program Review and the State Responsibility for Higher Education." *Journal of Higher Education,* 1981, *52* (1), 67–80.

Green, K. C. *Government Support for Minority Participation in Higher Education.* AAHE-ERIC Higher Education Research Report No. 9. Washington, D.C.: American Association for Higher Education, 1982.

Green, K. C., and others. *The American College Student, 1982: National Norms for 1978 and 1980 College Freshmen.* Los Angeles: American Council on Education and the Higher Education Research Institute, University of California, 1983.

Hackerman, N. "Science Is Universal—the Practitioners Are Not." *Science,* 1984, *225,* 577.

Hanson, G. R. (Ed.) *New Directions for Student Services: Measuring Student Development,* no. 20. San Francisco: Jossey-Bass, 1982.

Harris, J. "Gain Scores on the CLEP General Examination and an Overview of Research." Paper presented at the annual meeting of the American Educational Research Association, Minneapolis, March 1970.

Heath, D. H. *Growing Up in College: Liberal Education and Maturity.* San Francisco: Jossey-Bass, 1968.

Henson, J. W. "Institutional Excellence and Student Achievement: A Study of College Quality and Its Impact on Educational and Career Achievement." Unpublished doctoral dissertation, University of California at Los Angeles, 1980.

Higher Education Research Institute. "Value-Added: A New Approach to Institutional Excellence." Proposal submitted to the Fund for the Improvement of Post-Secondary Education, 1984.

Hodgkinson, H. L. *Institutions in Transition.* New York: McGraw-Hill, 1971.

Hofstadter, R., and Hardy, C. D. *The Development and Scope of Higher Education in the United States.* New York: Columbia University Press, 1952.

Horowitz, I. L. *Professing Sociology: Studies in the Life Cycle of Social Science.* Chicago: Aldine, 1968.

Hughes, R. M. *A Study of Graduate Schools in America.* Oxford, Ohio: Miami University Press, 1925.

Hunt, D. E. "Teachers Are Psychologists, Too: On the Application of Psychology to Education." *Canadian Psychological Review,* 1976, *17,* 210-218.

Hunt, D. E. "How to Be Your Own Best Theorist." *Theory into Practice,* Autumn 1980, *19,* 287-293.

Husen, T. (Ed.) *International Study of Achievement in Mathematics.* New York: Wiley, 1967.

Hutchins, R. M. *The Higher Learning in America.* New Haven: Yale University Press, 1936.

Jencks, C., and Riesman, D. *The Academic Revolution.* New York: Doubleday, 1968.

Jones, L. V., Lindzey, G., and Coggeshall, P. H. (Eds.) *An Assessment of Research—Doctorate Programs in the United States.* Washington, D.C.: National Academy Press, 1982.

Karabel, J., and Astin, A. W. "Social Class, Academic Ability, and College 'Quality.' " *Social Forces,* March 1975, *53* (3), 381-398.

Keller, F. F., and Koen, B. V. *The Personalized System of Instruction: State of the Art.* Austin: Engineering Institute, University of Texas, 1976.

Kells, H. R. "Factors Influencing and Attitudes About Macro-Level Outcome Analysis in Higher Education." *North Central Quarterly,* in press.

Klemp, G., and McClelland, D. "What Characterizes Intelligence Functioning Among Senior Managers." In R. Sternberg and R. Wagner (Eds.), *Practical Intelligence: Origins of Competence in the Everyday World.* Cambridge: Cambridge University Press, 1984.

Knapp, R. H., and Goodrich, H. B. *Origins of American Scientists.* New York: Russell and Russell, 1952.

Knapp, R. H., and Greenbaum, J. J. *The Younger American Scholar: His Collegiate Origins.* Chicago: University of Chicago Press, 1953.

Kohlberg, L. "Stages of Moral Development." In C. M. Beck, B. S. Crittenden, and E. V. Sullivan (Eds.), *Moral Education.* Toronto: University of Toronto Press, 1971.

Lanier, J. Untitled news release of the Johnson Foundation, Racine, Wisc., October 13, 1983.

Lawrence, J. K., and Green, K. C. *A Question of Quality: The Higher Education Ratings Game.* AAHE-ERIC Higher Education Research Report No. 5. Washington, D.C.: American Association for Higher Education, 1980.

Learned, W. S., and Wood, B. D. *The Student and His Knowledge.* New York: Carnegie Foundation for the Advancement of Teaching, 1938.

Levi, E. H. *An Adventure in Discovery.* Chicago: University of Chicago Press, 1971.

Levin, H., Glass, G., and Meister, G. "Cost-Effectiveness of Educational Interventions." Stanford, Calif.: Institute for Research on Educational Finance and Governance, 1984.

Levine, A. *Handbook on Undergraduate Curriculum.* San Francisco: Jossey-Bass, 1978.

Lindquist, J. "An Interview with Jack Lindquist." Newsletter of the National Clearinghouse for Commuter Programs, University of Maryland, in press.

Loevinger, J. "The Meaning and Measure of Ego Development." *American Psychologist,* 1966, *21,* 195–206.

Lyman, R. W. "Excellence, Quality . . . and the New Economy." *American Association for Higher Education Bulletin,* April 1982, pp. 3–5.

McCabe, R. H. "Excellence Is for Everyone: Quality and the Open Door Community College." Paper presented at the annual meeting of the American Association for Higher Education, Washington, D.C., March 1982.

McClain, C. J. *Degrees of Integrity: A Value-Added Approach to Undergraduate Assessment.* Washington, D.C.: American Association of State Colleges and Universities, 1984.

McDill, E. L., and Rigsby, L. C. *Structures and Process in Secondary Schools: The Academic Impact of Educational Climates.* Baltimore: Johns Hopkins University Press, 1973.

Manning, W. "Conceptual Critique." *La Red/The Net,* Fall Supplement 1982, pp. 3-6.

Marcus, L. R., Leone, A. O., and Goldberg, E. D. *The Path to Excellence: Quality Higher Education.* ASHE-ERIC Research Report No. 1. Washington, D.C.: Association for the Study of Higher Education, 1983.

Mayhew, L. B. *The Carnegie Commission on Higher Education: A Critical Analysis of the Reports and Recommendations.* San Francisco: Jossey-Bass, 1973.

Mentkowski, M., and Doherty, A. *Careering After College: Establishing the Validity of Abilities Learned in College for Later Careering and Professional Performance.* Final Report to the National Institute of Education: Overview and Summary. Milwaukee: Alverno College, 1984.

Middle States Association of Colleges and Schools. *Characteristics of Excellence in Higher Education and Standards for Middle States Accreditation.* Philadelphia: Middle States Association, 1978.

Middle States Association of Colleges and Schools. *Educational Excellence: Aspirations and Realities.* Program for 97th annual meeting, Philadelphia, December 1983.

Morgan, D. R., Kearney, R. C., and Regeus, J. L. "Assessing Quality Among Graduate Institutions of Higher Education in the United States." *Social Science Quarterly,* December 1976, *57,* 670-679.

National Center for Education Statistics. *The Condition of Education, 1983.* Washington, D.C.: National Center for Education Statistics, 1983.

National Commission on Excellence in Education. *A Nation at Risk: The Imperative for Educational Reform. A Report to the Nation and the Secretary of Education.* Washington, D.C.: U.S. Government Printing Office, 1983.

Ortega y Gasset, J. *Mission of the University.* Ed. and trans. by H. L. Nostrand. New York: Norton, 1944.

Pace, C. R. *Measuring Outcomes of College: Fifty Years of Findings and Recommendations for the Future.* San Francisco: Jossey-Bass, 1979.

Pace, C. R. "Achievement and the Quality of Student Effort." Unpublished report prepared for the National Commission on Excellence in Education. U.S. Department of Education, May 1982. (ED 227 101).

Pace, C. R. *Measuring the Quality of College Student Experiences.* Los Angeles: Higher Education Research Institute, University of California, 1984.

Patullo, E. L. "The Case for a Different Kind of Harvard." *Harvard Bulletin,* December 1972, p. 26.

Peng, S. S. "Education Attracts Fewer Academically High Achieving Young Women." *National Center for Educational Statistics Bulletin,* December 1982, pp. 1-9.

Perkins, J. A. "Organizations and Functions of the University." In J. A. Perkins (Ed.), *The University as an Organization.* New York: McGraw-Hill, 1973.

Perry, W. G. *Forms of Intellectual and Ethical Development in the College Years.* New York: Holt, Rinehart and Winston, 1970.

Peters, T. J., and Waterman, R. H. *In Search of Excellence: Lessons from America's Best-Run Companies.* New York: Harper & Row, 1982.

Rees, M. "The Ivory Tower and the Market Place." In S. M. McMurrin (Ed.), *On The Meaning of the University.* Salt Lake City: University of Utah Press, 1976.

Riesman, D. *Constraint and Variety in American Higher Education.* New York: Doubleday, 1956.

Roose, K. D., and Andersen, C. J. *A Rating of Graduate Programs.* Washington, D.C.: American Council on Education, 1970.

Rosenshine, B. *Teaching Functions in Instructional Programs.* Washington, D.C.: National Institute of Education, 1982.

Rossmann, J. E., and others. *Open Admissions at the City University of New York: An Analysis of the First Year.* New York: Prentice-Hall, 1975.

Rotter, J. "Generalized Expectations for Internal Versus External Control of Reinforcement." *Psychological Monographs,* 1966, *1* (609), entire issue.

Rudolph, F. *The American College and University: A History.* New York: Vintage, 1962.

Sanford, N. *Where Colleges Fail: A Study of the Student as a Person.* San Francisco: Jossey-Bass, 1968.

Schudson, M. S. "Organizing the 'Meritocracy': A History of the College Entrance Examination Board." *Harvard Educational Review,* February 1972, *42* (1), 34–69.

Snyder, M. B. "An Assessment of Quality in Undergraduate Education." Unpublished doctoral dissertation, University of California, Los Angeles, 1983.

Solmon, L. C. "The Definition of College Quality and Its Impact on Earnings." *Explorations in Economic Research,* Fall 1975, pp. 537–587.

Solmon, L. C., and Astin, A. W. "Departments Without Distinguished Graduate Programs." *Change,* September 1981, *2* (4), 23–28.

Southern Association of Colleges and Schools. *Criteria for Accreditation (Proposed).* Atlanta: Commission on Colleges, Southern Association of Colleges and Schools, 1982.

Southern Regional Education Board. *Meeting the Need for Quality: Action in the South.* Progress Report to the Southern Regional Education Board by Its Task Force on Higher Education to the Schools. Atlanta: Southern Regional Education Board, 1983.

Study Group on the Conditions of Excellence in Higher Education. *Involvement in Learning: Realizing the Potential of American Higher Education.* Washington, D.C.: National Institute of Education, 1984.

Touraine, A. *The Academic System in American Society.* New York: McGraw-Hill, 1974.

Ulan, A. *The Fall of the American University.* New York: Library Press, 1972.

University of the State of New York. *The Bulletin of the Re-*

gents Statewide Plan for Postsecondary Education 1984. Albany, N.Y.: State Education Department, 1982.

" 'Up to Half of Teacher Education Programs Should Be Closed,' Critic Says," *Chronicle of Higher Education,* September 15, 1984, p. 19.

Veblen, T. *The Higher Learning in America: A Memorandum on the Conduct of Universities by Business Men.* New York: Sagamore Press, 1957.

Veysey, L. "Undergraduate Admissions: Past and Future." In *Marketing in College Admissions: A Broadening of Perspectives.* New York: College Entrance Examination Board, 1980.

Walzer, M. *Spheres of Justice: A Defense of Pluralism and Equality.* New York: Basic Books, 1983.

Warren, J. R. "The Measurement of Academic Competence." Final report submitted to the Fund for the Improvement of Postsecondary Education, December 1978.

Webster, D. S. "The Origins and Early History of Academic Quality Rankings of American Colleges, Universities, and Individual Departments, 1888-1925." Unpublished doctoral dissertation, University of California, Los Angeles, 1981.

Webster, D. S. "America's Highest-Ranked Graduate Schools, 1925-1982." *Change,* May-June 1983, pp. 13-24.

Weiner, B. A. "Theory of Motivation for Some Classroom Experiences." *Journal of Educational Psychology,* 1979, *71,* 3-25.

"Why Teachers Fail." *Newsweek,* September 24, 1984, pp. 64-70.

Willie, C. V. "Educating Students Who Are Good Enough: Is Excellence an Excuse to Exclude?" *Change,* March 1982, pp. 16-20.

Winter, D. G., McClelland, D. C., and Stewart, A. J. *A New Case for the Liberal Arts: Assessing Institutional Goals and Student Development.* San Francisco: Jossey-Bass, 1981.

Wise, S. L., Hengstler, D. D., and Braskamp, L. A. "Alumni Ratings as an Indicator of Departmental Quality." *Journal of Educational Psychology,* 1981, *73,* 71-77.

Wolff, R. P. *The Ideal of the University.* Boston: Beacon Press, 1969.

Index